T0396838

THE OXFORD EDITION OF CHARLES DICKENS

General Editor
DAVID HEWITT

THE LIFE AND ADVENTURES OF NICHOLAS NICKLEBY

THE OXFORD EDITION OF CHARLES DICKENS

CHARLES DICKENS

The Life and Adventures of Nicholas Nickleby

VOLUME 2

Essay on the Text and Notes

Edited by

ELIZABETH JAMES

and

JOEL J. BRATTIN

with

J. H. ALEXANDER

OXFORD
UNIVERSITY PRESS

OXFORD
UNIVERSITY PRESS

Great Clarendon Street, Oxford, OX2 6DP,
United Kingdom

Oxford University Press is a department of the University of Oxford.
It furthers the University's objective of excellence in research, scholarship,
and education by publishing worldwide. Oxford is a registered trade mark of
Oxford University Press in the UK and in certain other countries

Published in the United States of America by Oxford University Press
198 Madison Avenue, New York, NY 10016, United States of America

British Library Cataloguing in Publication Data
Data available

Library of Congress Control Number: 2023942390

ISBN 978–0–19–888824–6

Printed and bound in the UK by
Clays Ltd, Elcograf S.p.A.

CONTENTS

Volume 2 Essay on the Text and Notes

ABBREVIATIONS, SHORTENED FORMS OF REFERENCE, AND CONVENTIONS

39	The first edition in both its physical forms (see 39A and 39B, and 861, 895–6 below).
39A	*The Life and Adventures of Nicholas Nickleby*, 20 numbers in 19 (London, 1838–9).
39B	*The Life and Adventures of Nicholas Nickleby* (London, 1839).
48	*The Life and Adventures of Nicholas Nickleby* (London, 1848). The Cheap Edition.
58	*The Life and Adventures of Nicholas Nickleby* (London, 1858). The Library Edition.
67	*The Life and Adventures of Nicholas Nickleby* (London, 1867). The Charles Dickens Edition.

Forster	John Forster, *The Life of Charles Dickens*, ed. J. W. T. Ley (London, 1928).
Kirkpatrick	Robert J. Kirkpatrick, *Charles Dickens, 'Nicholas Nickleby', and the Yorkshire Schools: Fact v Fiction* (Snaisgill, 2017).
Letters	*The Letters of Charles Dickens*, ed. Madeline House, Graham Storey, Kathleen Tillotson, and others, 12 vols (Oxford, 1965–2002).
ODEP	*The Oxford Dictionary of English Proverbs*, 3rd edition, rev. F. P. Wilson (Oxford, 1970).
OED	*The Oxford English Dictionary*; online edition (www.oed.com).
Opie	*The Oxford Dictionary of Nursery Rhymes*, ed. Iona and Peter Opie (Oxford, 1951, corrected 1952).
Parrott	Jeremy Parrott, *The Collected Dickens: A bibliography of the lifetime U.K. editions of Charles Dickens's works* (Szeged, Hungary, 2020).
Patten	Robert Patten, *Charles Dickens and his Publishers*, 2nd edition (Oxford, 2017).
Schlicke	Charles Dickens, *Nicholas Nickleby*, Oxford World's Classics edition, ed. Paul Schlicke (Oxford, 1990).
Slater 1978	Charles Dickens, *Nicholas Nickleby*, Penguin edition, ed. Michael Slater (Harmondsworth, 1978).
Slater 2009	Michael Slater, *Charles Dickens* (New Haven and London, 2009).

The following conventions are used in transcriptions from Dickens's manuscript. Deletions are enclosed <thus> and insertions ↑thus↓. A deletion within a deletion is indicated <<thus>>, and an insertion within an insertion

↑↑thus↓↓. The changing of one character or word to another is indicated by '→'. New paragraphs are indicated by '*n.p.*'. The same conventions indicate variants between the printed editions, as appropriate, and where there is space for a missing printed character this is denoted by a caret (^). A vertical bar (|) indicates a line break.

ESSAY ON THE TEXT

1. THE TEXT OF *NICHOLAS NICKLEBY*

This is the first critical edition of *Nicholas Nickleby* to be founded on a rigorous textual examination of the manuscript, where it survives, and the authorized printed editions. This examination has led the editors to concur with the general policy of the Oxford Edition of Charles Dickens in basing their text on the first printed version, published in twenty parts (as nineteen) in 1838–9, and bound for its issue in volume form in 1839.

When a manuscript is complete, or largely so, one might consider using it as one's copy-text, though its processing by highly skilled compositors to prepare it for public consumption would still weigh heavily in favour of following the printed texts. In the case of *Nicholas Nickleby* the surviving portions of the manuscript make up only one-tenth of the total, effectively ruling it out of consideration except by advocates of a composite copy-text.

As the relevant section of this essay will show (897–903) two of the three authorized editions subsequent to the first (the Cheap in 1848, and the Charles Dickens in 1867) tend to make the 1838–9 text more formal: the punctuation is generally much heavier, the sentence structure is regularized, perceived redundancy and tautology are ironed out, and melodramatic language is toned down. There are many small verbal changes, but most of them are unremarkable. Dickens would certainly have been involved in preparing the Cheap Edition, where most of the changes took place, but there is very little there that can be called distinctively authorial. He may not have been active in the Library Edition in 1858, but in the Charles Dickens Edition he continued his 1848 revisions, though on a reduced scale: in both the punctuation continues generally to acquire weight, though more commas are deleted than inserted. It should be noted that Dickens was not, evidently, involved in revising the *whole* novel in either 1848 or 1867 (see 897–8 and 902 below).

The later editions corrected errors in the 1838–9 text (as well as introducing new ones), and corrections of obvious errors are accepted as emendations in the present edition. But the editors have chosen to base their text on that first published in monthly parts and the original volume, whose comparative lightness and looseness may be felt to match the structural freedom of the narrative. They emend from the manuscript on the rare occasions where the copy-text is in error, and on those occasions when its compositors appear to have misread or misinterpreted the manuscript, most often in matters of punctuation. They accept corrections—but not, normally, other changes, whether those involve wording, punctuation, spelling, or capitalization—from later English editions published in Dickens's lifetime. And on a small number of occasions they emend without the authority of a later edition to correct a persistent error.

2. INCEPTION

The formal inception of *Nicholas Nickleby* can be dated precisely, to 18 August 1837 when a draft agreement was drawn up between Charles Dickens and Chapman and Hall for a new work of fiction. The crucial opening sentence reads as follows:

> Whereas the said Charles Dickens is the author of a Book or Work intitled The Posthumous Papers of the Pickwick Club—lately published in parts or numbers and which the said Edward Chapman & William Hall have printed & published And whereas the said Charles Dickens intends to write and compose another and new Book or work the title whereof has not yet been decided on of similar character and of the same extent and contents in point of quantity as the said work entitled "The Posthumous Papers of the Pickwick Club" and the publication and sale of the last-mentioned work having proved very profitable the said Edward Chapman & William Hall are desirous of printing and publishing the said new Book or work in the same manner as they have hitherto printed and published the said former Work And the said Charles Dickens is willing that they should do so upon the terms hereinafter expressed.[1]

The Pickwick Papers had appeared in monthly parts from March 1836 to November 1837 and proved phenomenally popular: sales of the early numbers were modest (some 500 copies), but they had risen to

[1] *Letters*, 1.659–62 (659). For the full agreement, in its final form, dated 18 November 1837, see Appendix 1 (916–21).

nearly 40,000 shortly after the work's completion.[2] *Pickwick* had its origin as an accompaniment to a series of engravings depicting Cockney sporting life, an assignment which Dickens developed into an essentially picaresque narrative, unified mostly by marvellously distinctive and memorable characters participating in a seemingly inexhaustible sequence of richly comic episodes. Understandably Chapman and Hall wanted more of the same for the new fiction, and they were prepared to pay well: £150 per issue meant a total of £3,000, whereas Richard Bentley had agreed to pay only £500 for the manuscript of *Oliver Twist* (though this was in addition to the payments for the serial appearance of that work in his *Miscellany*, where each instalment attracted a fee of £21).[3] Chapman and Hall were not to be disappointed: with a sale of 50,000 for the first number, *Nickleby* immediately surpassed *Pickwick*. In the second chapter Dickens provided a Pickwickian comic sketch with the public meeting 'to take into consideration the propriety of petitioning Parliament in favour of the United Metropolitan Improved Hot Muffin and Crumpet Baking and Punctual Delivery Company' (15.25–7). But the new work, though still recognizably picaresque, is far less episodic overall than *Pickwick*.[4]

The contract drafted in August and finalized in November 1837 is the formal inception. But it is possible that *Nickleby* was stirring in Dickens's imagination as much as four years before. In a fascinating note Edgar Rosenberg has pointed out that Dickens signed a letter, dating probably from October 1833, to one Miss Urquhart, an amateur actress, 'Charles. I.B.L.K.Y.N. Dickens'.[5] The signature puzzled the editors of the correspondence, but Rosenberg notes that if the letters are reversed they read 'N.Y.K.L.B.I'. There are still puzzles, but, if the suggested dating of the letter is correct, it seems that in 1833 there was some connection in Dickens's mind between his amateur theatrical activities and the name of his future hero. *Nickleby* made another embryonic appearance just one year before the draft contract, when on 4 November 1836 Dickens concluded an agreement

[2] Patten, 52. [3] Patten, 59–60.

[4] For the picaresque nature of this novel see Sister Mary Cleopha Cipar, O. S. U., 'Picaresque Characteristics in *Nicholas Nickleby*', *Dickensian*, 84 (1988), 43–6.

[5] *Letters*, 1.31: to Miss Urquhart, [?October 1833]. For the article see Edgar Rosenberg, 'Nickleby's Pilgrimage: Footnote to a Footnote', *Dickensian*, 99 (2003), 32–3.

to act as editor and principal contributor for Bentley's *Miscellany*. The sixth clause runs as follows:

> It is mutually understood between the parties hereto that the said Charles Dickens Esq shall not enter into any arrangement to conduct or write for any other periodical publication whatever with the exception of the "Pickwick Club" now publishing by Messrs Chapman & Hall and a similar work which he has undertaken to write for the same publishers upon the completion of the "Pickwick Club."[6]

In fulfilment of the requirement implied in the 1837 contract, Dickens certainly continued to make his readers laugh, but he also introduced the exposure of what he took to be a deeply serious social problem. We do not know whether, when the agreement was drafted in August, or perhaps even when it was finalized in November, he had any idea how the new novel would begin. In the event he focused the first four numbers pre-eminently on a school in Yorkshire designed to represent a class of establishments which he understood to be receptacles for illegitimate and otherwise unwanted boys who would be provided with extremely basic accommodation and education, at a distance, without vacations, on attractive financial terms and often with scant regard for their welfare or happiness. It is not surprising that the subject should have aroused a strong reaction in Dickens. His own erratic education made him acutely aware of the misery and harm caused by inadequate schooling, and throughout his career he was to return to the subject as part of his revolutionary positioning of children at the heart of much of his fiction, as well as in his journalism.[7] He decided to undertake an investigative journey to Yorkshire, in the depths of winter, clearly with his new fiction in mind. On Thursday 25 January 1838 he wrote to the novelist Harrison Ainsworth: 'I should have written to you before, but my month's work has been dreadful—Grimaldi, the anonymous book for Chapman and Hall, Oliver and the Miscellany. They are all done, thank God, and I start on my pilgrimage to the cheap schools of Yorkshire (a mighty secret of course) next Monday Morning.'[8] The horrendous workload undertaken by Dickens, to which he was about to add the composition of the new

[6] *Letters*, 1.649–50 (650).

[7] See Philip Collins, *Dickens and Education* (London, 1963), 1.

[8] *Letters*, 1.358–60 (359): to W. Harrison Ainsworth, [25 January 1838].

novel, consisted of his editorship of Bentley's *Miscellany* including the serialized *Oliver Twist*; *Memoirs of Grimaldi*, a hack-work editorial job also for Bentley; and *Sketches of Young Gentlemen*, a series of sketches produced for anonymous publication by Chapman and Hall, since Dickens had agreed not to write for any publisher other than Bentley, an exception being made for *Nicholas Nickleby*.

Unfortunately there is very little hard information about what Dickens had heard of the northern schools before his expedition, or exactly who or what he saw during his brief visit. His own statements are often of questionable accuracy, and over the years Yorkshire has produced an extraordinary variety of contradictory testimonies. The evidence has been assembled and judiciously assessed by Robert J. Kirkpatrick.[9]

In his Preface to the 1848 Cheap Edition Dickens claims that his information about the Yorkshire schools dates back to his childhood:

> I cannot call to mind, now, how I came to hear about Yorkshire schools when I was a not very robust child, sitting in bye-places, near Rochester Castle, with a head full of PARTRIDGE, STRAP, TOM PIPES, and SANCHO PANZA; but I know that my first impressions of them were picked up at that time, and that they were, somehow or other, connected with a suppurated abscess that some boy had come home with, in consequence of his Yorkshire guide, philosopher, and friend, having ripped it open with an inky pen-knife. The impression made upon me, however made, never left me. I was always curious about them—fell, long afterwards, and at sundry times, into the way of hearing more about them—at last, having an audience, resolved to write about them. (854)

It seems likely that Dickens's childhood knowledge of the Yorkshire schools came, at least in part, from a former pupil at Bowes Hall, an establishment run by George Clarkson. After a year at this establishment John Crosse Brooks moved to Dickens's old school in Chatham shortly after Dickens had left for London in 1822, but over sixty years later he divulged that he himself, rather than Clarkson, had attempted the misguided surgical procedure. According to Brooks he imparted this information in the course of Dickens's subsequent return visits

[9] Robert J. Kirkpatrick, *Charles Dickens, 'Nicholas Nickleby' and the Yorkshire Schools: Fact v Fiction* (Snaisgill, 2017).

to Chatham, though whether he misinformed Dickens or Dickens misunderstood or misremembered is not clear.[10] Whatever the case, a further twist is added by Dickens's ascription of the procedure to William Shaw of Bowes Academy, discussed below.

Dickens left London by coach on 30 January 1838 with his illustrator Hablot Browne, bearing, in a 'pious fraud', a letter from a colleague of his close friend the solicitor Thomas Mitton purporting to enquire into the availability of a place at a Yorkshire school (as recounted in a communication to John Forster used for the Preface to the Cheap Edition of 1848: see 854 above).[11] On the evening of Thursday 1 February they arrived at Greta Bridge, from where Dickens sent a vivid report of the journey to his wife. Always on the alert for promising material he recorded two encounters that were to suggest details for the new work:

> We reached Grantham between 9 and 10 on Tuesday night, and found everything prepared for our reception in the very best Inn I have ever put up at. It is odd enough that an old lady who had been outside all day and came in towards dinner time turned out to be the Mistress of a Yorkshire School returning from the holiday-stay in London. She was a very queer old body, and shewed us a long letter she was carrying to one of the boys from his father, containing a severe lecture (enforced and aided by many texts from Scripture) *on his refusing to eat boiled meat*. She was very communicative, drank a great deal of brandy and water, and towards evening became insensible, in which state we left her.
>
> Yesterday we were up again shortly after 7 and came on upon our journey by the Glasgow Mail which charged us the remarkably low sum of *six pounds, four* for two places inside. We had a very droll male companion until seven oClock in the evening, and a most delicious lady's maid for twenty miles who implored us to keep a sharp look-out at the coach windows as she expected her carriage was coming to meet her and she was afraid of missing it. We had many delightful vauntings of the same kind; and in the end it is scarcely necessary to say that the Coach did not come, and a very dirty girl did.[12]

[10] Kirkpatrick, 67–8, citing *Newcastle Courant*, 24 December 1886.

[11] Mitton's colleague is identified by the editors of the correspondence as Charles Smithson (?1804–44): *Letters*, 1.427n. In the Cheap Edition Preface Dickens refers to 'some letters of introduction', but writing to his wife on 1 February 1838 he says he will 'deliver the letter', suggesting there was only one: *Letters*, 1.365–6 (366).

[12] *Letters*, 1.365–6 (365): to Mrs Charles Dickens, 1 February 1838.

One has little difficulty in recognizing here the inspiration for Mobbs's mother-in-law (100.21–6) and the 'very fastidious lady' who expected a green chariot (57.25–36).

In the Preface to the Cheap Edition Dickens writes that he proceeded to visit several schools in the neighbourhood ('I went to several places in that part of the county where I understood these schools to be most plentifully sprinkled'), before eventually presenting his letter to a local contact. There is no record of any other details of the investigation. In this Preface Dickens maintains 'that Mr. Squeers is the representative of a class, and not of an individual', but it is generally thought likely that the character bears a particular relationship to William Shaw, the proprietor of Bowes Academy, whom Dickens and Browne met on 2 February, as Dickens records in his diary: 'Mem. Shaw the schoolmaster we saw to-day, is the man in whose school several boys went blind sometime since, from gross neglect. The case was tried, and the Verdict went against him. It must have been between 1823 and 1826. Look this out in the Newspapers.'[13] None of the Dotheboys students is blind, but it is significant that Shaw had 'a slight scale covering the pupil of one of the eyes', according to a former pupil, possibly a result of the severe outbreak of ophthalmia at the Academy that led to Shaw being successfully sued by two sets of parents in the trial Dickens refers to, back in 1823.[14] By describing Squeers as one-eyed, Dickens made it inevitable that Shaw should be identified as the original. We do not know with any certainty how Shaw received Dickens and Browne, how much if any of Bowes Academy they were able to inspect, or who else they talked to during their stay, with the exception of an initially evasive local attorney who eventually heartily advised against sending a boy to a Yorkshire school (see note to 112.33). It is also unclear what other schools in the area they may have visited. There were eight of them at the time in the area around Bowes.[15]

Dickens must have known of the Bowes Academy before his Yorkshire visit, as he produces only a slightly parodied version of its prospectus in Chapter 3 (30.25–36). In January 1838, as it had done

[13] *Letters*, 1.632: diary, Friday, 2 February 1838. Dickens may well have looked up the press reports of the two prosecutions in 1823 (see Kirkpatrick, 84–91), but inevitably the testimonies centre on the ophthalmic infection and there are no details in the text that obviously derive from this source.

[14] Kirkpatrick, 112. [15] Kirkpatrick, 3.

in previous years, *The Times* published advertisements from a number of establishments, including Shaw's which asserts that 'YOUTH are carefully INSTRUCTED in the English, Latin, and Greek languages, writing, common and decimal arithmetic, book-keeping, mensuration, surveying, geometry, geography, and navigation, with the most useful branches of the mathematics, and provided with board, clothes, and every necessary, at 20 guineas per annum each. No extra charges. No vacations.'[16] Dickens confirms his acquaintance with the advertisements in a letter of 9 July 1838, a week after the appearance of the fourth number, to Lord Robert Grosvenor, the Whig MP involved with legislation aimed at improving the welfare of poor children: 'Mr. Charles Dickens presents his Compliments to Lord Robert Grosvenor and begs to inform him that Mr. Squeers and Do-the-boys Hall were originally suggested to him by such advertisements as Lord Robert Grosvenor has had the kindness to enclose. Those particular advertisements had never come under Mr. Dickens' notice before, although he was in the immediate neighbourhood of Mr. Twycross (as he finds by his printed address) in the course of a little tour among the Yorkshire Schools which he made last winter.'[17] It is also likely that in the course of his visit Dickens would have picked up one of Shaw's cards with a similar prospectus on one side and a list of required clothing on the other.[18]

Writing to the author Anna Maria Hall at the end of 1838, Dickens was in no doubt that he had toned down rather than exaggerated what he had learnt about the schools: 'Depend upon it that the rascalities of those Yorkshire schoolmasters *cannot* easily be exaggerated, and that I have kept down the strong truth and thrown as much comicality over it as I could, rather than disgust and weary the reader with its fouler aspects. The identical scoundrel you speak of, I saw—curiously enough. His name is Shaw.'[19] Dickens may have received reports of even worse conditions and treatment, and much was amiss in some of these establishments. But it is not obvious that they were worse than

[16] *The Times*, 12 January 1838, 2, col. a.

[17] *Letters*, 1.411: to Lord Robert Grosvenor, 9 July 1838. Thomas Twycross ran a school at Winton in Westmorland from 1834 until 1855: Kirkpatrick, 294–5.

[18] For a reproduction of the card see V. C. Clinton-Baddeley, 'Benevolent Teachers of Youth', *Cornhill Magazine*, 169 (1957), 361–82 (facing 363).

[19] *Letters*, 1. 481–3 (481): to Mrs S. C. Hall, 29 December 1838. As noted earlier in the essay the pedagogue wrongly alleged to have treated the suppurated abscess was not Shaw but George Clarkson.

schools elsewhere in England. A substantial body of positive testimonies suggests that the Yorkshire schools often fulfilled satisfactorily, according to the standards of the time, a need for practical rather than Classical education, at prices affordable by families of modest means for whom 'No vacations' meant no expensive coach journeys more than once a year. Dickens drew attention to real abuses. But he did so as part of an imaginative mythopoeic dystopia, drawing on bitter and haunting memories of his own later childhood fused with his inimitable comic genius and his immersion in fairy tales and narratives such as Smollett's *Roderick Random*, where in the fifth chapter the hero and his fellow student give their brutal schoolmaster a taste of his own medicine.

The immediate effect of the critique of the Yorkshire schools in *Nicholas Nickleby* was considerably less than Dickens claimed. In the Cheap Edition Preface of 1848 he asserts: 'There were, then, a good many cheap Yorkshire schools in existence. There are very few now.' In fact, of the eight schools active in 1838 only two had closed. Inevitably Bowes Academy was one of these, expiring late in 1840; the other, Startforth Hall Academy, run by Francis Clark, had closed a year earlier.[20]

The campaign against the Yorkshire schools is one of three principal originating components in the development of *Nicholas Nickleby*. It seems likely that the three came to Dickens entirely independently, the loose structure of the work easily accommodating them. The second component consists of the theatrical element centring on the travelling troupe run by Vincent Crummles which Nicholas joins for their run at the Portsmouth Theatre. In contrast to the Yorkshire scenes, those set in Portsmouth mark a shift to the more purely comic mode expected by many from the author of *Pickwick*.

The theatre had been a passion of Dickens from his childhood attendance at the Theatre Royal, Rochester which he was to recall in his 1860 paper 'Dullborough Town' in *The Uncommercial Traveller*. That passion led to a lifelong involvement with the amateur and professional stages, and a particular enthusiasm for popular entertainments.[21] Dickens likely found inspiration for Crummles and his company in the career of the actor-manager T. D. Davenport (1792–1851), whose

[20] Kirkpatrick, 92–3, 224–5.

[21] See Paul Schlicke, *Dickens and Popular Entertainment* (London, 1985).

company included Davenport's young daughter Jean. Dickens would have come across them at the Westminster Theatre in 1832 or at the Richmond Theatre, where the nine-year-old Jean's career was launched, when he was staying at nearby Petersfield in 1836.[22] He may also have seen an old playbill for their performances at the theatre in Portsmouth in the course of his retreat to the Isle of Wight for nine days in early September 1838 to complete *Oliver Twist*. He probably passed through Portsmouth (his birthplace), and he was certainly there at some stage during the composition of *Nickleby*.[23] Like the Crummleses, the Davenports sought fresh pastures in the United States, in April 1838.[24]

The last of the three major components contributing to the growth of *Nickleby* is the Cheeryble brothers, introduced at the mid-point of the narrative. Dickens himself acknowledges in the 1839 and 1848 Prefaces that they are drawn from life, and it is generally accepted that they are based on the admirable Manchester merchant brothers William Grant (1769–1842) and Daniel Grant (1782–1855).[25] It is likely that he made two investigative journeys to Manchester, in November 1838 and January 1839, with a view to highlighting in the second half of his novel the harsh conditions of child-labourers in the northern factories. On 29 December 1838 he wrote to the Irish journalist Edward Marlborough Fitzgerald:

> I went, some weeks ago, to Manchester, and saw the *worst* cotton mill. And then I saw the *best*.... There was no great difference between them.
>
> I was obliged to come back suddenly, upon some matters connected with the publication of "Oliver Twist", and saw no more. But on the 11th. of next month I am going down again, only for three days, and then into the enemy's camp, and the very head-quarters of the factory system advocates....

[22] See Malcolm Morley, 'Where Crummles Played', *Dickensian*, 58 (1962), 23–9; 'Dickens Goes to the Theatre', *Dickensian*, 59 (1963), 165–71; 'More About Crummles', *Dickensian*, 59 (1963), 51–6.

[23] Forster, 2. See Michael Slater's facsimile reproduction of *The Life and Adventures of Nicholas Nickleby*, 2 vols (London, 1982), 1, xlii. See also his reproduction there of the Portsmouth playbill with its prominent reference, in a variety of fonts, to the 'Great and Astonishing Success, of the most Celebrated Juvenile Actress! of the day Miss Davenport! Who was received with Cheers of Applause!' ([xlv]).

[24] Paul Schlicke, *Dickens and Popular Entertainment* (London, 1985), 85 and 258 (note 73).

[25] See R. R. Carmyllie, *Charles Dickens and the 'Cheeryble' Grants* (Ramsbottom, 1981). In the 1848 Preface Dickens states that both the brothers were dead: William had indeed died six years earlier, but Daniel lived on till 1855.

> ...So far as seeing goes, I have seen enough for my purpose, and what I have seen has disgusted and astonished me beyond all measure. I mean to strike the heaviest blow in my power for these unfortunate creatures, but whether I shall do so in the "Nickleby", or wait some other opportunity, I have not yet determined.[26]

Dickens met the Grant brothers at a dinner held in his honour during the first of these visits in early November.[27] In the event he decided against including further social criticism in this novel, so the Grants and their Lancashire connection remain a shadowy presence in the background while their fictional equivalents play a prominent role.

In the course of a dinner hosted by Chapman and Hall on 5 October 1839 to celebrate the completion of *Nicholas Nickleby*, Dickens stated that the work 'had been to him a diary of the last two years: the various papers preserving to him the recollection of the events and feelings connected with their production'.[28] Dotheboys, the Crummleses, and the Cheerybles are the most prominent entries in this metaphorical diary, but several other details derive from the author's experiences during the 'last two years'. Dickens asserted that Smike was suggested by a gravestone near Bowes Academy (see note to 82.33). The story of the 'The Five Sisters of York' was inspired by the great grisaille window in York Minster (see note to 62.28), to which Dickens's attention was drawn by the verger on his Yorkshire excursion: 'I went over York Cathedral the other day. I had scarcely set foot in the Nave when the Verger taking me by the shoulder led me to a particular pillar to contemplate a particular window. "There!" said the old man "*Mr. Britton the great artist and architect* says that's the first window in all Europe; and if Mr. Britton don't know a fine window when he sees it, who does,—as the Dean says." '[29] The character of John Browdie may be based on the attorney who advised Dickens against patronizing a Yorkshire school, and who features in the Preface to the Cheap Edition (see note to 112.33). The 'literary gentleman' of Chapter 48 was suggested by an unauthorized dramatization of the novel by William Thomas Moncrieff, first performed on 20 May 1839 (see note to

[26] *Letters*, 1.483–4: to [E. M.] Fitzgerald, 29 December 1838.

[27] See Slater 2009, 126 and Carmyllie, *Charles Dickens and the 'Cheeryble' Grants*, 14–20. Dickens's statement in the 1848 Cheap Edition Preface that he 'never exchanged any communication' with the brothers simply means that he never wrote to them.

[28] Slater 2009, 136.

[29] *Letters*, 1.375–6 (376): to George Cattermole, the painter, [?February 1838].

640.26): Dickens's response was immediate, the chapter appearing at the end of the June number published on 31 May, and Moncrieff immediately issued a long public defence of his action.[30] One detail that apparently failed to find a place in the novel was a jest transmitted by Forster: 'A thousand thanks for that joke (new!) respecting the Thames Tunnel. I shall certainly put it into Nickleby.'[31]

3. COMPOSITION

The timetable. Dickens's progress with the composition of *Nicholas Nickleby* in 1838 and 1839 can be traced in some detail chiefly through his surviving letters, many of them addressed to John Forster. Since it was Dickens's general practice at this period to give only the day of the week it is not always possible to date the letters precisely, but the editors of the first volume of the Pilgrim Edition of the letters, Madeline House and Graham Storey, have been remarkably successful in pinning down most of the dates. Thus we know that it was on Wednesday 21 February 1838 that Dickens, who had returned from his Yorkshire expedition by the 8th of the month,[32] informed Forster: 'The first chapter of Nicholas is done. It took time but I think answers the purpose as well as it could.'[33] The following evening he conveyed additional information to Chapman and Hall: 'I have been decoyed to the play, and seduced from Nicholas by a thousand blandishments, but the first chapter is ready, and I mean (God willing) to begin in earnest tomorrow night, so you can begin to print [i.e. set up the type] as soon as you like. The sooner you begin, the faster I shall get on.'[34] Dickens's intention to 'begin in earnest' was no doubt stimulated by the fact that, in terms of the agreement of 18 November 1837 (see above, 862, and Appendix 1 (916–21)), he was contracted to provide the first monthly copy on or before 15 March, despite the pressure of many other commitments, notably his work for *Bentley's Miscellany* (see 864–5 above), not to mention the birth of his daughter Mary on 6 March. Probably in early March he complained to Forster:

[30] S. J. Adair Fitz-Gerald, *Charles Dickens and the Drama* (London, 1910), 121–6.
[31] *Letters*, 1.407: to John Forster, [?24 June 1838].
[32] *Letters*, 1.368–9: to Mrs Henry Belcombe, 8 February 1838.
[33] *Letters*, 1.377: to John Forster, [?21 February 1838].
[34] *Letters*, 1.379: to [Chapman and Hall], 22 February 1838.

'No ride for me to-day. Sitting first, then a business appointment with Mitton (who remained here the other evening) then a hasty dinner, and then Nickleby who has scarcely advanced a jot. | I will be busy all tomorrow morning with Miscellany Papers.'[35] A similar note assigned to 8 March or thereabouts sounds a trifle more hopeful: 'Thank God, all continues to go on well—except Nickleby and he does *not* go on well, and therefore we do *not* dine together, but I stick to it, in thorough style until a late hour of the night, and hope I shall be able really to "report progress" tomorrow.'[36] Probably the following day Dickens informed Forster that the progress had duly been made: 'I wrote 20 slips of Nicholas yesterday, and only left 4 [of the current chapter] to do this morning. Up at 8 oClock too!'[37] If the editors of the correspondence are correct in their conjecture that a note to Charles Hicks, the foreman-printer at Bradbury and Evans, dates from the third week of March, Dickens managed to meet his contractual obligation and had received first proofs: 'As Nickleby is to be re-set, I send it you *un*corrected—or at least with only a very few corrections made; and one insertion. According to my calculation of the quantity, the number will not bear more, but if it should require anything to make up, I will insert it directly you send me the new proofs.'[38]

In his biography of Dickens, Forster records that the first (April) number was published on 'magazine day', the last day of March, attaining an astonishing sale of nearly 50,000 copies,[39] though Robert Patten qualifies this with 'in, at most, a few days' time',[40] presumably since it is unlikely that Chapman and Hall would print this many copies before testing the market. Once again the pale green numbers, familiar from *The Pickwick Papers*, were an eagerly-awaited phenomenon for book buyers and readers every month. Priced at a shilling (or two shillings for the final double number), each instalment consisted of two plates and thirty-two pages of text, sandwiched between 'The Nickleby Advertiser', typically containing sixteen pages of miscellaneous advertisements, and a varying number of advertising pamphlets,

[35] *Letters*, 1.381: to John Forster, [?March 1838]. The Pilgrim editors suggest that the reference to 'sitting' refers to an appointment for a portrait by either Samuel Lawrence (1812–84) or Ferdinand Pickering (1811–*c.* 1882).

[36] *Letters*, 1.385: to John Forster, [?8 March 1838].

[37] *Letters*, 1.385–6 (385): to John Forster, [?9 March 1838]. In the early numbers of *Nickleby* 24 slips would be a little over 4,000 words.

[38] *Letters*, 1.389: to Charles Hicks, [?March 1838].

[39] Forster, 109. [40] Patten, 70.

leaflets and announcements, all stitched into printed wrappers with a front cover design by Hablot Browne. The tantalizingly vague yet elaborate title, *The Life and Adventures of Nicholas Nickleby containing a faithful account of the fortunes, misfortunes, uprisings, downfallings, and complete career of the Nickleby family. Edited by "Boz." With illustrations by "Phiz"*, promised a story full of incident and high emotion—hinted at in the ups and downs of Browne's design—and not unlike the stimulating effect of the varied formats, sizes, typography, colour, and even words of the surrounding advertising material.[41]

Anticipating the excitement, on the eve of publication Dickens and his publishers issued a 'proclamation', dated 28 February, designed to deter potential producers of inferior imitations of *Nicholas Nickleby*, like those which had proved such an annoyance with *Pickwick Papers* and *Oliver Twist*.[42] This three-page pamphlet (a copy of which was inserted in No. 5 of the same day's serial instalment of *Sketches by Boz*), is reproduced as Appendix 2 (922–4). The 'Nickleby Proclamation', as it became known, adopts the slovenly and tasteless rhetoric of its targets in an attempt to warn them off. It had no effect, however, and for its first ten numbers the new work was remorselessly shadowed by *Nickelas Nickelbery*, edited by 'Bos', a pseudonym used by Thomas Peckett Prest, who continued to make his name with Dickensian imitations.[43]

We have seen that the first number presented Dickens with challenges. The same is probably true of the second, though the evidence is uncertain. In a note to Forster conjecturally dated 15 April, the

[41] The advertiser of Intense Diamine ink caught the mood as he addressed the 'Readers of *Nickleby*' directly in No. 17: 'You must have often envied the freedom and fluency with which the author gives expression to the most intense feelings, and fretted as you have tried in vain to make your own ideas flow with equal grace from the points of your pens. Did it never occur to you that there was something in the *Ink* that he uses?' For a recent study of the place of advertising in Dickens's serials see the second chapter of Sara Thornton, *Advertising, Subjectivity and the Nineteenth-Century Novel: Dickens, Balzac and the Language of the Walls* (London, 2009), 63–118: 'Reading the Dickens Advertiser: Merging Paratext and Novel'.

[42] Forster, 322.

[43] See Louis James, *Fiction for the Working Man, 1830–1850: A Study of the Literature Produced for the Working Classes in Early Victorian Urban England* (London, 1963), Ch. 4 (45–71, especially 63–4). The Proclamation was also printed in *Cleave's Penny Gazette of Variety. Late The London Satirist*, 1.21 (3 March 1838), p. 4, col. 5, followed later in the same column by an advertisement for Edward Lloyd's plagiarized *Oliver Twiss* imitating the style of Dickens's document.

deadline for the May number, he found himself seriously short of material: 'The cold, or the mulled wine, or the driving, made me as bad as you. I couldn't write a line 'till three oClock, and have yet 5 slips to finish, and don't know what to put in them for I have reached the point I meant to leave off with.'[44] The editors of the correspondence conjecture that Dickens may have inserted one or other of the two tales told at the inn, but five slips would be less than a thousand words and each of the tales is several times that length. A further conjecture placing a note to Bradbury and Evans in the third week of April is more convincing: 'As I am induced to think from your estimate that I have still a couple of pages or so to write, and consequently cannot correct the first sheets until I see the last, perhaps you will make another wonderful exertion not exhausting yourselves but having regard to your healths and the happiness of your wives and children.'[45] If this does indeed refer to the second number, it may possibly indicate an original ending at 87.19, before the company retire for the night, though additional material could have been inserted earlier in the narrative.

The evidence for the progress of the third (June) number is more certain, though it suggests that composition had not become any easier. In a letter dated 20 May to Thomas Noon Talfourd, Dickens writes: 'I am desperately hard up just now, having only written one chapter of Nickleby number three. I hope to make a great dash tomorrow, however, to proceed at rail-road pace.'[46] This leads the editors of the correspondence to observe rightly: 'From now on he apparently wrote *Oliver* before *Nickleby* each month, making no further attempt to finish *Nickleby* by the 15th.' Authorial duties had on occasion to edge out formal spiritual obligations: 'Not at church, but correcting proofs', Dickens informed Forster one Sunday morning, perhaps 24 June, and if so probably referring to *Nickleby*, which would make it the only surviving record of the fourth (July) number, apart from a note to Hicks at the end of the month indicating a mistake found in a hasty survey of the proofs.[47]

[44] *Letters*, 1.395–6: to John Forster, [?15 April 1838].

[45] *Letters*, 1.397: to Messrs Bradbury & Evans, [?April 1838].

[46] *Letters*, 1.400: to T. N. Talfourd, 20 May [1838].

[47] *Letters*, 1.407: to John Forster, [?24 June 1838]; 1.408: to Charles Hicks, [?29 June 1838].

Writing to Bentley, probably on 10 July 1838, Dickens is optimistic that the fifth (August) number of *Nickleby* can be fitted in between the monthly instalment of *Oliver Twist* for the *Miscellany*, completed on the 7th according to his short-lived diary for 1838–9,[48] and the composition of the following instalment later in the month: 'Wilson has Oliver for the Month. I have planned the tale to the close, and if I have any fortune in preparing the next No. of Nickleby expeditiously, hope to make a great start this month.'[49] In his diary Dickens notes that he began the fifth number on the 10th:[50] Chapter 15 which opens it seems to have been written fluently and with gusto (it includes the hilarious letter from Fanny Squeers), and at proof stage two passages of 16 and 26 lines (two leaves) were actually cut, probably because there was too much material for the number (see 926–7 below). A week later, though, Dickens had to inform the Philadelphia publishers Carey, Lea & Blanchard that his difficulty in meeting the printing deadlines meant he could not provide them with early proofs of the novel to enable them to be the first to publish it in the United States: 'I have never seen your Agent Mr. Miller upon the subject of Nicholas Nickleby, but if I had I should have been unable to have sent you early proofs of any Number that has yet appeared, as I have been rather behind-hand than in advance and have only completed each Number a day or two before its publication.'[51]

In a letter to Bentley, dated around 26 July by the editors of the correspondence, Dickens proposed that he should rest *Oliver Twist* for a month.[52] This must have been agreed, for the October issue of the *Miscellany* did not contain the normal instalment.[53] It did not give him more time overall: he was attempting to finish that novel (the letter refers to 'making a great start'), but it did allow the

[48] *Letters*, 1.633.

[49] *Letters*, 1.413: to Richard Bentley, [10 July 1838]. Wilson was manager for Samuel Bentley, who printed the *Miscellany* for his brother Richard. An agreement with Bentley dated 20 September 1837 required that Dickens finish *Oliver Twist* so it could be published in volume form before serialization was complete (*Letters*, 1.654–5 (654)). A revised agreement dated 22 September 1838 moved the date on to 25 October (*Letters*, 1.666–74 (669)).

[50] *Letters*, 1.633.

[51] *Letters*, 1.416–17 (417): to Messrs Carey, Lea & Blanchard, 18 July 1838.

[52] *Letters*, 1.421; to Richard Bentley, [?26 July 1838].

[53] *Oliver*'s place in September 1838 was occupied by 'Full Report of the Second Meeting of the Mudfog Association for the Advancement of Everything', a satire on the British Association for the Advancement of Science: a 'report' on the first meeting had replaced *Oliver* in October the previous year when Dickens was at loggerheads with Bentley (Slater 2009, 105).

reorganization of his timetable so that he could complete the next instalment of *Nickleby*, the sixth, early in August and leave himself a full month in which he could work towards the completion of *Oliver*. In a letter conjecturally dated 8 August he informs Forster: 'I worked pretty well last night—very well, indeed,—but although I did eleven close slips before half past twelve I have yet four to write to complete the chapter; and as I foolishly left them 'till this morning have the steam to get up afresh.'[54] A note tentatively assigned to Thursday 20 September indicates that Dickens sent Charles Hicks 'a chapter—12 pages I hope. You will have another (please God) either on Sunday Night, or Monday Morning': this most likely refers to the seventh instalment of *Nickleby*.[55] There seems to be no record of the composition of the eighth number which appeared at the end of October. The month must have been particularly stressful with the completion of *Oliver Twist* occupying the author's attention until the 22nd, when he wrote apologetically to the man of letters Samuel Laman Blanchard: 'I have been so incessantly occupied, night and day, that I have not opened a letter this month until today.'[56]

One might imagine that with *Oliver* out of the way Dickens would have found it easier to concentrate on *Nickleby*, now in need of its ninth (December) number, but November turned out to be another difficult month. The first week was occupied by the expedition to north Wales and on to Manchester where he met the Grant brothers, the originals of the Cheerybles who were to make their first appearance in the eleventh number, published on 31 January 1839. On his return Dickens found it difficult to settle down to composition: in the course of apologizing, probably on 19 November, to his actor friend W. C. Macready for his failure to complete a promised farce, *The Lamplighter*, he explained that 'I found myself compelled to set to work *first* at the Nickleby on which I am at present engaged, and which I regret to say—after my close and arduous application last month—I find I cannot write as quickly as usual. I *must* finish it at latest by the 24th.'[57] The following day, in a letter endorsed by Forster

[54] *Letters*, 1.425: to John Forster, [?8 August 1838].

[55] *Letters*, 1.437: to Charles Hicks, [?20 September 1838].

[56] *Letters*, 1. 442–3 (442): to S. Laman Blanchard, 22 October 1838. For the completion of *Oliver Twist* see the Clarendon edition of that novel, ed. Kathleen Tillotson (Oxford, 1966), xxiii.

[57] *Letters*, 1.456–7 (456): to W. C. Macready, [?19 November 1838].

'Nov. 20, 1838', he reports: 'I have just begun my second chapter—cannot go out to-night—must get on—think there *will* be a Nickleby at the end of this month, now, (I doubted it before) and want to make a start towards it, if I possibly can.' But he still suggests that 'I think I might adventure on an expedition to the Adelphi tomorrow night'.[58] It seems they went, and saw the dramatization of *Nickleby* by Edward Stirling. Despite his fierce objections to such abuses of his copyright, Dickens indicated to Forster on the 23rd that he approved of many aspects of this production. It is also clear that there was no let-up in the pressure of the monthly deadline: 'I was writing incessantly until it was time to dress; and have not yet got the subject of my last chapter, which *must be* finished to-night.'[59] In the event, Chapter 29 centred on Folair's absurd challenge to Nicholas.

The tenth (January) number had still not been begun by 12 December when Dickens was 'cogitating the next number'.[60] He had spent much of the time since the appearance of its predecessor completing *The Lamplighter* for Macready. Although it turned out to be unsuitable for production it was not time wasted: Dickens reworked it as a short story[61] and saved a memorable utterance for Mantalini in the eleventh number of *Nickleby* (see the explanatory note to 438.22). In a note to Forster tentatively dated mid-December the author announces that he 'got to the 16th. slip last night, and shall try hard to get [to] the 30th. before I go to bed', which would suggest that he anticipates completing Chapter 30.[62] On the 20th he has 'been at work all day' and hopes 'to finish this chapter by bed-time. Tomorrow I shall have a stiff job.'[63] That would be Chapter 31, leaving five pages for Chapter 32 to complete the number. Thus probably on the 21st he writes to Charles Hicks at 1 a.m.: 'If you can let me know in the course of the day, *exactly* how many more pages you want, it will greatly facilitate our progress. According to my calculation, five more will do it.'[64] The same morning he strikes an optimistic note for Forster: 'Five

[58] *Letters*, 1.457–8 (457): to John Forster, [endorsed 20 November 1838].
[59] *Letters*, 1.459–60 (459): to John Forster, [?23 November 1838].
[60] *Letters*, 1.467–8 (467): to R. H. Barham, [12 December 1838].
[61] See Joel J. Brattin, 'From Drama into Fiction: *The Lamplighter* and "The Lamplighter's Story"', *Dickensian*, 85 (1989), 131–9.
[62] *Letters*, 1.471: to John Forster, [mid-December 1838].
[63] *Letters*, 1.471–2: to John Forster, [20 December 1838].
[64] *Letters*, 1.473: to Charles Hicks, [?21 December 1838].

printed pages—or rather less I hope—to write. And I am getting on swimmingly.'[65]

A similar upbeat tone is evident when the new year saw Dickens begin the second half of the novel with the eleventh (February) number and writing, probably on 21 January 1839, to the antiquary John Noble: 'Accept my best thanks for the Highland Whiskey, which, as in honor bound, I intend trying this very night. As I shall be at work on Nickleby, you will know what has inspired me, if the next Number should contain anything specially good.'[66] There turned out, though, to be a problem with 'underwriting' at the end of the number. Late in the month Dickens wrote to Hicks:

> I felt quite certain when I received your note last night, that there must be some mistake. However, it put me out of heart, and instead of sitting up and finishing as I should otherwise have done, I left off at 3 O'Clock this morning and went to bed.
>
> I shall write 5 slips more in addition to what I now send, which will be amply sufficient. If you send up for them about *2* o'Clock, I have no doubt I shall have them ready for you.
>
> When you send the proofs, be good enough to send a duplicate—never mind waiting until it's revised—I am obliged to go to a public dinner to-night, but if they arrive this evening or tomorrow morning, I will lose no time on their correction and return.[67]

Judging from the content of Chapter 36 it seems likely that the additional page and a half were to be inserted in the course of the narrative rather than at the end.

Dickens severed his connection with *Bentley's Miscellany* after the January 1839 number, and got out of his contract to serialize *Barnaby Rudge*, which he had tentatively begun at the beginning of the month.[68] This left him comparatively free to concentrate on the completion of *Nickleby*, and his progress reports become resolute and positive in tone. On 9 February he recorded in his diary that he was 'thinking about' it, that is to say about the twelfth (March) number.[69] Probably by 14 February 1839 composition was in full swing, as he reports to

[65] *Letters*, 1.473: to John Forster, [21 December 1838].
[66] *Letters*, 1.493: to John Noble, [?21 January 1839].
[67] *Letters*, 1.496: to Charles Hicks, [?26 January 1839].
[68] Slater 2009, 128–30; *Letters*, 1.490–1 (491): to John Forster, [4 January 1839].
[69] *Letters*, 1.640.

Forster: 'I have gallantly refused dinner Invitations from Talfourd, Milnes, Elliotson, and two others, and really begin to hope that I shall be able to *keep on* at Nickleby. Tomorrow we are obliged to go to [the composer] Hullah's, which makes it the more necessary that I should stick like a leech to Nicholas to-night. | I will report progress on Sunday if you dine here.'[70] On the 22nd he writes triumphantly: 'Nickleby is finished—and (I think) as good a Number as the last.... I begin again (God willing) on Monday!!!'[71] It is not recorded whether or not he began the thirteenth (April) number as early as this. In any case, it was still in progress in the middle of March when he wrote to Forster on a Friday, probably after his return from a week in Devon arranging country accommodation for his parents in what turned out to be a vain attempt to exile his father from the capital so that he would run up fewer debts: 'I must be alone in my glory to-day and see what I can do. I perpetrated a great amount of work yesterday and have every day since Monday, but I must buckle to again and endeavour to get the Steam up. If this were to go on long, I should "bust" the boiler. | I think Mrs. Nickleby's love scene will come out rather unique.'[72] A week later he was still 'busy finishing' the number,[73] and the rest of the month was to involve 'a hard week's work and very late hours at my Desk',[74] partly with the preparation of copy for *The Pic-Nic Papers*, a set of stories and occasional papers by various hands to be published in aid of John Macrone's widow and children, partly with *Nickleby* proof correction.[75]

On Sunday 7 April 1839 Dickens was making rather slow progress with the fourteenth (May) number, having to sort out a potential conflict between the demands of serial publication and the best conduct of the narrative for eventual continuous reading in volume form: 'I am doing the Snail at present—not the Railroad, and if I finish the next No. by next Saturday shall consider myself well off. The devil of it is, that I am afraid I must spoil a number now and then, for the sake of the book. It's a hard case, but I *ought* to be hard as iron to my own

[70] *Letters*, 1.508: to John Forster, [?14 February 1839].

[71] *Letters*, 1.511–12: to John Forster, [?22 February 1839].

[72] *Letters*, 1.527: to John Forster, [15 March 1839].

[73] *Letters*, 1.529: to W. C. Macready, [22 March 1839].

[74] *Letters*, 1.529: to Frank Stone, [?23 March 1839].

[75] *Letters*, 1.529: to Henry Colburn, 25 March 1839; 1.533: to John Forster, [?26 March 1839]. John Macrone (1809–37), Dickens's first publisher, had died prematurely on 9 September 1837 leaving his widow and three children in straitened circumstances.

inclinations and do so.'[76] This number advances several plot lines at once, perhaps moving the action along at a faster pace than Dickens would have liked. The first chapter (43) sets the rather hectic pace with its title 'Officiates as a kind of gentleman usher, in bringing various people together' and its repeated emphasis on the unlikely coincidence of Nicholas encountering Frank Cheeryble for the first time in a fracas with the register-office clerk. The number also introduces Brooker and Snawley, as well as accommodating contrasting domestic scenes involving the Mantalinis and Nicklebys. Four days later Dickens informs Macready: 'Nicklebeian fetters bind me here to-night. I may not sup abroad.'[77] The hard work paid off, though, and by 15 April not only was the number evidently complete but the first chapter of the June number had been composed, as Dickens announces in a triumphantly italicized postscript to a letter to Thomas Mitton: '*15th:* end *of 1st. chapter in next No.*'[78]

At the end of April Dickens arranged the rental of a cottage for his family and himself at Petersham in Surrey (now in the London Borough of Richmond) for four months, to enable him to finish *Nickleby* with a minimum of interruption.[79] The first fruits were the early delivery of copy for the fifteenth (June) number, as evidenced in amused terms by a letter, probably of 10 May, to Charles Hicks:

> The copy which precedes that now inclosed has gone to Mr. Browne, who will send it to Chapman and Hall who will send it to you. In the first half of slip 20, "Cray" is written for "Bray", and "Janet" for "Madeline". Perhaps you will alter this, if you remember it, and save your readers some botheration. Please to be careful of the MS.
>
> Send me the proof, if you please, by the twopenny post. I hope to get on like a house on fire, and will of course come up to town to correct the last chapters, and lose no time in sending copy as I write it.
>
> My compliments to Mr. Evans and ask him *what* will be his feelings when he gets the copy on the 10th.[80]

[76] *Letters*, 1.540: to Thomas Mitton, [7 April 1839].

[77] *Letters*, 1.542: to W. C. Macready, [11 April 1839].

[78] *Letters*, 1.544: to Thomas Mitton, [15 April 1839]. The editors of the correspondence wrongly take the postscript to refer to the first chapter of the May number, leading them to conclude that Dickens had taken over a week to write it.

[79] *Letters*, 1.640 (diary). Dickens was still at Doughty Street on 8 May (*Letters*, 1.548), so the diary entry for 30 April probably refers to the signing of the lease.

[80] *Letters*, 1.549: to Charles Hicks, [?10 May 1839].

This is the number incorporating Dickens's revenge on Moncrieff for his shameless dramatization *Nicholas Nickleby and Poor Smike*, which opened at the Strand on 20 May (see note to 640.26). The smooth initial progress in the country faltered somewhat with the sixteenth (July) number (Chapters 49–51). On 18 June, finding himself late again with copy, Dickens wrote humorously to Bradbury and Evans:

> I am quite astonished to find that you have not received the whole copy of the next No. which I can only conclude *must* have been stolen by some blackguard coachman.
>
> Always ready to spare you trouble and uneasiness, I have rewritten the first chapter and will with great pleasure re-write the rest. The number will be a *leetle* later than I could wish, but this you will attribute (I know) to my good nature and friendliness, and the immorality of the Richmond coachmen, who are very benighted indeed. I know you are overflowing with gratitude, but that you needn't mention I assure you.
>
> I send the first chapter with this.[81]

Evidently Dickens had left himself no choice, as he confessed to another correspondent, but to 'shut myself up for my monthly labours, and remain shut up for ten days to come'.[82]

The composition of the last four numbers of *Nickleby* (19 and 20 being issued as a double number for October) seems to have proceeded comparatively smoothly. It was not an easy task, as Dickens explained to Blanchard on 11 July while he was at work on No. 17 (August: Chapters 52–4): 'I am very glad to read what you say about Nicholas. It is very difficult indeed to wind up so many people *in parts*, and make each part tell by itself, but I hope to go out with flying colours notwithstanding. I have been at work all day, so if this note is illegible it's not my fault, but number seventeen's, which is yet an infant.'[83] Planning negotiations with Chapman and Hall for post-*Nickleby* arrangements made it difficult for him to devote his full attention to the task in hand, as he informed Forster: 'You will see that I have been thinking the subject over. Indeed I have been doing so to the great stoppage of Nickleby and the great worrying and fidgetting of myself.'[84] But on the 26th he was able to send Mrs Macready,

[81] *Letters*, 1.556: to Messrs Bradbury & Evans, 18 June 1839.
[82] *Letters*, 1.556: to Mary Berry (of Twickenham), [?June 1839].
[83] *Letters*, 1.560–1 (561): to S. Laman Blanchard, [11] July 1839.
[84] *Letters*, 1.562–5 (562): to John Forster, [14 July 1839].

newly delivered of a son, 'an early proof of the next Number', which includes Chapter 52 featuring Mr Kenwigs's baby.[85]

On 3 September 1839 Dickens moved with his family from Surrey, where he must have completed No. 18 (September), to Broadstairs on the east coast of Kent for the month, and the next day he was 'Getting to rights, and thinking of the end of Nickleby'.[86] He communicates his detailed calculations for the final straight to Hicks on Sunday 15 September:

> I send you 60 slips of copy, and the preface. I shall write 105 which will about settle your business—perhaps not more than 100, and perhaps between the two. I hope I *may* finish on Thursday—at latest on Friday—I will send you another parcel before the last, and dispatch the very last one with all possible speed.
>
> You had better send proofs (I think) by Dovor Coach from the Golden Cross Charing Cross. Be sure that I will correct the last proofs without an instant's delay, and find speedy means of returning them to you. Let me have duplicates of all the proofs you send, and send them as often as you please. The titles of 2 chapters are wanting in the copy inclosed. I will supply them when I correct.
>
> On Saturday morning Mr. Forster is coming down to me. Anything sent to him on Friday night, he will bring.[87]

Three days later he elaborates to Forster:

> I plainly see that I must come to town on Saturday, or I shall delay the proofs terribly, and perhaps endanger the appearance of the No.... I am very anxious that you should see the conclusion of Nickleby, the preface &c before it finally leaves my hands. I have therefore written to Hicks telling him to send proofs to your chambers on Saturday evening, and a note beforehand, saying when they may be expected. If you don't object, we will devote the evening to a careful reading.... I shall not finish entirely, before Friday—sending Hicks the last 20 pages of MS by the Night coach. I have had pretty stiff work as you may suppose, and I have taken great pains.[88]

[85] *Letters*, 1.571–2 (571): to W. C. Macready, 26 July 1839.

[86] *Letters*, 1.641 (diary).

[87] *Letters*, 1.580: to Charles Hicks, [15 September 1839]; compare 1.642 (diary), where Dickens also notes that he wrote the Preface to *Nicholas Nickleby* on 15 September.

[88] *Letters*, 1.581–2 (581): to John Forster, [18 September 1839].

At last, on 20 September, Dickens recorded in his diary: 'Finished Nickleby this day at 2 o'Clock, and went over to Ramsgate with Fred and Kate, to send the last little chapter to Bradbury and Evans in a parcel. | Thank God that I have lived to get through it happily.'[89] The following day he met Forster according to appointment: 'To town to day (by steam from Ramsgate) to correct proofs. Dined with Forster, and went carefully through the whole No. with him. We did not finish 'till past midnight. Slept at home. Wet through, weary, and happy to have finished.'[90]

The final, double, number was published ten days later. Between the now-familiar pages of advertisements, it contained four plates—three illustrations for the last two chapters, and a portrait of Dickens engraved after a specially-commissioned painting by Daniel Maclise—followed by four pages of publisher's announcements, the first for proof impressions of the portrait and the fourth for the forthcoming one-volume issue. (For further discussion of the portrait, see Appendix 4, 933–4). These pages were followed by the final chapters 59 to 65, amounting to 48 pages, and by 16 pages of traditional preliminary material—the half-title, title page, dedication, preface, contents, and list of plates—for purchasers who might wish to bind their monthly numbers into book form. The first readers, who had followed the adventures of the Nickleby family month by month, were now able to read Dickens's Preface, in effect an Afterword, written in retrospect to explain and clarify certain misunderstandings, and to say 'farewell' to those who had followed him so faithfully. He writes as a 'periodical essayist', yet the sharp-eyed might have noticed that the new title page, with the simplified title *The Life and Adventures of Nicholas Nickleby*, inspired by the running heads of the monthly numbers, reads, not 'Edited by "Boz"' but 'By Charles Dickens'.

At the beginning of October, Dickens resumed residence at Doughty Street after a four-month absence from town, intending to go 'forthwith tooth and nail' at *Nickleby*'s long-delayed successor *Barnaby Rudge*.[91] Meanwhile, *Nicholas Nickleby* was published in volume form on the 23rd, and on the 25th Dickens was able to send

[89] *Letters*, 1.642.

[90] *Letters*, 1.643 (diary: Saturday, 21 September 1839).

[91] *Letters*, 1.589: to George Cruikshank, [?3 October 1839]. In the event, *The Old Curiosity Shop* intervened.

the dedicatee William Macready a finely bound presentation copy: 'The book, the whole book, and nothing but the book (except the binding which is an important item) has arrived at last, and is forwarded herewith. The red represents my blushes at its gorgeous dress; the gilding all those bright professions which I do *not* make to you; and the book itself my whole heart for twenty months, which should be yours for so short a term, as you have it always.'[92]

Two more aspects of the *Nickleby* compositional process merit additional notice. First, each number normally contained two illustrations produced by Hablot Browne in consultation with the author. An extended treatment of these is to be found in Appendix 4, 929–35. And secondly there is the version of scenes derived from Chapters 7, 8, 9, 12, and 13, which Dickens prepared specially for his immensely popular reading tours in later years. Despite reservations about the initial draft,[93] he persevered over a long weekend in August 1861 with an adaptation of the school scenes from *Nickleby*, beginning with Squeers and the boys breakfasting at the Saracen's Head and ending with Nicholas's flight south with Smike. Somewhat to his surprise, it was received with enormous enthusiasm during his first season in the autumn of that year when it was usually paired with the trial scene from *Pickwick*. After a triumphant evening at Norwich he wrote to Wilkie Collins:

> [t]he people were really quite ridiculous to see, when Squeers read the boys' letters. And I am inclined to suspect that the impression of protection and hope, derived from Nickleby's going away protecting Smike, is exactly the impression—this is discovered by chance—that an Audience most likes to be left with.[94]

Five years later, in order to accommodate a companion reading of *Dr. Marigold*, Dickens produced a shorter version omitting Fanny Squeers's tea-party (which involved rewriting the opening of the next section in which Smike is found to be missing), and cutting some of the descriptive passages, as well as many small changes of wording. This adaptation met with less success, the audiences having responded

[92] *Letters*, 1.593–4 (593): to W. C. Macready, 25 October 1839.
[93] *Letters*, 9.447: to Wilkie Collins, 28 August 1861.
[94] *Letters*, 9.489–90: to Wilkie Collins, 31 October 1861 (490).

particularly to Fanny, 'Tilda, and John Browdie, and it was not repeated in subsequent years.[95]

The manuscript. Approximately one-tenth of the manuscript of *Nicholas Nickleby* is known to have survived. Six chapters from the first third of the novel (9, 10, 15, 16, 17, and 20) are complete or nearly so, along with a few smaller fragments from the final chapters. Details appear in 'Textual Witnesses' (940–3).

Dickens writes on small leaves, or 'slips', averaging some 175 words per leaf in the manuscript that survives from the earlier part of the novel, rising to around 300 words towards the end.[96] His handwriting at this early stage in his career is fairly easy to read. He writes fluently: some leaves have no changes at all, and few have more than ten, mostly involving single words; across the surviving manuscript the average is five or six. (The changes in question are verbal: purely punctuational changes are by their nature usually difficult to identify in manuscript.) There are a small number of false starts or minor changes of direction locally, but no sign of any major second thoughts in spite of the relaxed narrative structure: there may, of course, have been substantial shifts elsewhere in the manuscript, but that cannot now be known. It is clear from internal evidence that many of the changes were made in the course of the initial composition whereas others were introduced on a subsequent reading through, perhaps before resuming composition after a break. Some passages seem to have been written with particular ease: for example Fanny and 'Tilda dressing for the tea-party in Chapter 9, the stunned reaction to Fanny Squeers's letter in Chapter 15, the encounter between Mr Gregsbury and Pugstyles in Chapter 16, Miss Knag's introduction to Kate in Chapter 17, and Miss La Creevy's reunion with Nicholas in Chapter 20.

In the surviving manuscript there are approximately one thousand verbal changes; presumably there might have been ten times that number if it had been complete. The most frequent reason for the alternatives is stylistic enhancement, a broad category accounting for roughly half the total. Sometimes a clumsy repetition of a word is

[95] Philip Collins, 'The Texts of Dickens' Readings', *Bulletin of the New York Public Library*, 74 (1970), 360–80 (372–3); Philip Collins, 'The Dickens Reading-Copies in Dickens House', *Dickensian*, 68 (1972), 173–9 (178).

[96] See Patten, 71n.: Patten's calculation is confirmed by the sole surviving complete leaf from the later part of the manuscript held by the Morgan Library.

eliminated: at 126.21–4 Dickens avoids repeating 'tears' by replacing the first instance of the word with 'traces of emotion'; and at 202.8–9 he changes 'get into . . . get it into' to 'get into . . . put it in'. Dickens introduces one alternative in a string of 'said's at 122.19–28: 'said Ralph . . . said Miss La Creevy . . . said Ralph . . . <said> ↑replied↓ Miss La Creevy . . . said Ralph'; for the last two speeches in the exchange he avoids ascriptions altogether, and at proof stage he was to improve the still rather awkward sequence by substituting 'cried Ralph' for the third ascription. On occasion, though, Dickens actually introduces repetition for rhetorical enhancement: at 180.24 'I could take no other part than I have chosen' becomes 'I could take no other part than I have taken'; at 197.12 'all along the passage, and all up the narrow stairs' becomes 'all along the narrow passage, and all along the narrow stairs'; and at 198.18–19 Gregsbury is made to address Pugstyles as 'my worthy friend . . . my dear friend' rather than 'my worthy friend . . . my dear fellow'. Sometimes Dickens replaces an adequate word with a sharper *mot juste*: Miss Squeers speaks 'archly' rather than 'playfully' (111.24); an iron door opens 'with <fierce> ↑slow↓ obstinacy' (131.21); Mr Gregsbury is '<glad> ↑rejoiced↑' to see the delegation (197.38); and Miss La Creevy says that 'head-aches don't <cause> occasion red eyes' (252.15–16). In a more complex example Nicholas is 'a proud, haughty, <supercilious> ↑consequential↓, <beggarly> turned-up-nosed <young fellow."> <young dog> ↑peacock↓' (104.23–4). Examples demonstrate Dickens's simple but effective enhancement of rhetoric: 'It's ↑all↓ along of you Mr. Nickleby' (115.35); 'The word slipped from my lips, I <didn't> ↑did not↓ mean it indeed' (128.7); and 'beg him to love you <always> all his life ↑through↓' (185.20–1). Other typically effective stylistic enhancements appear in the following: 'young ladies . . . will <be jealous of> ↑jostle↓ each other <(though that [?]> in the race to the altar' (117.9–10); Mrs Nickleby '<With> ↑Pouring forth↓ these, and a perfectly wonderful train of other disjointed expressions of regret' (261.15–16); and Miss La Creevy bitterly observing that Ralph has gone forth 'on some ↑kind,↓ charitable business I dare <swear> say' (255.18–19). One can observe the cumulative effect of a series of small stylistic sharpenings in the passage where Mantalini is introduced: 'His name <had b> was originally Muntle <which> ↑but it↓ had <become> ↑been converted↓, by an easy transition, <Mantolini> into <Mantalini> Mantalini' (130.3–5).

Not all Dickens's changes are enhancements. Some seem at best neutral or evenly balanced: 'And <accordingly> ↑so↓ Miss Squeers made up her mind…' (107.11–12); Nicholas and 'John Browdie shook hands across the table with <great solemnity> much gravity' (113.36–7); 'a fever or some unpleasantness of that <kind> ↑sort↓' (186.28–9); 'a tendency to cultivate mustachios and look <ferocious> fierce' (208.2); and 'London is as <great> <a desert> ↑complete a solitude↓ as the plains of Syria' (253.28).

Rather more than 150 of the changes made in the manuscript may be said to add nuance and flavour. Dickens can change the tone, as when he deletes 'poor' before 'Kenwigs' (185.9), or when he eliminates 'very' twice: 'This was wholly unintelligible to Nicholas who had no other distinct impression on his mind at the moment, than that Miss Squeers was a→an <very> ordinary looking girl, and her friend Miss Price a <very> pretty one' (114.32–4). A small but important shift results in Nicholas having a 'young and ardent' rather than 'proud and ardent' spirit (261.7, 'young' being substituted above the line). On the same page Kate speaks 'with honest anger', rather than merely 'angrily', a change made as the phrase was being written (261.20); shortly afterwards, when Nicholas speaks to Kate, Dickens adds the adverb 'tenderly', and then (the word now being appropriate) 'proudly' (261.37, 262.3). Dickens inserts or alters details of description or action: Mantalini wears a morning gown 'with ↑a waistcoat and↓ Turkish trousers of the same pattern' (129.7); Pugstyles is a 'plump <little> ↑old↓ gentleman' (198.12); as Gregsbury prepares to dismiss Nicholas, Dickens makes him ring the bell by adding 'ringing' after 'said Mr. Gregsbury' (205.26); 'Miss La Creevy ↑had a hearty laugh, and↓ went home to breakfast, in great good humour' (253.17–18); Kate is described as 'throwing herself on her brother's shoulder ↑and clasping him in her arms↓' (261.32–3).

On at least two occasions Dickens had second thoughts about characters' names: for a second or two 'Tilda was Mary Anne (at 110.8), and John Browdie was briefly Browder (from 112.33 to 113.21). Two false starts involve rejected chapter titles: Chapter 9 (103) was originally to be headed (in part at least) 'Mrs. Squeers takes a dislike to Nicholas, and another lady takes a liking to him', and Chapter 20 (252) first read 'Nicholas ↑at length↓ encounters his uncle who exhibits great composure'.

Dickens does not usually cut material in the manuscript, but there are some thirty occasions when he strikes out a detail. He originally wrote: 'A decent annuity would have restored her [Mrs Nickleby's] thoughts to their old train and her husband would have become again a martyr to unmerited misfortune'; but he trimmed the passage so that 'train and her husband ... misfortune' reads simply 'train at once' (125.6–7). Later in the same chapter Kate says she will pay no attention to Mantalini 'with so much quiet contempt that the gentleman seemed rather put down', which Dickens again abbreviates, to 'with quiet contempt' (131.29). When Gregsbury is dismissing Nicholas, Dickens seems to have considered another speech before abandoning it: ' "Door, <Toby"—said Mr> Matthews"—said Mr. Gregsbury as the boy appeared. <"Door for a gentleman who thinks fifteen shillings a week> <'not mu>'. A few lines later he omits a phrase: ' "Door, Matthews—cried Mr Gregsbury. <with angry emphasis.>' (205.28, 33). At her workshop Madame Mantalini 'led the way down ↑a flight of <old>↓ stairs ↑and↓ through a <long> passage' (215.8–9).

Some fifty of Dickens's changes in the manuscript can be attributed to a desire to clarify points. This may involve the insertion of a single word: Miss Squeers at 23 was presumed to have possessed the normal graces of a woman of 'that ↑particular↓ period of life' (103.27–8); Squeers goes 'to fetch three <boys> new boys and dun the relations of two old ones' (110.14–15); Mantalini will ride a fine new horse 'in the park before the very chariots of the ↑rejected↓ countesses' (214.15–16). Dickens adds small directional pointers: 'and ↑furthermore↓ the allusion to Nicholas's nose, which was not intended to be taken in its literal sense, but ↑rather↓ to bear a latitude of construction according to the <?respe> fancy of the hearers' (104.27–30); 'Newman had parried these questions as long as he could, but being ↑at length↓ hard pressed and driven into a corner ...' (207.2–4). Some clarifications are more elaborately explanatory: 'whoever was ↑first↓ engaged to be married <first should> should straightway confide the mighty secret to the bosom of the other, before communicating it to any living soul ↑and bespeak her as bridesmaid without loss of time↓; in fulfilment of which pledge the miller's daughter ↑when her engagement was formed↓ came out express at eleven o'clock at night' (108.37–109.3); '<Tired> Exhausted as I am, ↑and standing in no common need of rest↓ I <could> ↑can↓ not ↑hope to↓ close my eyes all night unless you <had told> tell me everything' (180.19–20).

On another fifty or so occasions Dickens exhibits a tendency to hesitation in composition, a feature that became more pronounced in his later years. He will write, or begin to write, a word, delete it, and then reinstate it, sometimes after trying an alternative, or eventually reject it: 'try <things> things on for people' (215.30–1); 'Kate's part in the <pag> pageant' (220.11); 'the finery <that> ↑<which> that↓ bedecks the thoughtless and luxurious' (210.17–18); 'Nicholas had husbanded his <scant> scanty stock of money' (179.10); '<being> <feeling> ↑<being> feeling↓ uncertain' (118.13).

In some forty instances, Dickens runs ahead of himself and steps back to insert a point before returning to his original train of thought. Thus, when Squeers anticipates 'such time as little Wackford is able to take charge of the school', Dickens starts a speech by the lad ('"Oh! won't I ?re'), then deletes it for an additional exchange of two speeches before allowing the boy to detail his anticipated treatment of the pupils (105.11–19). Towards the end of the same chapter there is a similar instance where, after Miss Squeers has retorted 'making another face', Dickens has Miss Price respond 'You needn't make yourself uglier than you are Ma'am': he deletes this and substitutes above the line the printed response beginning '"You are monstrous polite' and follows it with Miss Squeers's reply before reviving Miss Price's original speech, now with 'plainer' for 'uglier' (117.21–7). Examples of stepping back on a smaller scale include Mantalini's 'Two demd fine <real> women, real countesses and splendid fortunes' (213.31–2) and 'but <freezes up the> extending its influence to <hollow> summer friends, freezes up the sources of good-will and kindness' (219.8–9).

On over thirty occasions Dickens seems to have had difficulty working out how a passage should run. This is often the case in his later manuscripts, but it is rare in these early years. In Chapter 9 Mrs Squeers 'got up outside the coach as it stopped to change at Greta Bridge, <with> <a little basket> ↑<taking <bearing> with her a <certain ?net bag> small bundle↓ containing <a brandy> ↑something in a↓ bottle and ↑some↓ sandwiches' (110.17–19). In Chapter 17 the narrator says of Kate in her unhappiness at the Mantalini establishment: '<but as she h> <as she had> but she was too young <and too much hurt> for such consolation, and her honest <pride was hurt> feeling was hurt' (220.30–1). And in Chapter 20 he observes of Miss Knag 'Here was one of the advantages of <being> ↑having lived↓ <so much> alone ↑so long <for <<years>> so many years>↓ <One of the many who from the absence of any early associations connected with>' (253.19).

In seventy or so instances Dickens starts in a new direction but immediately has second thoughts. These backtrackings tend to be on a small scale: as when Miss Squeers says '"...it would be a pity to interrupt wouldn't it Mr. Browdie? He! he! he!"' and Dickens starts a new paragraph with '"I deant know' (116.11–12). What Browdie was going to say will never be known, as Dickens rejects the idea and deletes the three words. Shortly afterwards he continues another of Fanny Squeers's speeches: '"I scorn your words, minx" said Miss Squeers. <"—coming into people's houses>' (117.39). Some twenty of these second thoughts appear at the beginning of a new leaf where Dickens abandons not only what he has written but the whole leaf, usually resuming the writing on the other side which now becomes the recto. Most of the examples are again small-scale, so that it is difficult to see why he did not simply continue writing after the deletion: perhaps he simply preferred not to start a new leaf with a crossing-out. Sometimes the difference between the deleted version and the final manuscript version is very slight: thus 'Nicholas Nickleby' becomes 'Nicholas' (104.7), and in a more extensive false start a little later in the same chapter the only difference between the final text of the rejected version and that on the new recto ('Squeers's life...The infantine appeal' at 105.20–4) is that the former has 'This infantine app[eal]' and the latter 'The infantine appeal' (a repeated 'burst' is changed to 'shout' in a revision of the new recto). In some cases Dickens has a more fundamental change of mind, though always on a local level. Where one of Gregsbury's speeches first continued at a leaf end 'land, I admit the full justice of the <accusation> remark. I am proud of <my free> this free and happy country, <and my bones> beneath whose soil my bones will one day', the new recto has 'land, I admit the full justice of the remark. I *am* proud of this free and happy country. My form dilates...' (199.6–8). In a similar transformation Miss Knag originally said on the new leaf 'who had such small feet that they were no bigger than those they put upon wooden legs. He had been rather wild as a boy Madame Mantalini, as a great many men are, you know, more or less,': on the new recto this reads 'who had such <small> small feet that they were no bigger than those which are usually <put upon> ↑joined to↓ wooden legs—the most symmetrical <?sh> feet Madame Mantalini that even you can imagine' (216.7–10).

There are two examples of more substantial second thoughts. The first occurs in the account of Gregsbury's reception of the delegation in Chapter 16. After 'read the questions.' (199.17–18) the manuscript has:

> "'Question Number one'"—said Mr Pugstyles reading slowly, and in something of a <gre> snoring tone as most men in spectacles do "'Did you ↑not↓ Sir, give a voluntary pledge to vote for <annual parliaments and> universal suffrage and <bian> triennial parliaments<[?]">?'"
>
> "No" replied Mr Gregsbury.
>
> "Oh!" groaned the deputation. It made quite a little couplet.
>
> "No. I did not"—said Mr Gregsbury <amiably> ↑warmly.↓ "An illiterate voter in the crowd, enquired if I would vote for universal suffering and triangular parliaments, to which I replied (jestingly) 'by all means'."
>
> Another <suppr> half-suppressed groan.
>
> "'Question Number two. Did you not Sir

At this point Dickens breaks off and deletes everything before taking a fresh slip to write the final version starting with 'This done'. Probably he found the humour in the rejected passage below par. The other substantial change of mind resulted in the deletion of a concluding sentence for Chapter 20, after Nicholas tells Smike 'we will be poor together." (264.14): '"I tell you"—said Nicholas "that the same fate shall be ours in life, and the same grave shall hold us both in death."' Even with *Nickleby*'s loose structure, Dickens probably knew this was unlikely to be the case.

Changes between manuscript and first edition. Between the surviving portions of the manuscript of *Nicholas Nickleby* and its first appearance in print there are approximately one hundred verbal differences and over two thousand non-verbal (mostly punctuation). There are no surviving proofs, so it is impossible to know for certain if a particular change was authorial or made in the printing house: for more detail, see 'The Present Edition' (905–8).

In spite of their large number, which would suggest as many as 20,000 in the complete novel, the non-verbal differences require little discussion. In the early nineteenth century it was generally understood that it was part of the compositors' job to provide the punctuation. Thus in the case of the Waverley Novels, originally published between 1814 and 1831, Walter Scott provided only indicative punctuation, with extensive use of the dash, knowing that the compositors would provide his manuscripts (actually copies of the original made to maintain his theoretical anonymity as the Author of Waverley) with the punctuation necessary for their public appearance.[97] Although Dickens's manuscript punctuation is much more assiduous than Scott's, it is clear that for *Nicholas Nickleby* he too expected, and indeed relied on, his printers to upgrade it for public consumption. Most obviously he could afford to be cavalier about handwriting idiosyncrasies, such as the omission of some 150 full stops in the surviving manuscript. Printers render Dickens's manuscript dashes as commas on some 250 occasions, particularly at the end of speeches. No doubt Dickens expected the compositors to augment his manuscript punctuation: in the first printed text derived from the surviving manuscript portions, over 1,250 commas are added (with only 25 or so deleted), more than 100 commas become semicolons, and nearly 50 semicolons are added. The additional punctuation is partly grammatical, partly rhetorical, in the usual period fashion. One short paragraph boasting five inserted commas will illustrate the procedure: '"If that is all you want↑,↓" said Nicholas↑,↓ pointing to the pen↑,↓ and smiling↑,↓ in spite of himself↑,↓ at the affected embarrassment of the schoolmaster's daughter, "perhaps I can supply his place."' (107.34–6). There are also some 75 instances of initial capital letters being changed to lower case, mostly when a speech continues after the ascription, and nearly 150 spelling changes.

The hundred or so verbal changes made between the surviving manuscript and the first printed text parallel to some extent the alterations Dickens made in the course of composition, and the vast majority are likely to be authorial. Nearly half of them seem to have been intended as stylistic improvements. Clumsy repetitions are amended: as at 132.16–18, where Madame Mantalini originally 'looked at the door as if <ind> she wished to be gone, but hesitated notwithstanding as if unwilling to leave to Mr Mantalini the sole honor of shewing them down stairs', 'as though' replacing the second

[97] See David Hewitt's General Introduction to the Edinburgh Edition of the Waverley Novels (30 vols, Edinburgh, 1993–2012), Vols 1–23b.

'as if'; and at 221.8–9, where the printed text reads 'I think she was; indeed, now I come to think of it, I am sure she was', the manuscript twice has 'it' for 'she', resulting in three neighbouring occurrences of that word. In general the stylistic enhancements are very modest. In one speech by Nicholas 'What could I be hardly expected to undergo?' becomes 'What could I hardly be expected to undergo?', matching the preceding speech by Newman, and 'assistant to the brutal pedagogue' is changed to 'assistant to a brutal pedagogue' (206.20, 27). When Kate says 'It is some base conspiracy which carries its <?on> own falsehood along with it' the published version slims 'along with it' down to 'with it' (256.25–6), and the same thing happens shortly afterwards when Nicholas asks 'Who speaks in a tone as if I had done wrong and brought disgrace on those I love?' (257.38–9), 'those I love' becoming 'them'. There are two instances where a more precisely appropriate word is substituted for the manuscript original: 'steam-boats' for 'steam ships' (on rivers) at 198.28, and 'complicated' for 'extraordinary' in the 'most complicated state of perplexity' attributed to Mrs Nickleby (256.35–6).

A handful of the verbal changes in the transition from manuscript to print were evidently made to clarify things for the reader: 'then' is inserted in Madame Mantalini's 'Miss Knag the forewoman shall ↑then↓ have directions to try you with some easy work at first' (132.11–13); an ambiguity is eliminated when Kenwigs refers to 'that pound or two which I shall <have to> leave among your children when I die' (185.17–18); and a temporal locator is inserted when Ralph says 'I hold out no threat ↑now↓' (260.29).

On several occasions manuscript errors were observed and rectified for the first edition, including three curious instances of 'gentleman' for 'gentlemen' (197.25, 27; 207.38) and 'overstopping' for 'overstepping' (203.3). Differences in verbal forms which may arguably be classed among the verbal variants occur when the manuscript's 'anything' becomes 'any thing' (107.28, 111.26, 252.21) and 'Hallo' becomes 'Hollo' (129.1): the present text emends these. The handful of likely misreadings of, or inadvertent omissions from, the manuscript by Dickens's original compositors are discussed under 'The Present Edition' (907–8).

Changes in the sense are rare, and small in scale. Dickens probably deleted 'simple' from Newman's 'Such simple preparations' because he thought the adjective redundant (179.15), and a similar deletion in 'a few moments <deep> reflection' responds to an illogicality (182.19). The deletion of 'and villainy' from 'malice and villainy' and the substitution of 'poverty or suffering' for 'poverty and suffering' have minimal effects on the sense (180.10, 27). The most telling change in the sense involves the upgrading of the amusing disapproval by Lillyvick of the French language, where the manuscript reads: '"What's water in French Sir?" | "<*L'eau*> ↑*Eau*↓" replied Nicholas. | "Ah!" said Mr Lillyvick shaking his head "I thought as much. I don't think anything of that language—nothing at all." The first edition has 'the water', recovers Dickens's original conception with '*L'Eau*', and inserts 'mournfully,' and 'Lo, eh?' (209.32–6). The manuscript actually had '*L'Eau*' originally but Dickens replaced it with '*Eau*', so that in the first edition he is recovering his initial concept through a change he must have introduced at proof stage.

Ten passages of significant length were cut at proof stage, presumably because Dickens had overwritten the normal allocation for 32 pages of print. The first five of these occur in No. 3: three from Chapter 9 being short additional exchanges between Nicholas and 'Tilda Price, and Fanny Squeers and 'Tilda, in the same vein as much of the dialogue in this scene; two from Chapter 10 involving a particularly bitter set of remarks by Ralph, and a brief two-sentence exchange between Kate and her mother. The sixth and seventh, much longer, passages are from the conclusion to the exuberantly-written Chapter 15 in No. 5, where there was no room for an extended description of Miss Petowker's rendering of the 'Blood Drinker's Burial' or Mrs Kenwigs's alarm on behalf of her children. The remaining three passages, from No. 6, Chapter 20, are arguably of most interest, emphasizing Nicholas's new self-awareness, and Smike's increasing reliance on him. All of these passages are printed in Appendix 3 (925–8).

Over the course of the edition a number of variant readings appeared, often progressively and by no means consistently, with the result that none of the copies seen (whether fully collated or in other cases spot-checked) were identical, and all exhibited a different combination of variant states.[98] It is likely that further copies might

[98] In addition to the four copies of 39A and two of 39B collated and listed under 'Textual Witnesses', three further copies of 39A (two at the British Library and one personal copy in possession of Elizabeth James) have been spot-checked for known variants.

contain additional variants but, leaving aside printing flaws such as quod and plate marks, around 100 seems a reasonable estimate. The majority—almost two-thirds—involve printing defects, such as broken letters (the ascenders of 'h' and 'd' being particularly vulnerable) and missing punctuation (especially full stops and quotation marks), most of which tended to occur in later impressions due to the deterioration of type or plates. The one-volume issue, for example, contained over 50 defects of this kind. At the same time, some fifteen amendments to punctuation were introduced at various stages (amongst them a curious one-off variant observed in some copies of the 1839 volume which places the title of the first story of Chapter 6 within double quotation marks as "THE FIVE SISTERS"), and including eleven corrections of obvious errors which have been adopted as emendations in the present edition, as well as four verbal changes (170.4, 221.14, 235.14, and 632.36) correcting manuscript misreadings. By beginning our investigations with early impressions of the monthly numbers it has proved possible to trace the evolution of some of these changes: so, for example, the single quotation mark before 'My' (89.1) was first altered to two single quotes before eventually being replaced by a double quotation mark. An intriguing question is raised by the first verbal variant where 'visiter' was corrected to 'sister' in response to Dickens's remonstrance with the printer shortly before publication.[99] Evidently his note arrived too late to prevent early issues of No. 4 appearing with the incorrect reading, but the copy sent to the British (Museum) Library on 6 July 1838, barely a week after publication on 30 June, has the correct reading of 'sister'. This suggests either that a replacement leaf was issued for purchasers to substitute for the erroneous page or that the printers acted very quickly to reprint the entire number.[100] In contrast, the second verbal correction from 'latter' to 'letter' in No. 5 appears to have been made relatively late, perhaps only shortly before publication in volume form in October.[101] That issue, comprising the monthly numbers without wrappers and advertisements,

[99] *Letters*, 1.408: to Charles Hicks, [?29 June 1838].

[100] An unbound second copy in the British Library contains both the incorrect and corrected leaf, supporting the likelihood of a cancellans having been issued although further confirmatory evidence would be needed to rule out the possibility of a collector having removed the page from a later printing.

[101] Our findings agree with E. H. Strange's observation that the second issue of No. 5 is 'by no means common as a monthly number'. See his 'Notes on the Bibliography of *Nicholas Nickleby*', *Dickensian*, 33 (1937), 30–3 (32).

with the prelims and portrait published with No. 19 and 20 bound at the front, marked a far-reaching change, arguably as significant as any verbal variant: the transition from monthly serial to novel.

4. LATER EDITIONS

The Cheap Edition

In March 1847 a Prospectus was issued for a collected edition of Dickens's works to be known as the Cheap Edition. Neatly printed in double columns with new prefaces and frontispieces, and published in a range of formats and prices, this was an enterprising scheme designed to reach a wide variety of new readers. The Prefaces, a feature of the edition, were seized upon by Dickens as a means of showing 'what important social improvements have taken place' since the books were originally written.[102] *Nicholas Nickleby* followed *Pickwick* as the second title in the series, appearing in weekly instalments from October 1847 to May 1848, and as a bound volume, using the stereotype plates, on 27 May 1848.[103] It was reissued several times between 1850 and 1866:[104] a collation of the 1857 issue has revealed a few corrections but also a number of new printing defects.

The copy-text for the Cheap Edition was probably an early issue of 1839, at least for Numbers 4 and 15. Both contained erroneous readings—'visiter' for 'sister' (170.4) and 'No' for 'Do' (632.36)—which were quickly corrected for later printings of the original numbers but not picked up, or simply accepted, for the Cheap Edition. Indeed, 'visiter' becomes 'visitors' in tacit acceptance of the mistake. Numerous changes were made for the Cheap Edition text, but by no means consistently. They are heaviest in gatherings B to N (from the beginning to 330.11 in the present text). In contrast, gatherings O to R (330.12–437.12) and Y to BB (542.17–648.28) have only minor compositorial changes (such as 'Sir' to 'sir'),

[102] *Letters*, 5.161 and note: to John Forster, [7 September 1847].

[103] See Simon Nowell-Smith, 'The "Cheap Edition" of Dickens's Works [First Series] 1847–1852', *Library*, 5th series, 22 (1967), 245–51. An incomplete set of weekly parts is held by the Bodleian Library (Vet. A6 e. 574). Nowell-Smith states (249) that the identifying imprints set vertically upwards along the fold of the outermost leaves of each weekly part were removed for the volume, but they are often discernible in the copy belonging to Clive Hurst. A set of monthly parts is held by the Beinecke Library, Yale University (Gimbel/Dickens D5 Set 1, pts 8–16).

[104] Parrott, 39

strongly suggesting that Dickens did not revise these sections and that his attention was concentrated on the first third of the book.

The Cheap Edition makes over 5,000 accidental or non-verbal changes, the general effect being to contribute to the formalization of the text by introducing weightier, more consistent, punctuation. More than 4,000 commas are added, over 500 commas become semi-colons, and more than 200 become colons. Over 150 full stops and commas are upgraded to exclamation marks. In some 70 cases the Cheap Edition breaks compound sentences into two by removing the connecting 'and', while creating more than 120 further new sentence divisions without verbal change. Some of this regularization may have been due to changing fashions in printing, but the introduction of new sentence divisions is likely to have been Dickens's work, or at least not to have raised objections on his part, and we know from his practice in the surviving proofs of other novels that he liked to add commas. The Cheap Edition also corrects 35 errors of punctuation together with 10 or so instances of typographical error or misspelling and a few lapses in spacing.

There are more than 600 substantive or verbal changes and, while there is no firm evidence, most of them were probably the work of Dickens himself. He indicated in an advertisement of 1847 that 'the whole Text' of each title would 'be carefully revised and corrected throughout, by the Author'.[105] One of the first variants eliminates a jocular reference to Russell Square, which Dickens may have found forced: 'a farm, which, exclusive of house and paddock, is about the size of Russell Square, measuring from the street-doors of the houses' (7.3–5) becomes 'a farm, which was as small a landed estate as one would desire to see'. Shortly afterwards one finds the removal of a topical allusion to Mr Seguin, the box-office manager at Her Majesty's Theatre, 'Mr. Seguin gives away the orders' changing to 'they give away the orders' (11.1), and later the name of an inn is altered from 'the George the Fourth' to the perhaps more chronologically appropriate 'the George the Third' (227.11). On four occasions 'Lord Verisopht' becomes 'Lord Frederick' or 'Lord Frederick Verisopht' (243.37, 244.6, 498.2–3, 501.11): Michael Slater plausibly suggests that this change of nomenclature, carried through more consistently in the Charles Dickens Edition, is made because the relentless use of

[105] Parrott, 22.

the satirical 'Verisopht' came to seem inappropriate for 'this character whom in the text the reader is increasingly asked to take seriously, even to admire a little'.[106] One of the last variants, a pointed clarification that Mantalini's partner at the end of the novel is not his wife, is a response to two enquiries Dickens had received on the subject, in 1839 and 1841:[107] he changes 'a buxom female, the proprietress of the concern' to 'a buxom female—not the lawful Madame Mantalini but the proprietress of the concern' (823.39–825.1).

The overall tendency of the revisions, many of them small and involving only single words, is to tighten and formalize, curbing some of the vitality of language and introducing a more restrained narrative style. Much of this effect is achieved by removing redundant words, as in 'murmur <forth> something' (29.10) and '<rather> disposed' (207.37), and adjectives or adverbs in phrases such as 'so much <honest> composure' (261.22) and 'Ralph <sternly> bade' (750.17). Dickens eliminates ten instances of 'very', most of them unnecessary in their context, and often with beneficial results, e.g. 'your remarks are <very> offensive' (113.25–6); 'with the speed of <very> light itself' (284.30–1); 'without attracting any <very> marked attention' (301.32). Words or phrases interpreting speeches are cut on more than twenty occasions, when, for example, 'said Nicholas, smiling' is reduced to 'said Nicholas' (154.31), 'muttered Ralph, gnawing his fingers' to 'muttered Ralph' (787.29), and 'answered Kate, weeping' to 'answered Kate' (219.18), incidentally helping to inject her character with a little of the spirit which becomes more noticeable as the novel progresses. A less welcome deletion of what might be regarded as tautology occurs with the removal of the nicely poetic second sentence from Lord Frederick's hazy recollections of the night of the brawl: '. . . he could not separate the transactions of one time from those of another. <Last night seemed a week ago, and months were as last night.>' (674.8–9). Some fifty changes are intended to tone down melodramatic language, particularly associated with the bitter encounters between Ralph Nickleby and Nicholas but also in the dramatic revelations of the final chapters. Thus Ralph 'went' rather than 'reeled' back into his house (252.3), and regarded his nephew with a 'scowl' instead of a 'scowl of deadly hatred' (257.25–6), while Nicholas

[106] 'A Note on the Text' in the Penguin edition of *Nicholas Nickleby*, 36.
[107] See *Letters*, 1.590–1 and note: to Dr J. H. Hutton, [October 1839].

justified his intervention to save 'a miserable creature from the vilest cruelty' rather than 'a miserable wretched creature from the vilest and most degrading cruelty' as in the first edition (258.18–19). Much later Nicholas is shocked by Madeline's 'clear transparent whiteness' on the day before her wedding, in this case a judicious pruning of 1839's overwrought 'clear transparent cold ghastly whiteness' (703.6). For similar reasons of refinement 'God' is replaced by the more moderate 'Heaven' on eight occasions (e.g. 85.13, 104.12), and once 'damn' is softened to 'curse' (204.14).

There are occasional attempts to improve grammar, and especially to address chronology with the use of the pluperfect. So, for example, within the space of a couple of pages describing the Kenwigs's anniversary party, 'put' becomes 'had put' (169.2), 'kept' becomes 'had kept' (169.6), and 'was' becomes 'had been invented' (171.10). Elsewhere errors are corrected: 'there was present' becomes 'there were present' (301.12–13), 'gentleman were there' becomes 'gentleman was there' (534.2), 'previously' is substituted for 'previous' (267.37), and 'obstacles that' replaces an ugly repetition in 'obstacles which' (701.15). The most consistent change, which may have been the work of a compositor, is the substitution of 'till' with 'until' (e.g. 153.33, 239.24) and 'upon' with 'on' (e.g. 509.8, 731.11–12). Perhaps associated also with a desire for correctness, there are new thoughts on the representation of Yorkshire dialect although these are by no means systematic: 'yours' becomes 'yourn' (141.13) and 'sort' becomes 'sart' (828.12); but in other places 'Draat' becomes 'Drat' (511.6), 'wont' becomes 'want' (511.7), and 'thot' becomes 'that' (513.33).

The 1857 reissue of the Cheap Edition corrected some of the faults of the 1848 printing, but around thirty remain, including two erroneous verbal changes which were carried forward into the Library and Charles Dickens editions. There are at least 150 incidental differences between the two issues, mostly affecting punctuation, and almost all the result of worn and damaged plates or poor printing. As a result copies appear to vary, with some printing faults in one copy less apparent or not present at all in another.

The Library Edition

The Library Edition was designed as a handsomely printed collected edition for wealthier readers, though, lacking illustrations and drably bound, it was not a commercial success.[108] *Nicholas Nickleby* was the second title, published as volumes three and four of the edition in February and March 1858, in a print run of 2,000. The text was based closely on the Cheap Edition, with few alterations and no obvious authorial involvement: on 6 December 1857 Dickens wrote to the printer Frederick Evans: 'Your printing from the Cheap Edition, had best go on without waiting for me. If I see anything wrong in the sheets you send me, I will let you know of it promptly.'[109]

Only a limited number of non-verbal changes from 1848 appear, most noticeably the addition of nearly 150 commas and the deletion of some 200. Amongst them are a few which might be considered improvements, such as the restoration of the first-edition comma in 'You are, my love' (276.25) and the deletion of another comma after 'who' in the phrase 'found out a man, who plainly . . . ' (685.24). One remaining misspelling of 'Snevellicci' is corrected (637.32), and the use of single and double quotation marks in Kate's reading from the mock silver-fork novel is rationalized (367.30–368.3).

There are some 33 verbal variants, mostly of marginal benefit, if any: thus 'poor dear Mr. Nickleby' becomes 'my poor dear Mr. Nickleby' (362.5), and 'out at the window' becomes 'out of the window' (506.20). Some dialect renditions are standardized, such as 'roonaway' to 'runaway' (558.23), 'Weel' to 'Well' (163.10), and 'soom' to 'some' (828.29). Almost a third of the revisions are arguably inferior or clearly wrong, amongst them 'youth' for 'use' (700.31) and 'It shall be done' for 'I shall be done' (695.15). Ironically in an edition marked by a sharp increase in the number of hyphenated words (partly the result of adopting many end-of-line hyphens necessitated by the double-column lay-out of the Cheap Edition), the two hyphens in 'con-sarn' (267.27) and 'ow-dacious' (754.22), which had captured idiosyncrasies of speech so effectively, are removed.

The Illustrated Library Edition

In 1861 the unsold stock of the Library Edition of *Nicholas Nickleby*, augmented by copies newly printed from the original stereotype plates, was reissued with the first-edition illustrations as

[108] Parrott, 76–7.

[109] *Letters*, 8.487: to Frederick Evans, 6 December 1857.

part of the Illustrated Library Edition. Reprinted several times between 1862 and 1869/70,[110] the edition has no textual significance.

The People's Edition

In 1865 the stereotype plates of the Cheap Edition of *Nicholas Nickleby* were used for the novel's appearance in two volumes as part of the People's Edition, designed principally for sale at railway bookstalls. The selling price was 2*s.* per volume. Again, the edition has no textual significance.

The Charles Dickens Edition

Nicholas Nickleby appeared in 1867 as the sixth volume in the Charles Dickens Edition, a project celebrated in its Prospectus as marking the twenty years 'since the first stereotype plates were cast for cheap editions' by 'reprinting them in a far more agreeable and remarkable form'. The author's involvement, symbolized by the facsimile of his signature on the half-title, is most obvious in the descriptive headlines and slight revisions to the Preface. The edition is known to have been reprinted in 1868, 1869, and 1870.[111]

The first third of the volume has only a handful of variants from the Library Edition, and there is no reason to think that Dickens was responsible for any of them. Appropriately, he appears to have begun revising at the point where he had, for whatever reason, first left off work in the Cheap Edition. Changes in the first of the two sections not revised in 1848 (330.12–437.12) are relatively light, and more than half of them are devoted to correcting the many remaining occurrences of 'Lord Verisopht' to 'Lord Frederick' or 'Lord Frederick Verisopht'. Changes in the second of the unrevised sections (542.17–648.28) are more comprehensive and continue through the final numbers to the end of the novel.

In the volume as a whole there are approximately 3,500 non-verbal alterations, in addition to spelling changes. Most significant is the conversion of dashes to full stops and new sentences in over 300 cases, to semicolons in over 100, and to commas in about 220. A further 160 or so commas are added, but twice as many are deleted, including some 165 first inserted in the Cheap Edition. A number of corrections

[110] Parrott, 109. [111] Parrott, 218.

are made, including the removal of a misleading comma in 'poor petty tradesman' (601.38), but many more typographical errors involving damaged letters and missing or imperfectly-printed punctuation mar an otherwise well-considered edition. Some of these flaws are likely to be the result of worn plates, and may not appear in all copies.[112]

The almost 300 verbal changes broadly continue the revisions Dickens had made for the Cheap Edition, with similar proportions in the categories identified and to similar effect. In around 80 instances single words are eliminated, of which almost half involve the deletion of 'and' with the creation of new sentence divisions. Other single word changes continue the replacement of 'God' by 'Heaven' or 'Lord' (332.22, 484.38), and the removal of some instances of an over-emphatic 'very' (617.18, 661.1, 808.14), as well as unnecessary interpolations such as 'Ah' (398.31) and 'Eh' (440.39, 780.33, 781.3). Of the longer excisions, one of the more interesting occurs in the abbreviated description of Lord Frederick as he faces Sir Mulberry for the last time: pale and dishevelled as he was, we no longer need to be told that it was 'all most probably the consequences of the previous day and night' (674.30–1). There are a few corrections such as 'she' for 'he' (172.10) which had escaped previous scrutiny, and, once again, a number of small clarifications, so that we are assured in the final paragraph of Chapter 61, for instance, that the reader must follow 'Ralph's' footsteps rather than the vaguer 'his' (806.7). A remaining over-specific (and obscure) reference, this time to the game of '*La Merveille*' (662.35, '*La Morveille*' in the Library Edition), is generalized to 'other games'. The narrative style, already formalized by the removal of dashes, is tightened, especially in the fluently-written final chapters, by the inclusion of verbs which had been left understood: thus, for example, 'his eyes so prominent, and his face so convulsed' becomes 'his eyes were so prominent, and his face was so convulsed' (722.28). As before, there are a small number of dialectical changes, and occasional modifications to grammar and usage.

Foreign editions

The editions of *Nicholas Nickleby* published in Europe and America have no textual significance, but they merit a brief overview.

[112] At 69.8 'friar's' was correctly printed initially but appears in at least one copy as 'frair's'.

In 1839 *Nicholas Nickleby* was included in Baudry's European Library, published in Paris. The edition follows the London 1839 text very closely, with a few verbal errors and minor changes in the punctuation. In 1839 and 1840 the novel was published by Frederick Fleischer in Leipzig as Vols 4 and 5 in an early collected edition of Dickens's works. The text follows the original numbers very precisely, except that the Preface appears at the beginning of the second volume, possibly because it was not available in 1839 when Fleischer's first volume appeared. Four years later *Nicholas Nickleby* appeared, again in Leipzig, in Bernard Tauchnitz's Collection of British Authors, 1843 being the year in which Dickens began to negotiate payment for his works with this publisher.[113] The edition follows the London text with scrupulous fidelity.

It was observed above (876) that in July 1838 Dickens was in negotiation with the Philadelphia publishers Carey, Lea & Blanchard but that his difficulty in meeting the printing deadlines meant he could not provide them with early proofs of the novel to enable them to be the first to publish it in the United States. Lea & Blanchard (as the firm had become) brought out *Nicholas Nickleby* in 1839: the text follows the London edition closely, with light changes to the punctuation and wording. The Philadelphia edition was followed by William H. Colyer in New York the same year, with additional changes to the punctuation and verbal variants. New York saw a rival edition, again in 1839, by James Turney Jr, evidently set from the London edition, following the pagination closely, but with a tendency to verbal approximation. The Turney edition was reissued by two further New York publishers, J. Van Amringe in 1840 and Robert P. Bixby & Co. in 1842.[114]

In 1867 Dickens reached an agreement whereby Ticknor & Fields of Boston became his official American publishers.[115] In that year they

[113] Patten, 123n.

[114] The edition by (Carey,) Lea & Blanchard, and that by Turney, originally appeared in numbers in 1838–9. The novel was also serialized in periodicals: *Albion* (New York), *Museum of Foreign Literature, Sciences, and* Art (Philadelphia), and *Boston Notion*. See Walter E. Smith, *Charles Dickens First American Editions: A Bibliography* (Calabasas, CA, 2012), 118–50 for the foregoing items and other American editions during the next two decades. On 9 November 1839 the *Boston Notion* announced (p. 9) that '[b]y the assistance of an enterprising friend in New York, we have obtained Nos. XIX and XX of "*The Life and Adventures of Nicholas Nickleby*," by Boz. Only three copies came out in the Great Western, and we have obtained one of them.'

[115] Slater 2009, 557.

re-issued the Library Edition and, also in 1867, followed its text for their own Diamond Edition, with changes in punctuation and spelling.

5. THE PRESENT EDITION

The present edition of *Nicholas Nickleby* follows the monthly numbers published between March 1838 and September 1839, and attempts to offer the same experience as the first readers would have encountered. It begins with the front wrapper to No. 1, and the text opens with the drop-head title and chapter heading to the introductory Chapter 1, as it did in the original serialization. Thereafter each monthly instalment begins on a new page so as to emphasize the part structure of the novel, until the final double number containing the concluding chapters 59 to 65. Only then was the original reader supplied with the preliminary material—the half-title, title page, dedication, preface, contents, and list of plates—customarily found at the beginning of a book. We believe that retaining this arrangement not only honours the editorial aim to present Dickens's text in its earliest form, but demonstrates vividly the evolution of the novel, and of Dickens as an author, even as it was being written.

The copy-text for this edition is an early set of the original numbers in the possession of one of the editors. Manuscript survives for only about 10 per cent of the main text, and there are no proofs. The printers did their work with commendable efficiency, and Dickens's manuscript is in general clear. Only a small number of emendations have been deemed necessary: fewer than 200 in all for a very long novel.

The manuscript is the source of some 75 of the emendations. Two-thirds of these restore original punctuation. As noted above, the printers were expected to interpret and supplement Dickens's punctuation, and they did this with great skill; but occasionally, so the present editors believe, the original movement of thought, usually in speeches, has been lost, or potentially confusing punctuation has been introduced, and in these cases they have adopted the manuscript readings. Two such emendations are typical of the way in which it has been possible to recover the speech dynamics that Dickens is likely to have heard as he wrote: '"Well, my dear," said Squeers, drawing up his chair. "What do you think of him by this time?"' (where the copy-text has 'chair, "what': 104.9–10); '"Demmit, you don't mean to say you want me, do you demmit?"' (where the copy-text ends 'do you, demmit?' and the manuscript 'do you<,> demmit?': 129.11). Two examples of potentially misleading printed commas in the narrative deleted because they are absent in the manuscript are: 'which bright salmon flesh-tint was considered by Miss La Creevy's chief friends and patrons<,> to be quite a novelty in art' (119.5–7), and 'an assumption of kindness which sat worse upon him<,> even than his usual manner' (122.35–6). However, the vast majority of the many commas inserted by compositors or at proof stage may be regarded as helpful, or at least not harmful. We know from novels with surviving proofs that Dickens was much more likely to insert than delete commas, and so the editors have restored most of the small number deleted from the manuscript in the serial parts of *Nicholas Nickleby*, as for example (now in speeches): 'it will save his time if I thank him and say what I wish to say to him↑,↓ as we walk along' (126.19–20); 'walk as fast as you can, and you'll get into the step that you'll have to walk to business with↑,↓ every morning' (126.34–6); 'Why↑,↓ your poor dear papa's cousin's sister-in-law' (221.3–4); 'Now↑,↓ I'll tell you what' (254.14); and 'all I have to say about that↑,↓ is' (255.3). In general, the editors wish to avoid the excesses of a member of Vincent Crummles's company, Mr Curdle, who had 'proved, that by altering the received mode of punctuation, any one of Shakespeare's plays could be made quite different, and the sense completely changed; it is needless to say, therefore, that he was a great critic, and a very profound and most original thinker' (318.18–22). While Mr Curdle is quite right that punctuation can significantly affect meaning, the editors carefully retain the punctuation of the 1838–9 copy-text unless we find either a distortion of Dickens's meaning as expressed in his manuscript, or absolute error which must be corrected.

Although the spelling of words fell within the purview of the compositors the manuscript forms have been restored in the present text where they might be significant for the meaning of the text: most notably two of Fanny Squeers's mis-spellings ('recuvvor' rather than 'recuvver' and 'tortorshell' rather than 'tortershell': 181.17, 30), but also 'anything' for 'any thing' (107.28, 111.26), 'anybody' for 'any body' (109.10), 'everything' for 'every thing' (115.13), and the phonologically distinct 'Hallo' for 'Hollo' (129.1). On the other hand 'villany' at 127.23 has been retained as a period spelling although the manuscript has the normal modern form: there is no distinction in sound. An interesting case is presented by the copy-text's reference to

Miss Knag being her own 'confident' (253.21). In manuscript the word is spelt 'confidant' and this form is also found in the Cheap and subsequent editions. Given the phonological implications the editors have chosen to follow Dickens's manuscript spelling.

A very few apparent misreadings of the manuscript have been corrected: 'your father has got [for 'get' in the copy-text] some nonsense in his head' (106.11); 'Miss Price in rejoinder congratulated herself upon not being possessed of the envious feelings [for 'feeling'] of other people' (117.29–31); 'this great and free and happy country, whose power [for 'powers'] and resources are, I sincerely believe, illimitable' (200.37–201.1); 'You have no connexion with any of those [for 'these'] rascally papers, have you?' (202.7–8); and 'There are many warm hearts in the same solitary guise as poor Miss La Creevy [for 'La Creevy's']' (253.32–3).

Several small words seem likely to have been changed inadvertently or overlooked by the compositors. The editors have restored these via emendation: 'which [for 'the' in the copy-text] two causes of merriment taken together' (112.11); 'a new sitter, transfixed by admiration of [for 'at'] the street-door case' (253.37–8); and 'she nodded her head and said, "Very true," with a great [for 'with great'] appearance of satisfaction' (125.36–7). More substantial words, and one clause, are likely to have been accidentally omitted or transposed: 'Nicholas opened his eyes rather at this', where 'rather' was omitted in the first edition (111.25); 'she had loved him dearly for many years, and was warmly attached to her children, and had no greater share of selfishness than is the usual lot of mortals', where the middle clause was overlooked and omitted in the first edition (125.4–6); and 'I will twist his nose off his demd countenance' which appears in the copy-text as 'I will twist his demd nose off his countenance' (214.34). On one occasion it seems that the compositor missed an authorial joke, and on another that he failed to follow a construction. In the first instance Nicholas echoes Miss Price's 'dressed so beautiful and looking so well', replying '"My dear girl, what have I got to do with her dressing beautiful or looking well?"' (114.20–3): the copy-text has 'beautifully'. And in a later chapter, where Nicholas says 'I tell you if I had stood by, tame and passive, I should have hated myself' (180.28–9), a similar change was made to 'tamely and passively'. At 119.3–4 the compositor has failed to observe Dickens's manuscript instruction to delete a word, so that 'a <very pink> ↑bright salmon

<-coloured>↓ flesh-tint <which> she had originally hit upon' appears in the copy-text as 'a bright salmon flesh-tint which she had originally hit upon': the editors omit 'which' in the present text (avoiding a repeated occurrence of the word in line 5).

Two unusual cases call for particular mention. At 120.30 the word 'introduced' appears in the 1838–9 copy-text. The present text emends to 'preserved'—a word at first encounter quite difficult to read in the manuscript, but clear once it has been recognized. Both words are effective. While it is possible that Dickens changed his manuscript reading in proofs, the editors think it more likely than not that the compositor made a guess at a word that would fit the context, or left a blank for Dickens to fill in. At 128.21 the copy-text gives 'otto of roses'. In manuscript Dickens used the same form, deleted it, and substituted 'Attar of Roses'. Though he may well have changed his mind again in the now lost proofs, the editors, considering it slightly more likely that a compositor chose what he understood to be a more conventional form, emend the copy-text in favour of the form Dickens originally settled on in manuscript.

The editors acknowledge that some of the emendations may result in readings rejected by Dickens in the now lost proofs. However, their experience of his practice in works where proofs survive has encouraged them to believe that it is possible to judge with a reasonable degree of confidence which changes are likely to be authorial, or to have been made in accordance with Dickens's procedures, and those that were probably introduced without authority or simply as the result of error.

Nearly one hundred emendations have been made from editions subsequent to the 1838–9 copy-text. These correct clear errors in the original, and most of them would have been required to be emended editorially if there had been no authorized source. More than half the corrections derive from the Cheap Edition, the majority addressing obvious problems with punctuation such as single quotation marks where double are required, easily identifiable in the Emendation List (991–6). Punctuation in the 1830s was extremely flexible, but a few really eccentric punctuation marks crept into the copy-text, and the editors delete them when they disappear in 1848: e.g. 'all the speeches put together did exactly what<,> they were intended to do' (20.31–2), and 'However striking such a contrast as this<,> may be to lookers-on' (28.24).[116] The Cheap Edition also renders consistent the spelling of appellations: 'Madame' (231.38), 'Chowser' (245.16, 669.13), 'Snevellicci' (397.2, 399.35: the occurrence at 637.32 had to wait till 1858), and 'Grogzwig' (826.19).[117] It corrects typographical errors which resulted in strange words like 'provi-vision', 'quanty', 'preremptory', and 'suprise' (306.5–6, 676.34, 748.4, 783.15). And it provides two speeches with concluding commas (13.11 and 13.13): although such commas are sometimes omitted in early editions of Dickens their absence is anomalous in *Nicholas Nickleby*. Fewer punctuational emendations derive from the Library Edition, and even fewer from the Charles Dickens Edition, most of the problems having been identified and corrected in 1848. The Library Edition spotted two potential ambiguities and changed 'You are my love, you know you are' to 'You are, my love, you know you are' (276.25), and 'I will live at least, in peace' to 'I will live, at least, in peace' (380.2–3). Its other contributions include correcting 'for twenty-years' to 'for twenty years' (370.38), and 'a man, who, plainly knows' to 'a man, who plainly knows' (685.24), and changing the final punctuation after 'how do you find yourself to-night' from a full stop to a question mark (732.23–4). It was not until the Charles Dickens Edition that two redundant and potentially confusing commas were eliminated in 'a poor<,> petty tradesman' (601.38), and 'if he had examined his own heart a little more carefully, he would have found<,> he could not resist' (611.4–5). A handful of corrections of punctuational and other small errors were actually made in the course of printing the copy-text: see for example the entries in the Emendation List for 63.19, 90.18, and 398.31.

Ten verbal corrections are taken from variants in the 1838–9 printing and from 1848 and 1867. As noted above, in the course of printing the numbers Mrs Kenwigs's 'visiter' was corrected to 'sister' (presumably the manuscript had been misread: 170.4), 'her brother's latter' to 'her brother's letter' (221.13–14), 'Miss Knag inmost soul' to 'Miss Knag's inmost soul' (235.14), and 'No you think not?' to 'Do you

[116] A similar emendation at 215.25–6 is made on the authority of the surviving manuscript, though it is also corrected in the Cheap Edition: 'although it was a great deal of trouble<,> to have young people<,> who were wholly unused to the business'.

[117] A similar emendation, 'Madam' to 'Madame', at 215.39 is made on the authority of the surviving manuscript, though it is also corrected in the Cheap Edition.

think not?' (632.36). In the Cheap Edition several apparent misreadings of the manuscript were corrected: 'a hackney-coachmen's knock' to 'a hackney-coachman's knock' (15.39), the dialect 'deame' to 'deane' (59.2), 'excited' to 'exerted' (143.2), and 'developed' to 'enveloped' (237.3). Something is amiss in the copy-text at 461.6–7, where Charles Cheeryble gives the instruction 'cheque for Mr. Linkinwater, Tim'. Linkinwater and Tim are of course the same person, so the Cheap Edition reasonably corrects to 'cheque for Mr. Trimmers, Tim'. (The Library Edition, and following it the Charles Dickens Edition, prefer 'cheque from Mr. Linkinwater, Tim', which is an improvement on 1838–9 but still sounds odd.) One obvious error at 172.6–10, 'Mrs. Kenwigs . . . did as he was desired', was not corrected to 'as she was desired' until 1867.

Editorial emendations—involving the introduction of readings which do not appear in any authorized text—are rarities. There are seven in the present text. A strange comma that survived in all the authorized editions is eliminated: 'a fat, elderly, large-faced<,> clerk' (460.13). Another odd comma is also deleted: 'Peg<,> expressing her acquiescence in this arrangement, Mr. Squeers turned the box bottom upwards' (761.4–5). Insertion of a comma in such a context is not unknown, but the Cheap Edition deleted one a few pages earlier ('Squeers<,> shaking his head, Ralph accompanied him to the street-door': 752.36–7), and this has confirmed the editors in their view that it should be regarded as erroneous, along with that after 'Nicholas' at 637.29. The editors regularize ''Tilly' to 'Tilly' twice (516.38, 549.19) and 'Tilda' to ''Tilda' (831.34). Finally, some action is called for by the strange question mark at 814.16 in '"No, Sir?" replied Kate. "Not once."' The question mark is retained in 1848: 1858 substitutes a full stop, 1867 an exclamation mark. The full stop is clearly wrong, but the exclamation mark hardly seems called for. The editors have decided that a comma is the most appropriate response.[118] In addition to these seven editorial emendations there are a further nine where the present text involves editorial interpretation of the manuscript readings: these are designated 'MS derived' in the Emendation List.

Not all editorial decisions are easy ones. Before concluding this essay, the editors wish to highlight some of the cases where we have

[118] The present edition follows the Cheap Edition's correction of a similarly foolish question mark to a comma at 83.19.

considered emendation but have decided to retain the copy-text reading. We hope that this will cast some further light on our editorial process.

As indicated in the first section of the essay, the goal of the present edition is to present Dickens's 1838–9 text, corrected with readings from the manuscript where the editors judge that the copy-text is likely to have distorted his intentions, with readings from subsequent editions which amount to corrections of errors in the copy-text, and with a small number of corrections without the authority of a later edition where we have found persistent error. Because we aim to present the text most closely approximating what Dickens would have chosen to publish in 1838–9, we do not restore passages from the manuscript that Dickens rejected for reasons of space (see Appendix 3: 925–8). For similar reasons, we do not adopt revisions that Dickens or a compositor made in the Cheap, Library, or Charles Dickens editions—except where such revisions amount to corrections of errors in the 1838–9 copy-text.

On quite a number of occasions the editors have considered adopting a punctuational mark from manuscript or from a later edition but have decided that there is not a compelling case for emendation. Thus at 104.23–32 where the manuscript has 'turned-up-nosed peacock . . . a peacock with a turned-up nose' the copy-text ends with 'a turned-up-nose'. It may be that the compositor simply standardized the two occurrences, ignoring logic, but it may also be that in proof Dickens inserted the final hyphen as a touch of humour. Adjustment of punctuation was one of the roles of the compositors, and although it can occasionally lead to distortion of Dickens's intentions we have allowed most of the changes made by the compositors (or in proof) to stand. This is the case with several commas inserted after initial short words which we know from novels with surviving proofs that Dickens himself tended to favour: e.g. 'Now↑,↓ I will say' (124.4), 'Oh↑,↓ you're not going' (184.31), 'No↑,↓ my dear' (218.15), and 'What↑,↓ if I am steeped in poverty?' (264.13). It may also involve retaining a comma inserted later in a sentence: 'I don't mind telling you↑,↓ Kenwigs' (184.2). Although we have tended to restore manuscript commas that we judge significant, where we do not perceive any clear significant loss resulting from the removal of a comma we have allowed the reading of the copy-text to stand: 'it may be necessary to state that the friend from whom she had so recently returned<,> was a miller's daughter of only eighteen' (108.31–3); 'after he had sat staring at Nicholas a long time<,> over the empty plate' (113.11–12); and 'the first ideas called up in Mrs. Nickleby's mind by the words milliner and dressmaker<,> were connected with certain wicker baskets lined with black oilskin' (125.29–31). Noting that in the earlier nineteenth century question marks and exclamation marks were often interchangeable, the copy-text has been allowed to stand in a case such as the following, where it differs from the manuscript: 'What can be the matter?' rather than 'What can be the matter!' (117.15). At 686.11 the question mark after 'Sad story' has been accepted as a plausible interpretation of Newman's appalled reaction, although its transformation to an exclamation mark in the Cheap Edition is perhaps more obvious. We have of course accepted the compositor's adjustment of the manuscript's punctuation in cases where the only reason for emendation would be an editor's personal preference for the original reading: 'I must know it sooner or later,→; and what purpose can be gained . . .' (180.11–12); 'I don't wish to alarm Mrs. Kenwigs,→; but I hope they haven't come from any jail or hospital' (186.26–8); 'they wondered how Madame Mantalini could have such people about her,→: requested they might see . . .' (220.19–20).

The Cheap, Library, and Charles Dickens editions often introduce punctuational and other errors, but they also sometimes make the punctuation of the 1838–9 copy-text more readily understandable, especially for a modern reader. Even where this is so, the editors have resisted accepting stylistic revisions from the later editions, except where there is a correction of error. Thus the present text has: 'here you are, Sir?' rather than the reading introduced in the 1848 Cheap Edition 'here you are, Sir!' (51.37); 'No; but *do* you think so, Kate,' rather than 1858's 'No; but *do* you think so, Kate?' (537.33); and 'why don't you praise the neatness and prettiness with which it's kept,' rather than 1867's version with a concluding question mark (538.34–5). Occasionally a later edition changes the meaning, deliberately or inadvertently, by repunctuating, but if the editors judge that the copy-text makes sense it has been allowed to stand. A case in point is the following sentence at 738.15–17: 'I ask you if you don't see it, but I need not say that, I know you don't, or you would have been more strictly upon your guard.' The Cheap Edition moves the comma after 'that' back so that it follows 'say', plausibly but probably unnecessarily. It follows a similar procedure at 796.23, omitting the first comma in 'besides that, his griefs were theirs, they mourned with him the death of one...'. At 486.23–4 the Charles Dickens Edition repunctuates 'free, generous, spirited masters' as 'free, generous-spirited masters', which may recover the intended meaning, but since equally it may not the present editors have not emended. The word 'did'nt' appears in the present text, unemended, at 154.8, as well as in the 1848 preface (854.24). Though Dickens more frequently uses the familiar form 'didn't', the editors have been unwilling to impose consistency here, given that the word appears in both forms in the early nineteenth century. Similarly, we have accepted 'wont', where one might expect 'won't' (618.30). A different punctuational issue arises at 441.34, where subsequent editions agree with the copy-text in referring to a 'private-madhouse-sort' of manner. The second hyphen there may seem undesirable, but to omit it would require an editorial emendation, and since it is not an undeniable error the editors have opted not to regularize. The same principles have guided the editors' considering of variants between copies of the 1838–9 text, as at 18.18–20: 'he would also prove, that these men corresponded with each other by secret words and signs, as, "Snooks," "Walker," "Ferguson," "Is Murphy right?" and many others'. Here the commas after 'prove' and 'as' disappear in later issues and editions (though the former is present in the Cheap Edition). Since neither comma is clearly in error we have allowed them both to stand.

Many instances of changes in wording in the Cheap, Library, and Charles Dickens editions which are substantial, significant, or both have called for editorial scrutiny, but (while recording them in the variant list) we have followed the copy-text whenever we judge them to be revisions rather than corrections. A few examples must suffice. Mrs Nickleby vaguely remembers a public house, 'the Old Boar or the George the Fourth' (227.1). The Cheap and subsequent editions alter the name of the latter to 'the George the Third', a more likely possibility historically, given that George the Fourth's reign began only in 1820, that the novel is set in the 1820s, and that Mrs Nickleby refers to a time when Kate was less than 3 years old. But there is also Mrs Nickleby's own unreliability to consider, so we have allowed the copy-text to stand. In the 1848 Cheap Edition, references to 'Lord Verisopht' are frequently revised to 'Lord Frederick' or 'Lord Frederick Verisopht' (starting at 243.37). This change can be understood as a stylistic revision or as a correction of extrinsic detail, and, while it may well be a change Dickens intended or sanctioned, the editors have decided to accept the original copy-text readings as an integral part of the novel as it first appeared: readers are unlikely to be confused. Later in the novel, Mrs Nickleby hears boots in the hall and guesses that it 'must be "the two Mr. Cheerybles"' (571.30). The editors suspect, because of the interior quotation marks, that Dickens may have intended Mrs Nickleby to refer, as she did at 488.34, to the brothers as the 'Cherrybles', and that the compositor missed the joke, regularizing the name to 'Cheerybles'. Emending to 'Cherrybles' on the basis of a presumed lost manuscript reading is tempting, but the editors felt the weight of evidence too weak to merit this kind of editorial intervention without support from any of the later editions.

Finally, the editors have had to consider how to treat Dickens's attempts to represent Yorkshire dialect. We have decided to leave dialect words in the form in which they appear in the copy-text, resisting the impulse to regularize. Dickens was inconsistent when writing dialect, and obviously developing his own ideas of how Yorkshire speech should be rendered.[119] Attentive readers will find on a single page instances of 'beant' (113.3), 'weant' (113.10), and 'deant' (113.19 and 113.31; the word 'Deant' also appears later, at 514.23), along with a more regular form 'dean't' with the apostrophe (113.15). In some cases, later editions attempt to bring dialect forms closer to standard English—changing, for example, 'hart' to 'heart' (164.14), 'anythink' to 'anything' (269.37), 'mun' to 'man' (511.4), 'thot' to 'that' (513.33), and 'Telle'e' to 'Tell'ee' (878.22). In other cases, they try to increase dialectical consistency by altering standard readings to what may be understood as conventionally unconventional ones—changing 'lad' to 'lod' (59.2), 'convulsions' to 'conwulsions' (174.9 and 174.11), 'runaway' to 'roonaway' (558.23), 'comfortable' to 'coomfortable' (559.30–1), and, charmingly, 'a hand, a heart, a highway' to 'a and, a art, a ighway' (756.26), among others. Attractive as these may be, the editors have consistently resisted any impulse to alter the copy-text's

[119] Walter Castle Railton finds that 'Dickens's hold of the elusive dialect of North-West Yorkshire was deplorably insecure', that the representation of dialect becomes even less convincing in the final part of the novel, and that it is restricted to John Browdie with no attempt to apply it to the speech of 'Tilda Price. In two of his examples, Railton suggests that 'Dang my boans and boddy, if I stan' this ony longer. Do ye gang whoam wi' me' (116.24–5) would be more plausibly rendered 'Ding mi b'yans an' body, if Ah stan' this onny lang-er! Thoo gan yam wi' ma', and 'Dost thee know where thee livest? Thee dost?' (516.13–14) as 'Diz tha knah wheer thoo lives? Thoo diz?' ('Dialect in *Nicholas Nickleby*', *Dickensian*, 27 (1931), 107–8).

dialect forms by adopting revisions from the Cheap, Library, or Charles Dickens editions. Many of these variants appear in the variants list, though others, as representing changes in spelling or punctuation without implications for meaning or pronunciation, do not.

The text of *Nicholas Nickleby* offered in the Oxford Edition is by no means revolutionary. It will present readers familiar with the novel with few surprises. The errors it corrects are neither legion nor seriously damaging. But the editors hope that the recovery (albeit unavoidably very partial) of a lighter punctuation and less formal syntactical system will enhance the stylistic spontaneity characteristic of this youthful and exuberant novel.

APPENDIX I

AGREEMENT FOR THE PRINTING AND PUBLISHING OF *NICHOLAS NICKLEBY*

DATED 18 NOVEMBER 1837

[Taken from A. S. W. Rosenbach, *A Catalogue of the Writings of Charles Dickens in the Library of Harry Elkins Widener* (Philadelphia, 1918), 40–5. For a draft of this agreement dated 18 August see *Letters*, 1.658–62.]

ARTICLES OF AGREEMENT Indented made and concluded this eighteenth day of November one thousand eight hundred and thirty seven Between CHARLES DICKENS of No. 48 Doughty Street in the County of Middlesex Esquire of the one part and EDWARD CHAPMAN and WILLIAM HALL of the Strand in the same County Booksellers and Publishers of the other part.

WHEREAS the said Charles Dickens is the author of a Book or Work intituled "THE POSTHUMOUS PAPERS OF THE PICKWICK CLUB" lately published in parts or Numbers and which the said Edward Chapman and William Hall have Printed and Published AND WHEREAS the said Charles Dickens intends to write and compose another and new Book or Work the Title of which has not yet been decided on of similar character and of the same extent and contents in point of quantity as the said work intituled "The Posthumous Papers of the Pickwick Club" and the Publication and Sale of the last mentioned Work having proved very profitable the said Edward Chapman and William Hall are desirous of printing and publishing the said New Book or Work in the same manner as they have hitherto printed and published the said former Work and the said Charles Dickens is willing that they shall do so upon the terms hereinafter expressed and for the purpose of accurately stating and defining the terms on which the said Edward Chapman and William Hall shall print and publish such intended New Work the said parties hereto have agreed to make and execute these presents NOW THEREFORE THESE PRESENTS WITNESS AND the said Charles Dickens Doth hereby for himself his heirs executors and administrators in consideration of the several payments hereinafter stipulated to be made to him by the said Edward Chapman and William Hall their heirs executors and administrators and of the covenants and agreements on their parts herein contained covenant promise and agree with and to the said Edward Chapman and William Hall their executors and administrators that he the said Charles Dickens shall and will compose and write a New Work the Title whereof shall be fixed upon and determined by him of a similar character and of the same extent and contents in point of quantity as the said Work intituled "The posthumous papers of the pickwick club" and that the said New Work shall consist of twenty parts or numbers and shall be terminated and completed in the twentieth part or number thereof and that he the said Charles Dickens shall and will write and deliver to the said Edward Chapman and William Hall their executors or administrators the Manuscript of the first number or part of the said intended New Work on or before the fifteenth day of March one thousand eight hundred and thirty eight and shall also write and deliver to the said Edward Chapman and William Hall their executors and administrators the Manuscript of the other and continuing Numbers or Parts of the same Work in regular succession on the fifteenth day of each of the nineteen Months next following the said fifteenth day of March one thousand eight hundred and thirty eight so as that the said intended New Work and the respective parts or numbers thereof from the first part or Number thereof to the twentieth and last number thereof may be Published by the said Edward Chapman and William Hall on the last day of the Month of March one thousand eight hundred and thirty eight and on the respective last days of the several months thence next ensuing AND THESE PRESENTS FURTHER WITNESS that the said Edward Chapman and William Hall do hereby for themselves their heirs executors and administrators in consideration of the right and licence hereby agreed to be granted to them and of the covenants and agreements on the part of the said Charles Dickens his heirs executors and administrators herein contained covenant promise and agree with and to the said Charles Dickens his executors administrators and assigns that they the said Edward Chapman and William Hall their executors or administrators shall and will Print and Publish the said New intended Work and the respective parts and Numbers thereof in the same form manner and Style in all respects as they have heretofore

Printed and Published the respective Parts and Numbers of the said Work intituled "The Posthumous Papers of the Pickwick Club" And that they also shall and will procure to be designed engraved and Printed and Published with each of the Parts or Numbers of the said intended New Work two Etchings or Engravings on Steel or Copper Plates in the like Style and manner as the Etchings or Engravings which have been Printed or Published with the Parts or Numbers of the said Work intituled "The Posthumous Papers of the Pickwick Club" which have been hitherto Published And that they the said Edward Chapman and William Hall their executors and administrators shall at their own proper costs defray and pay for all the Costs and Expences of and attendant upon or incidental to the Designing Engraving Printing Publishing Advertising and Selling the said New intended Work and the respective Parts or Numbers thereof and each and every of them AND shall and will duly and regularly Print and Publish the said New intended Work and the respective parts or Numbers thereof on the last day of the Month of March one thousand eight hundred and thirty eight and on the last day of every succeeding Month in due and regular succession until the twentieth or last Number thereof shall have been so Printed and Published as aforesaid AND ALSO shall and will pay to the said Charles Dickens his Executors or Administrators the sum of one hundred and fifty pounds Sterling on the delivery of the Manuscript of the first and every other of the parts or Numbers of the said intended New Book or Work AND IT IS HEREBY MUTUALLY AGREED by and between the Parties hereto that in consideration as well of the Costs Charges and Expences which are to be and shall be borne and laid out by the said Edward Chapman and William Hall in and about the Engraving Printing Publishing Advertising and Selling the said New intended Work and the Plates thereof as of the said twenty successive Payments of one hundred and fifty pounds to be respectively made by the said Edward Chapman and William Hall their Executors or Administrators to the said Charles Dickens his Executors Administrators or Assigns at the respective times and in the manner hereinbefore mentioned and provided for (making in the whole the sum of Three thousand pounds Sterling) They the said Edward Chapman and William Hall their Executors Administrators and Assigns shall have and enjoy AND the said Charles Dickens doth hereby give and grant to them their Executors Administrators and Assigns full licence and the sole and exclusive right of Printing Publishing and Selling the said intended New Book or Work and all the Number and Parts thereof and shall receive and be entitled to all and every the Gains and Profits which can or shall be made by the Publication and Sale of the said intended New Book or Work for and during and until the end and expiration of the full term of five years to be computed from the day on which the last Number or Part of The Said intended new Book or Work shall be published and that immediately from and after the end and expiration of the said term of five years the entire Copyright of and in the said intended new Work or Book and all the right title and interest therein or thereto shall belong and remain solely and exclusively to the said Charles Dickens his executors administrators and assigns and be held possessed and enjoyed by him and them as his and their absolute property for and during all the remainder which shall be to come and unexpired in the Copyright of the said intended New Book or Work of any term or terms of years which according to the Laws now in force or according to any Laws or Law hereafter to be made concerning Copyright in Books shall be granted or belong to or become vested in the said Charles Dickens as the author of the said intended new Book or Work his executors administrators or assigns And that at the expiration of the said term of five years the said Charles Dickens his executors administrators or assigns shall be at liberty if he or they shall think fit so to do to purchase the whole of the stock and printed Copies of the said intended new Book or Work and of the Engravings published therewith beyond the number of Five hundred which the said Edward Chapman and William Hall shall be entitled to retain and the said Edward Chapman and William Hall their executors administrators and assigns shall sell and deliver to the said Charles Dickens his executors administrators or assigns the whole of the said Stock printed Copies Engravings (except as aforesaid) at the cost price thereof and shall not demand or require from the said Charles Dickens his executors administrators or assigns any larger or other price for the same than the said Stock printed Copies and Engravings shall actually have cost them

AND IT IS HEREBY FURTHER AGREED that if the said Edward Chapman and William Hall their executors or administrators shall at any time during the said term of five years be desirous of selling or disposing of the license and exclusive right of printing publishing and selling the said intended new Book or Work during the said term of five years or the then residue of that term then they the said Edward Chapman and William Hall their executors or administrators shall in the first instance offer to transfer or relinquish the interest which they shall so desire to sell or dispose of to the said Charles Dickens his executors administrators or assigns and shall not sell dispose of or transfer the said right of printing publishing and selling any part thereof to any other person or persons than the said Charles Dickens his executors administrators or assigns unless and until the said Charles Dickens his executors administrators or assigns shall have declined to purchase the same at a price to be fixed on (in case the parties cannot agree) by two indifferent persons the one to be chosen by the said Edward Chapman and William Hall their executors or administrators and the other by the said Charles Dickens his executors administrators or assigns or if such two persons differ then at a price to be fixed by a third person or Umpire to be chosen by the two persons first appointed or unless and until the said Charles Dickens his executors administrators or assigns shall have refused or neglected to name one of the said two persons for the space of seven days after he or they shall have been requested so to do by the said Edward Chapman and William Hall their executors or administrators or unless and until the said Charles Dickens his executors administrators or assigns shall have neglected to pay the said price for fourteen days after the same shall have been so agreed upon or fixed AND IT IS HEREBY FURTHER AGREED that if the said Charles Dickens his executors or administrators shall be desirous of selling or disposing of the Copyright of the said intended new Work or Book or any part thereof then he or they shall in the first instance offer to transfer or relinquish the interest which he or they shall so desire to sell or dispose of to the said Edward Chapman and William Hall their executors administrators or assigns and shall not sell dispose of or transfer such Copyright or any part thereof to any person or persons other than the said Edward Chapman and William Hall their executors administrators or assigns unless and until the said Edward Chapman and William Hall their executors administrators or assigns shall have declined to purchase the same at a price to be fixed on (in case the parties cannot agree) by two indifferent persons or an Umpire to be chosen in the same manner as is hereinbefore provided in case of the said Edward Chapman and William Hall being desirous of selling or unless or until the said Edward Chapman and William Hall their executors administrators or assigns shall have refused or neglected to name one of the said two persons for the space of seven days after they shall have been requested so to do by the said Charles Dickens his executors or administrators or unless and until the said Edward Chapman and William Hall their executors administrators or assigns shall have neglected to pay the said price for fourteen days after the same shall have been agreed on or fixed PROVIDED ALWAYS AND IT IS HEREBY DECLARED and AGREED by and between the parties hereto that they the said Edward Chapman and William Hall their executors administrators or assigns shall not nor will print the said intended new Book or Work or any of the parts or numbers thereof in any other form or at any less price than the form and price in and at which the said Work intituled "the Posthumous Papers of the Pickwick Club" has hitherto been published and sold And shall not nor will print publish or sell any abridgement of the said intended new Book or Work or any selection therefrom without the previous consent in writing of said Charles Dickens his executors administrators or assigns IN WITNESS whereof the said parties to these presents have hereunto set their hands and seals the day and year first above written.

Charles Dickens   Edward Chapman   William Hall

Signed sealed and delivered by all the within named parties in the presence of

Wm. Chapman   Richmond   Charles Molloy   Lincoln's Inn

APPENDIX 2

THE *NICKLEBY* 'PROCLAMATION'

(SEE 'ESSAY ON THE TEXT', 874)

THE NEW WORK BY THE AUTHOR OF " THE PICKWICK PAPERS."

ON *the Thirty-first of March will be published, to be continued Monthly, price One Shilling, and completed in Twenty Parts, the First Number of* " THE LIFE AND ADVENTURES OF NICHOLAS NICKLEBY ;" *containing a faithful account of the Fortunes, Misfortunes, Uprisings, Downfallings, and Complete Career of the Nickleby Family—Edited by* " BOZ."—*And each Monthly Part embellished with Two Illustrations by* " PHIZ."

Whereas we are the only true and lawful " **BOZ.**"

And Whereas it hath been reported to us, who are commencing a New Work, to be called—THE

LIFE & ADVENTURES

OF

NICHOLAS NICKLEBY

THAT some dishonest dullards, resident in the by-streets and cellars of this town, impose upon the unwary and credulous, by producing cheap and wretched imitations of our delectable Works. **And Whereas** we derive but small comfort under this injury, from the knowledge that the dishonest dullards aforesaid, cannot, by reason of their mental smallness, follow near our heels, but are constrained to creep along by dirty and little-frequented ways, at a most respectful and humble distance behind.

And Whereas, in like manner, as some other vermin are not worth the killing for the sake of their carcases, so these kennel pirates are not worth the powder and shot of the law, inasmuch as whatever damages they may commit, they are in no condition to pay any.

FIRSTLY,

TO PIRATES.

THAT we have at length devised a mode of execution for them, so summary and terrible, that if any gang or gangs thereof presume to hoist but one shred of the colours of the good ship NICKLEBY, we will hang them on gibbets so lofty and enduring, that their remains shall be a monument of our just vengeance to all succeeding ages; and it shall not lie in the power of any Lord High Admiral, on earth, to cause them to be taken down again.

B M

SECONDLY,

TO THE PUBLIC.

THAT in our new work, as in our preceding one, it will be our aim to amuse, by producing a rapid succession of characters and incidents, and describing them as cheerfully and pleasantly as in us lies; that we have wandered into fresh fields and pastures new, to seek materials for the purpose; and that, in behalf of NICHOLAS NICKLEBY, we confidently hope to enlist both their heartiest merriment, and their kindliest sympathies.

THIRDLY,

TO THE POTENTATES OF PATERNOSTER-ROW.

THAT from the THIRTIETH DAY OF MARCH next, until further notice, we shall hold our Levees, as heretofore, on the last evening but one of every month, between the hours of seven and nine, at our Board of Trade, Number ONE HUNDRED AND EIGHTY-SIX in the STRAND, LONDON; where we again request the attendance (in vast crowds) of their accredited agents and ambassadors. Gentlemen to wear knots upon their shoulders; and patent cabs to draw up with their doors towards the grand entrance, for the convenience of loading.

Given at the office of our Board of Trade aforesaid, in the presence of our Secretaries, EDWARD CHAPMAN & WILLIAM HALL, on this Twenty-eighth day of February, One Thousand Eight Hundred and Thirty-eight.

(*Signed*)

APPENDIX 3

PASSAGES DELETED AT PROOF STAGE

The following ten passages appear in the surviving manuscripts but were cut at proof stage, probably because Dickens had 'overwritten': that is, written more than would fit into 32 pages, the length of a normal monthly serial instalment. They are here transcribed from manuscript.

Chapter 9

114.29 fault. Come] fault. *n.p.* "What do you suppose Fanny has to do with me?" asked Nicholas wondering much how this delusion came about. *n.p.* "Oh <? much more> ↑I know well enough↓"—<repl> rejoined Miss Price "there's John looking black at our talking so long. *n.p.* Come

115.35–6 I think. I should like] I think. *n.p.* "I hope so"—said Nicholas gallantly. *n.p.* "Are you always <so> lucky?" enquired Miss Price *n.p.* "At cards" replied Nicholas. *n.p.* "Dear me I should like

117.37 with a jerk. "You'll cry] with a jerk. *n.p.* "I pity and despise you ↑'Tilda↓"— said Miss Squeers. *n.p.* "You are beneath both of them" replied Miss Price. *n.p.* "I haven't words to tell you what I think of you"—said Miss Squeers. *n.p.* "I'm very glad to hear it" rejoined Miss Price. *n.p.* "An ungrateful, ill-disposed, bad-minded, good for nothing creature—" said Miss Squeers. "You'll cry

Chapter 10

122.20 portrait. "Is that] portrait. *n.p.* "Where's your mother? In bed?" *n.p.* "No Sir, she has been up for hours." <replied Kate> *n.p.* "I wonder at that—so early in the day—barely twelve o'clock"—said Ralph "Is she at home?" *n.p.* "In <her> our own room Sir" replied Kate timidly. *n.p.* "I want to see her↑—with you↓"—said

Ralph <"I have found out something for you> "Can you spare me a few minutes?" *n.p.* "Oh uncle, <—> of course my time is yours." answered Kate. *n.p.* "You'll excuse ↑us↓ Ma'am will you?" <said> ↑growled↓ Ralph turning <round> to Miss La Creevy. *n.p.* "Oh! Don't mention it Sir, pray" *n.p.* "Is that

126.15–16 directly." *n.p.* "Have you nothing] directly." *n.p.* "Kate my dear"—said Mrs Nickleby "What do you think?" *n.p.* "Certainly Mama"— replied Kate *n.p.* "Have you nothing

Chapter 15

183.25–6 detention. *n.p.* "Lor] detention. *n.p.* "It's ↑a↓ very remarkable thing," said Mr. <Ken> Kenwigs. "Do you know I thought I see him turn pale about five minutes before he heard he was wanted." *n.p.* "Did you though?" exclaimed the unmarried sister of Mrs. Kenwigs "—*I* did, seriously." *n.p.* "So did I" observed Miss Petowker "but I thought it might be the effect of those two ↑last↓ awful lines in the Blood Drinker's Burial <that> ↑which↓ often as I have gone through that recitation always make me shudder myself, I declare." *n.p.* This was a line <for a> to catch a little more applause, or perhaps an encore which the bachelor friend had more than once obscurely hinted at, but the thoughts of the company had been directed into a new channel, and it failed dismally. *n.p.* "Lor

186.37–8 *sal volatile. n.p.* The ladies] *sal volatile. n.p.* "You should really be more careful, Mr. Crowl" said Miss Petowker reproachfully *n.p.* "Yes, upon my word you should"— urged Mr Kenwigs "She's very delicate, and if you gave her a shock which affected her constitootion, how would you ever be able to forgive yourself? How do you find yourself now my dear?" *n.p.* "Very faint"—replied Mrs Kenwigs "I shall never be happy or know a minute's peace of mind, <...> 'till it's found out who these people are, and whether it's safe to have them in the house. I can't help it Kenwigs, and so it's no use talking." *n.p.*

"Well I am sure that's very reasonable in you and nobody can object to that my love"—said Miss Petowker. *n.p.* "Nothing can be more proper, and Mr Kenwigs is far too kind and good a husband, and knows your value <too w> a deal too well I'm sure, not to satisfy you at once"—said the married visitor. *n.p.* "Poor thing, her anxiety for her children's very natural"—said Mrs. Kenwig's sister. *n.p.* "—And nobody can blame her for it, or if they did would be a brute"—added the <lady> ↑delegate↓ from the back parlour." *n.p.* The ladies

Chapter 20

263.4–5 for the best." *n.p.* But before] for the best." *n.p.* When he had quite decided that he had done the best that could be done some new doubt arose and then the question had to be mentally argued all over again. But <Nichol> Nicholas was young, and there was always one <recollection> ↑reflection↓ that came to his assistance, and turned the scale in his favor. He had shewn Ralph Nickleby that he was superior to the base and mercenary motives he had insinuated. He had shewn him that if his hatred originated in the difference of their dispositions he should have good cause for it. Nicholas would walk faster as he thought of this, and <walk with> ↑assume↓ a more resolved and determined air. *n.p.* But before

263.28–9 he could speak, "let me hear] he could speak, "I have been talking about your old friend this morning." *n.p.* "I have but one"—said Smike with his accustomed hesitation "and he—is" *n.p.* "Is here <I hope"> you mean?" said Nicholas pointing to himself. *n.p.* Smike <gave a> nodded and looked his delight at being so readily understood. *n.p.* "Aye, aye" said Nicholas "but I mean an acquaintance of longer standing—Mr. Squeers." *n.p.* The poor fellow shivered at the <mere> ↑bare↓ mention of the name, and shook his head with most expressive dislike. *n.p.* "Well;" said Nicholas "he is anxious I am informed to have you back again, and not a little enraged with me for taking you away. What do you say? Are you hard-hearted enough to disappoint Mrs. Squeers?" *n.p.* Smike seemed very uneasy under this jesting on so serious a subject, and made no answer. Nicholas <at> relapsed into silence and resumed his former position which he maintained for some time, occupied with his own thoughts. When he again looked round, Smike was seated on a chair by the bedside, looking attentively at him. *n.p.* "You spoke just now to please me, and not because you felt merry"—said Smike "You look ill and tired. What is the matter?" *n.p.* "Nothing my good fellow"—said Nicholas *n.p.* "Something I know"—rejoined Smike. *n.p.* "Something"—said Nicholas rising into a sitting posture, "that I am resolved to think no more of, so we will not talk about it and I shall forget it the sooner. Come. Let me hear

264.9–10 could give. The thought] could give. *n.p.* "You—you—do not mean it!" cried his charge *n.p.* "I do." rejoined Nicholas "The thought

APPENDIX 4

NOTE ON THE ILLUSTRATIONS

Hablot Knight Browne, who had illustrated *The Pickwick Papers* so successfully, was part of the 'mighty secret' of *Nicholas Nickleby* from the beginning.[1] When Dickens set out on his fact-finding journey to Yorkshire on 30 January 1838 Browne went with him as travelling companion, and in search of material and artistic inspiration for the illustrations. In due course he provided 39 of the 40 plates for the novel, two for each number, together with a design for the wrappers; the final illustration was a portrait of the author, engraved after a painting by Daniel Maclise.

This excursion, and another to the Midlands and Manchester in early November, must have provided ample opportunity for discussion. At other times, according to D. C. Thomson in his biography of the artist, Dickens might call on Browne to read a portion of the novel with his suggestions for illustration, or—if time were short—simply leave a copy of the relevant passage; very occasionally he would write out detailed and lengthy notes incorporating specific extracts from the text.[2] Whatever the degree of consultation, according to a timetable prepared by Browne and quoted by Thomson, copy for the first subject in a monthly instalment was usually expected by the 11th of the month, and a sketch sent to Dickens on the 13th. This would be returned, with copy for the second subject, on the 14th, and a sketch of the second subject would go to Dickens on the 15th, being returned the next day. The plates were generally finished ten days later.[3] Inevitably things were not so regular in practice, and for much of 1838 the first half of the month was dominated by *Oliver Twist*, with *Nickleby* postponed to the second, so it is unlikely that author and

[1] *Letters*, 1.359: to W. H. Ainsworth, [25 January 1838].

[2] D. C. Thomson, *Life and Labours of Hablôt Knight Browne, 'Phiz'* (London, 1884), 63.

[3] Thomson, *op. cit.*, 234, as summarized in *Letters*, 1.549n. Browne would send the copy on to Chapman and Hall, who in turn would send it to the printers Bradbury and Evans (*Letters*, 1.549: to Charles Hicks, [?10 May 1839]).

artist were able to settle into the kind of routine suggested by Browne's template until 1839. Even then there was slippage on both sides: as observed in the essay, Dickens's own practice was prone to irregularity, while Browne was prevented by a 'sudden indisposition' from producing the plates for Number 14 (the May number), so that an announcement had to be inserted in the 'Nickleby Advertiser' (see 873–4) promising four in the following month.

The first three numbers, when Dickens was still aiming but struggling to meet his mid-month deadline, appear to have allowed Browne opportunity to try out his own ideas for illustrations. Preliminary sketches in the Huntington Library include 'Sir Matthew Pupker in the chair', Mr Mantalini enjoying a leisurely breakfast, and a grotesquely simpering 'Miss Squeers wants her pen mended', as well as hastily drawn outlines of a heavily laden stagecoach and several studies for Mr Squeers, some of which may have been made on the spot during their visit to Yorkshire.[4] Years later, when Edgar Browne asked about the portrayal of Squeers in the illustrations his father replied he was 'not unlike' the man whom they had met, William Shaw.[5] Also among these sketches are four illustrating the travellers' tales, including two of the Baron of Grogzwig, providing further evidence that these episodes were not late insertions to make up the shortfall in the second number. The final plate in Number 3 was worked up from a preliminary sketch 'Miss La Creevy takes Kate Nickleby's portrait', in which Kate faces the painter, who has her back to the reader. A revised version, now showing Ralph peering out from behind the screen, was sent to Dickens for approval with a pencilled note: '[Will] you have the kindness to send back—(either home or C and H) early [tomorrow] morning?'[6] A similar progression can be traced for the first plate in Number 5, which seems to have evolved from a sketch of a line of little Kenwigs girls headed 'Mr. Kenwig's party' to the published plate 'Nicholas engaged as Tutor in a private family'. Morleena is no longer seated in the row as described in the text, but Dickens later revealed,

[4] Illustrations to *Nicholas Nickleby*, Huntington Library, HM 39999. The collection contains 49 sketches, some little more than rough outlines, many with titles in Browne's hand.

[5] Edgar Browne, *Phiz and Dickens as they Appeared to Edgar Browne* (London, 1913), 11–12. One of these sketches showing Squeers with one eye wide open and the other tightly closed is reproduced in Valerie Browne Lester, *Phiz: The Man who Drew Dickens* (London, 2004), 62.

[6] Charles Dickens Museum DH 326. Transcription taken from *The Catalogue of the Suzannet Charles Dickens Collection*, ed. Michael Slater (London, 1975), 46.

in reply to a query about the figures of Mrs Kenwigs and Miss Petowker, that he was more concerned that neither lady was correctly portrayed, Mrs Kenwigs being too large and Miss Petowker lacking 'personal attractions'.[7]

In a note to Forster tentatively dated 18 September 1838 (thus referring to the seventh number) Dickens wrote: 'I don't know what hour you sent Browne to bed, but he has done nothing.'[8] In fact, 'The Professional Gentlemen at Madame Mantalini's', the first of the number's illustrations, proved one of the most successful, not least for its close interpretation of the text. The second plate, 'The Country Manager rehearses a Combat', paved the way for several theatrical subjects in Numbers 7 to 10, although a preliminary sketch for Chapter 27 'Mrs. Nickleby's surprise at meeting Kate in the theatre' was not used. From February 1839 Dickens was free to concentrate on *Nickleby* so it may be no coincidence that he paid close attention to the second draft illustration for Number 12 (the apprehension of Smike in Chapter 38): 'I don't think Smike is frightened eno[ugh or Squeers] earnest enough—for my purpose'.[9] On the other hand, the draft drawing for the first illustration in the following number, 'Nicholas recognizes the Young Lady unknown', shows the artist feeling his own way towards a satisfactory image.[10] By July 1839, when Dickens had moved out of London to write without interruption, there was at least one occasion when Browne received his instructions in the form of an advance description of the scene for illustration, in this case the hairdresser's shop in Chapter 52 (the first illustration for Number 17). Although, as the editors of the correspondence rightly point out, 'The plate cannot have been drawn from these instructions only, as they do not mention the coal-heaver in the doorway, described in the text.'[11] On 8 September Chapman and Hall delivered what must have been Browne's draft sketches for the last

[7] *Letters*, 2.51: to Professor and Mrs de Morgan, 12 April 1840.

[8] *Letters*, 1.435: to John Forster, [?18 September 1838]. Compare the note to Bradbury and Evans dated in the range 1837–April 1839 (*Letters*, 1.547): 'I have one hundred slips of copy ready for you, but cannot send it 'till I see Mr. Browne whom I have expected these two days. If he comes today, I can send you *more than two sheets* tonight.'

[9] Charles Dickens Museum DH 328; Dickens's note, transcribed in *Letters*, 1.513: to H. K. Browne, [February 1839].

[10] Charles Dickens Museum DH 332. The drawing differs from the finished plate in significant ways, and there are three attempts at the figure of Madeline in the lower margin.

[11] *Letters*, 1.560n.

number,[12] presumably including the final plate 'The children at their cousin's grave' with its echoes of the emblematic structure of the wrappers.

The amount of work involved was considerably increased by the novel's success which demanded that, in order to avoid excessive wear to the plates and to keep up with the faster rate of letterpress printing, it was necessary to etch multiple copies of the steel plates. A similar experience with the increasing popularity of *Pickwick Papers* had led to confusion as new plates were made during publication; this time Browne took the decision to etch multiple plates from the start. The details are set out in Albert Johannsen's study *Phiz: Illustrations from the Novels of Charles Dickens* (Chicago, 1956), and examples of all the plates can be seen in the collection formed by John F. Dexter, now in the British Library. Interpretations vary slightly, but most authorities agree that at least nine plates were etched in duplicate, seventeen in triplicate, and fourteen in quadruplicate, making a minimum of 125 steels in total. Browne was remarkably accurate in his copying of the central characters and scenes; the main differences between the primary plates and their copies appear in the background and foreground details, and variations in Phiz's signature. All versions were printed simultaneously so there is no priority of issue.

Once the plates were etched, the engraved captions were added. These were probably taken from the titles supplied by Dickens on the approved drawings, as evidenced in 'Kate Nickleby sitting to Miss La Creevy', and 'Madame Mantalini introduces Kate to Miss Knag' where Dickens's suggestion replaces a pencilled heading 'Madame Mantalini's Establishment No. 1'.[13] The engraved captions probably formed the basis for the List of Plates published in the final double number, despite several anomalies of capitalization, spelling (Mulberry is spelled with one 'r' on the plate caption for 'The last brawl between Sir Mulberry and his pupil'), and punctuation ("breaking up" is within double quotation marks on the plate caption for 'The breaking up at Dotheboys Hall', and there is no comma in the plate caption for 'A sudden recognition, unexpected on both sides'). There are four verbal discrepancies, three of which arise out of multiple copies of the plates: in 'Nicholas instructs Smike in the Art of Acting', one version

[12] *Letters*, 1.578: to John Forster, 9 September 1839.
[13] Charles Dickens Museum DH 325.

of the plate lacks the word 'in'; in 'Nicholas makes his first visit to Mr. Bray' three of the four versions have the longer caption 'Nicholas makes his first visit to the lodgings of Mr. Bray'; and on three of the four plate captions 'Linkinwater intimates his approval of Nicholas' is corrected to 'Mr. Linkinwater intimates his approval of Nicholas'. The remaining discrepancy, 'The Professional Gentleman at Madame Mantalini's', has 'Gentlemen' in all versions of the plate, again a preferable reading. Finally, the positions of 'Reduced circumstances of Mr. Mantalini' and 'The breaking up at Dotheboys Hall' in the last number are reversed and incorrectly paginated in the List of Plates.

Although it never appeared in the List of Plates, the decision to include a portrait of the author as the fourth plate in the final number, and as the frontispiece to the one-volume issue, was bold and deliberate. Once the success of *Nicholas Nickleby* was assured the publishers Chapman and Hall commissioned Dickens's friend, the Irish artist Daniel Maclise, to paint his portrait. The work was completed by the end of June 1839 when Dickens informed the actor John Harley 'Maclise has made another face of me, which all people say is astonishing',[14] and was promptly passed to William Finden for engraving. An announcement was included in a publisher's advertisement leaf inserted between the plates and the first page of the text of Number 17, and (with additional information) Number 18. The painting itself was given pride of place at the Nickleby dinner, while the engraving signed 'Faithfully yours, Charles Dickens', caused a stir when it appeared in the novel and as a separately available print.[15] As William F. Long has pointed out, this was the first time a portrait of Dickens had appeared under his own name[16] and, as one who was

[14] *Letters*, 1.557–8 (558); to J. P. Harley, 28 June 1839.

[15] The portrait was hotly debated at the time and remains a frequent topic of discussion. See Robert L. Patten, *Charles Dickens and 'Boz': The Birth of the Industrial-Age Author* (Cambridge, 2012), 218–25, and Gerard Curtis, 'Dickens in the Visual Market', in *Literature in the Marketplace: Nineteenth-century British Publishing and Reading Practices*, ed. John O. Jordan and Robert L. Patten (Cambridge, 1995), 213–49 (238–42).

[16] William F. Long, 'An Irreverent Contemporary Comment on the Impact of the *Nickleby* Portrait', *Dickensian*, 112 (2016), 46–53 (49). In the course of this piece Long comments plausibly (52, n. 22) that Dickens's letter to Harley may not refer to his dislike of an earlier version of Maclise's portrait, as has usually been understood, but rather to a different, earlier portrait. However, the catalogue of the exhibition held at the Victoria & Albert Museum in 1970 states: 'During June 1839, Maclise paid Dickens many visits at Elm Cottage, Petersham, studying the novelist in countless sketches which he destroyed in dissatisfaction': *Charles Dickens: An Exhibition to Commemorate the Centenary of his Death* (London, 1970), 108.

highly protective of his image, he had taken a close interest in its selection.[17] It was also particularly appropriate for a novel which had much to say about authorship and the business of writing.

Extra illustrations, and other related material, were a well-established feature of the book market at this time: *Nicholas Nickleby*, with sales of around 50,000 each month, was an obvious focus for enterprising traders and to some extent encouraged them by advertising their wares in the monthly instalments.[18] The third number carried an announcement of the first part of a series of *Illustrations to Nicholas Nickleby* by Peter Palette, the pseudonym used by the artist Thomas Onwhyn, who had produced a similar set for *Pickwick Papers*, while Number 11 quoted enthusiastic press reviews: 'subscribers... will lose half the zest of Nickleby's story, if they fail to take Peter Palette'. Like the novel itself, Onwhyn's series consisted of forty plates—thirty scenes and ten portraits—published in shilling parts by Edward Grattan from June 1838 to October 1839.[19] The scenic subjects complemented Browne's original designs rather than duplicating or reinterpreting them, with a tendency to illustrate dramatic or visually appealing incidents. The fact that they did not appear in strict chronological order, but were closely keyed to the text by pagination and quotation, encouraged purchasers to relive favourite moments as the novel was proceeding.

The ten portraits were added in response to a competing series of extra illustrations, also first announced in Number 11, followed by an elaborate full-page advertisement in Number 12. '*Heads from Nicholas Nickleby... from drawings by Miss La Creevy*' was the work of the illustrator [Joseph] Kenny Meadows and published in six sixpenny parts by Robert Tyas. The 24 portraits, four in each part, professed to show the most interesting characters 'at the period when their very actions define their true characters and exhibit the inward mind by its outward manifestations', rather like Miss La Creevy's miniatures. Each, it was claimed, is 'a literal transcript from the accurate and vividly minute

[17] *Letters*, 2.74–5: to George Brightwen, 28 May 1840 ('I beg to inform you that the portrait originally published in Nicholas Nickleby, and since published separately by Messrs. Chapman and Hall is considered the best likeness that has been engraved of its author'). In later years Dickens was especially critical of many photographs; see for example *Letters*, 9.465–6: to John Watkins, 28 September 1861.

[18] For a discussion of the place of extra illustrations see Luisa Calé, 'Dickens Extra-Illustrated: Heads and Scenes in Monthly Parts (The Case of *Nicholas Nickleby*)', *Yearbook of English Studies*, 40 (2010), 8–32.

[19] F. G. Kitton, *Dickens and his Illustrators* (London, 1899), 234–5. The only complete set seen contains Parts 6–9 with the imprint of Gilbert & Grattan, [*c.*1841].

descriptions of this able and most graphic author', so challenging the reader to recognize the 'maiden simplicity' of Kate, the 'depravity' of Sir Mulberry, the 'heartless villany of the calculating Ralph', and 'the broken spirit' of Smike. An advertisement for the complete series, carefully printed in uniform size and style for those who wished to have them bound with the novel, appeared in the final double number, strategically placed immediately after the official List of Plates.

The visual appeal of *Nicholas Nickleby* extended beyond suites of extra illustrations to individual pictures in newspapers and magazines or as accompaniments to extracts and reviews. It is no longer easy to retrieve the evidence, and much would have been of incidental interest, but three examples may be representative. On 10 November 1838 *The Mirror of the World*, a short-lived newspaper subtitled an 'Illustrated Miscellany of Literature, Fine Arts, and the Drama', opened with an extract from Number 8, entitled 'The Bespeak of Miss Snevellicci'. The text was taken from the end of Chapter 24 but the page is dominated by a large woodcut captioned 'First Appearance of Nicholas Nickleby on the British Stage'. Whereas Browne's illustration of the same subject looks out from the stage at the audience, this view is taken from the wings with Nicholas and the company to the right behind the curtain, and the orchestra pit and part of the auditorium out front to the left.[20] On 3 November 1838 *The Penny Satirist* devoted its front page to fifteen captioned portraits of characters from the novel, the same set which reappeared later on the first page of *The London Free Press, and The Universal Library* for 11 May 1839. Smike is not present, but the coachman, 'an intelligent man of liberal principles' who had upset the Yorkshire-bound coach, is a surprising inclusion.[21]

THE CHEAP EDITION

The Cheap Edition was unillustrated, for obvious reasons of economy, and—so it was claimed in the prospectus—to avoid competition with

[20] *The Mirror of the World*, Vol. 1, No. 3, [17]. The only copy of this number known to survive is held by the British Library as the first item (not separately catalogued) in Dex. 313 (available as Mic. B. 613/90).

[21] The only copy of this number of *The London Free Press* known to survive is held by the British Library. It is not separately catalogued but can be found among the small collection of newspaper cuttings and similar material in section 14 of Dex. 310 (available on microfilm as Mic. B. 613/88).

the original edition; instead new frontispieces by 'eminent' artists were commissioned for each volume. On 26 November 1847 Dickens wrote formally to Thomas Webster, the recently appointed Royal Academician who specialized in painting children: 'I need not say to you that I should feel any attempt thus slightly to connect what is best in English Art, with these stories, as most incomplete if it did not include your name. And I am particularly desirous to have for Nicholas Nickleby, which is now in course of publication, a sketch of the Yorkshire School from your hand.' The sketch would be needed by February 1848, he continued, adding his personal request that it should be coloured 'in order that I may possess it, afterwards', and assuring Webster that it should be engraved 'with the greatest care'.[22] The work, depicting a grim and angry-looking Mrs Squeers dispensing brimstone and treacle to a line of dishevelled boys, was completed in good time; Dickens immediately welcomed it as '*most admirable*', urging Edward Chapman to proceed with the engraving as soon as possible so that the original could be returned to the artist for exhibition at the Academy.[23] By 25 March the drawing had been transferred to the block for engraving, Webster had declared himself 'quite satisfied' with the result, and everything was in hand for publication at the end of May.

Just as with the first edition of 1839, the Cheap Edition was shadowed by the appearance of extra illustrations. Both Dickens and his publisher were well aware of their appeal and shrewdly decided to compensate for the lack of illustrations in the text by issuing a set of accompanying plates for those who could afford the additional cost. The artist Frank Stone was commissioned to provide three portraits—''Tilda Price dressing for the tea party', 'Kate Nickleby sitting for her portrait', and 'Madeline Bray pausing in her work'—to be engraved on steel by Edward Finden, brother of William who had been responsible for the original frontispiece portrait of the author. Bound in similar green wrappers to the monthly fascicles of the edition, and priced at a shilling, these very attractive images were intended to be bound with the text, but many purchasers may have enjoyed them as wall decorations.[24] The unauthorized Plates to

[22] *Letters*, 5.203: to Thomas Webster, 26 November 1847. The engraving was carried out by Thomas Williams.

[23] *Letters*, 5.247: to Edward Chapman, 15 February 1848. The finished work, exhibited at the Academy later that summer, was purchased by Dickens for £50. After his death it was sold under the title 'Dotheboys Hall: the Brimstone and Treacle scene' for £535 10*s*.

[24] The original painting of 'Tilda Price remained in Dickens's possession until his death, when it was sold for £42. *Catalogue of the Beautiful Collection of Modern Pictures, Water-colour*

illustrate the Cheap Edition of *Nicholas Nickleby*, published by Edmund Appleyard, followed a similar set for *Pickwick Papers* in what was intended to be a complete series of illustrations to the Cheap Edition by John Gilbert. Of the 32 wood-engraved plates, only the first four—including portraits of Wackford Squeers and the Baron of Grogzwig—were by Gilbert; the remainder were by anonymous illustrators of the penny serials usually associated with Appleyard's imprint and largely followed the original choice of subjects. John F. Dexter described them as 'happily very scarce' and the series was discontinued.[25]

THE LIBRARY EDITION

The only illustrations in the Library Edition of 1858 were unsigned vignettes by Browne incorporated into the engraved title pages for each volume. The design for Volume 1 depicts Ralph Nickleby's first meeting with the Nickleby family: a more refined interpretation than the equivalent plate in the first edition, with Kate and Nicholas standing protectively either side of a seated Mrs Nickleby, while Ralph looks intently at Nicholas, instead of glowering at his helpless sister-in-law. The design for Volume 2 illustrates the gently humorous scene from Chapter 41 with the gentleman in small-clothes leaning over the garden wall to pay court to Mrs Nickleby, standing with Kate below.[26] Again, the image presents a more elegant version with a substantial villa in the background, a more genial figure on the wall, and round pumpkins and squashes instead of the suggestive cucumbers of the original. Both were intended to complement a dignified edition for wealthier readers.

THE ILLUSTRATED LIBRARY EDITION

The Library Edition did not sell well, prompting Chapman and Hall to reissue it in 1861 with the original illustrations, except the frontispiece

Drawings and Objects of Art, of Charles Dickens Deceased... Sold by Auction, by Messrs. Christie, Manson & Woods... On July 9, 1870, etc. [1870], 5 (Annotated copy in Bodleian Library 1706 d. 87).

[25] John F. Dexter, 'Hints to Dickens Collectors', in *Dickens Memento* (London, [1885]), 7–35 (19).

[26] Dickens had been pleased with this chapter, writing to Forster in March 1839 'I think Mrs. Nickleby's love scene will come out rather unique' (*Letters*, 1.527).

portrait. Volume 1 contains the first twenty plates, with 'The Yorkshire Schoolmaster at "The Saracen's Head"' promoted to the position of frontispiece; the nineteen remaining appear in Volume 2 with 'Mr. and Mrs. Mantalini in Ralph Nickleby's Office' as frontispiece and 'The "breaking up" at Dotheboys Hall' in its correct position following 'Reduced circumstances of Mr. Mantalini'. The list of illustrations in each volume was compiled from the 1839 preliminaries (minus final full stops) rather than the engraved legends on the plates themselves, so preserving the small verbal and incidental discrepancies of the original edition.

The experiment paid off, the edition achieving healthy sales and a regular profit from the outset.[27] Such was its success that all thirty volumes were republished between 1874 and 1876, and again as the de luxe edition of 1881–2 using a fine set of plates which had been touched up by Browne after Dickens's death.[28]

THE DIAMOND EDITION

Early in 1867 Ticknor & Fields of Boston began publication of their Diamond Edition, partly in the hope that it would help persuade Dickens to undertake a reading tour of America.[29] This ambitious enterprise was notable for its illustrations by Sol Eytinge, a prolific American artist whose work was much admired by Dickens in these later years for its 'most agreeable absence of exaggeration, a pleasant sense of beauty, and a general modesty and propriety'.[30] The sixteen illustrations for *Nicholas Nickleby* portray characters rather than episodes from the text, amongst them as frontispiece a sensitive study of Nicholas and Smike which was re-used for the Diamond reading text 'Nicholas Nickleby at the Yorkshire school' in 1868. Others included a wildly dramatic portrayal of Henrietta Petowker enacting 'The Blood-Drinker's Burial' with her hair streaming loose just as the text describes, the genial Cheeryble Brothers with Tim Linkinwater, and a lovely Madeline with her father.

[27] Parrott, 100–5. [28] Thomson, 108. [29] Slater 2009, 557.

[30] *Letters*, 11.349: to J. T. Fields, 2 April 1867. Dickens's appreciative comments were appropriated and slightly modified by Ticknor and Fields for their advertising blurb published at the beginning of each volume in the edition.

THE CHARLES DICKENS EDITION

Back at home, Chapman and Hall had no intention of repeating the mistakes they had made with the Library Edition. The celebratory Charles Dickens Edition, launched in May 1867 with an extensive publicity campaign, contained eight of the best of the original illustrations.[31] Although it is not known whether Dickens had a hand in the selection, it would seem likely given his involvement in many aspects of this edition and his interest in the illustrations in general. There is no list of plates, which are: 'Mr. Ralph Nickleby's first visit to his poor relations' as frontispiece, 'The internal economy of Dotheboys Hall', 'The Country manager rehearses a Combat', 'Emotion of Mr. Kenwigs on hearing the family news from Nicholas', 'Mr. Linkinwater intimates his approval of Nicholas', 'Nicholas congratulates Arthur Gride on his wedding morning', 'Reduced circumstances of Mr. Mantalini', and 'The children at their cousin's grave'.

THE PRESENT EDITION

The present edition opens with a reproduction of the wrapper, followed by the frontispiece. The portrait was originally published with the three other plates in the final double number, preceding the text in the position adopted for all the plates throughout the serialization. Although it was not included in the List of Plates, it appeared as the frontispiece to the one-volume issue and we have therefore followed the publisher's intention and placed it in its logical position. The rest of the plates are placed facing the words of the text they illustrate: because they are printed on the same paper as the text in this edition, it has been possible to position them more precisely than indicated in the original List of Plates (see 851–2), which has the disadvantage of containing a few errors of pagination as well as reversing the order of two of the final plates. Since our list in Volume 1 (ix–x) is not part of the copy-text, it rectifies the mistakes as well as providing the page numbers in this edition and modernising the presentation.

[31] According to the prospectus, published in the *Athenaeum*, 4 May 1867, 600.

TEXTUAL WITNESSES

A. MANUSCRIPTS

The manuscript of *Nicholas Nickleby*, like that of *Pickwick Papers*, survives only in fragments. No proofs are known to be extant. Of the whole manuscript, 166 leaves (plus a half leaf and a 4-line fragment) remain, almost exclusively from six chapters in Numbers 3 to 6:

Chapter 9 (leaves 37–75) 39 ff. Charles Dickens Museum, London
Chapter 10 (leaves 75–106) 32ff. Rosenbach Foundation, Philadelphia
Chapter 15 (leaves [1]–22) 22 ff. British Library, London
Chapter 16 (leaves 47–70) 26 ff. Rosenbach Foundation, Philadelphia
Chapter 17 (leaves 1–2, 4–19) 18 ff. Rosenbach Foundation, Philadelphia
Chapter 20 (leaves 67–94) 28 ff. Rosenbach Foundation, Philadelphia
Chapter 54, p. 539 (1 leaf) Morgan Library, New York
Chapter 55, p. 549 (4 lines) Private owner
Chapter 57, pp. 567–8 (half leaf) Free Library, Philadelphia

Dickens first mentioned his wish that the manuscript of his novels should be preserved in the course of writing *Nicholas Nickleby*. He wrote to Charles Hicks, the foreman-printer at Bradbury and Evans, probably on 20 September 1838: 'I send you a chapter—12 pages I hope. You will have another (please God) either on Sunday Night, or Monday Morning. When you have time be good enough to look me up all the old copy you have of mine, as I am very anxious to have it complete' (*Letters*, 1.437). Hicks's role in preserving what remains is confirmed by a note in the portion held by the British Library stating that the leaves were 'formerly in the possession of Hicks, foreman of the printers, Messrs. Bradbury and Evans'. The three fragments from the later part of the novel appear to have had a different history. They are variously cut down and customized, probably for presentation as souvenirs or for charity, and almost certainly by Dickens himself.

With the exception of the British Library fragment, all the sheets are now unbound although some bear the traces of former guards or previous stitching. The leaves, or 'slips', are of quarto paper, measuring approximately 23 by 18.5 cm (the last three fragments are slightly larger, with the only complete leaf measuring 24.5 by 19.5 cm), written on one side with the exception of a few versos containing deleted beginnings, or passages for insertion.

For the sake of consistency the folio numbers used in this description follow Dickens's numeration rather than those used by some, but not all, of the holding libraries.

Charles Dickens Museum Chapter 9

The portion consists of 39 leaves, numbered 37 to 75, comprising the whole of Chapter 9. Six leaves (ff. 37, 39, 42 (re-used as 45), 52, 56, and 74) bear false starts, which were deleted and the sheet turned over and reversed to begin again. Towards the end of the chapter there are three passages which do not appear in the printed text: Dickens presumably cut these passages at proof stage, to reduce the instalment to the normal size of 32 pages.

There are printer's marks, with the names of compositors, as follows:

f. 50 First new paragraph annotated 'Biggar' (before 'I never saw': 108.27);

f. 55 Two deleted light marks within line 16, followed immediately by a third (not deleted) mark 'G81 [' (before 'long gloves' (110.34), the number indicating the original beginning of p. 81, which in the printed number begins with 'Nicholas opened' at 111.25);

f. 65 Light mark '84 [' before the fourth paragraph, which was deleted from the printed text (immediately following 'my fault.' at 114.29, which is on p. 83 in the printed number);

f. 74 Light mark '87]' before the final paragraph on the leaf ('They were no sooner gone' at 118.9, which is at the bottom of p. 85 in the printed number).

Rosenbach Chapter 10

The portion consists of 32 leaves, numbered 75 to 106, comprising the whole of Chapter 10. Six leaves (ff. 78, 83, 90, 97, 99, and 100) bear false starts, which were subsequently deleted and the sheet turned over and reversed to begin again. The final leaf has been cut away, through what must have been a line of additional text, just visible. There are two instances of short passages having been omitted from the chapter at proof stage, most likely because of overwriting.

There are printer's marks as follows:

f. 91 Light square bracket inserted before 'Madame' in the fifth line (126.13);

f. 95 Vertical line through the sixth paragraph with instruction: 'To set to the end' (at 128.15: 'There was comfort in this'; the conclusion of the paragraph on f. 96 is not struck through, and the paragraph appears normally in the printed text);

f. 99 Light square bracket before 'was originally' in the third paragraph (at 130.4).

British Library Chapter 15 (Add. MS 57493)

The portion consists of 22 leaves, numbered [1] to 22, comprising the first two-thirds of Chapter 15 (up to 187.16). The leaves are bound with letters relating to the Yorkshire schools. Two leaves (ff. 8 (re-used as 16) and 17) bear false starts, both undeleted, which were turned over and reversed to begin again. There are two long passages of excluded text, neither of them deleted.

There are no printer's marks.

Rosenbach Chapter 16

The portion consists of 26 leaves, numbered 45 to 70, comprising the final two-thirds of Chapter 16 (from 197.11). Three leaves (ff. 49, 50, 56) bear false starts, all deleted with the sheet turned over and reversed to begin again.

There is one printer's mark, on f. 45: a light square bracket before 'voice was heard' in the second paragraph with the circled instruction '145L' (at 197.25). In addition on f. 53 the final paragraph of the Pugstyles letter is circled in a dark ink, perhaps by Dickens. The reason for this marking is unclear.

Rosenbach Chapter 17

The portion consists of 18 leaves, numbered 1 to 19, with 3 being missing, comprising the whole of Chapter 17 with the exception of the one leaf (212.10–28). Two leaves (ff. 11, 17) bear false starts, both deleted with the sheet turned over and reversed to begin again.

There are printer's marks, with the names of compositors, as follows:

f. 6 Beginning of second paragraph ('"Two countesses') annotated 'Lloyd' (at 213.30);

f. 10 Beginning of second paragraph ('"I think that') annotated possibly 'Green' (at 215.29): the name has been deleted.

Rosenbach Chapter 20

The portion consists of 28 leaves, numbered 67 to 94, comprising the whole of Chapter 20. Four leaves (ff. 67, 73, 76, 79) bear false starts, all deleted with the sheet turned over and reversed to begin again. One (f. 76) also carries a short paragraph for insertion ('"You are here already . . . on you."': 256.16–18).

There are printer's marks, with the names of compositors, as follows:

f. 77 Beginning of second paragraph ('"It would be my duty') annotated 'Woodbridge' (at 257.1);

f. 82 Beginning of second paragraph ('"You hear') annotated 'Carbary' (at 260.5);

f. 89 Last line ('surrounded') annotated 'Green' (at 263.11).

Morgan Library Chapter 54 (MA 109.28)

The portion consists of a single leaf, measuring 24.5 cm x 19.5 cm, comprising 720.17–39 ('"What seems a cruel thing . . . interpose a word.'). The page is headed in double quotes 'G' (or possibly 'C', or '6'). It is very creased and may have been cut down at the top. It has been cropped at the foot, but the text concludes with Dickens's characteristic paraph or flourish as if it were the end of the chapter, though it is not. Perhaps this is a replacement page or an insert. The letter at the top is similar to one just visible on the Philadelphia fragment described below, suggesting that Dickens himself may have been responsible for cutting up this portion of the manuscript, possibly as souvenirs or for charitable purposes.

Private owner Chapter 55

The portion consists of a fragment comprising 735.12–15 ('"Good-looking, too... to the utmost.'). The fragment is attached to an envelope addressed to Mr Bell postmarked 1843. It was sold to an anonymous buyer at Bonhams, New York on 9 December 2015, lot 25 as part of the Henry Gould collection, having been sold previously at Sotheby's on 22 July 1980, lot 497.

Free Library, Philadelphia Chapter 57 (DMS N514n) Benoliel gift

This portion consists of the top half of a leaf, numbered 4, comprising 757.28–758.3 ('Mr. Squeers... becoming reverence.'). The paper is cropped at the foot, just revealing the top of a letter or number within double inverted commas: it might be 'T', or another letter, or a '7', and is similar to the 'G', 'C', or '6' visible at the top of the Morgan fragment. Dickens may have cut this portion of the manuscript into pieces, possibly as souvenirs, each headed with a letter of the alphabet or number.

Manuscript of the Preface to the Cheap Edition, 1848 (National Art Library, V&A: MSL/1876/Forster/168 [item 6] and MSL/1876/Forster/170 [item 2])

The manuscript consists of two items in a bound volume. Four mounted leaves of quarto paper numbered [1], 2–4, measuring approximately 22.5 cm x 18.5 cm, comprise the manuscript of the first two pages of the Preface as printed in 1848 and extracts from the final two pages (853–7 in the present edition). This is supplemented by a four-page typesetting of the 1839 Preface, mounted on two leaves, marked up by Dickens to indicate the passages to be quoted in the 1848 Preface (855.27–856.25 and 856.31–857.5 in the present edition), with new linking material (856.26–30).

The first of the manuscript leaves has been trimmed at the inner edge; the second and third leaves have been cut across in three places, probably by Dickens and possibly in the course of composition. There are no printer's marks.

B. AUTHORIZED EDITIONS IN WHICH DICKENS WAS INVOLVED

For details of the illustrations in the printed editions see Appendix 4 to the Essay on the Text (929–39).

1. **39A**

The Life and Adventures of Nicholas Nickleby, 20 numbers as 19 (London, 1838–9).

Wrapper title: The Life and Adventures of Nicholas Nickleby containing a faithful account of the Fortunes, Misfortunes, Uprisings, Downfallings, and complete career of the Nickleby family. Edited by "Boz." with illustrations by "Phiz." London: Chapman and Hall, 186, Strand.

Printer: Bradbury and Evans, Printers, Whitefriars.

Issued: 31 March 1838 to 30 September 1839 at 1*s.* per number.

Copies collated: Copy in possession of Elizabeth James (copy-text, bound from the parts); British Library 838.h.35 (copyright copy, bound from the parts); British Library Dex. 281; Worcester Polytechnic Institute SPEC COLL DICKENS PR 4565 A1 1839.

Contents:

No. I Chapters 1–4 [31 March 1838]
No. II Chapters 5–7 [30 April 1838]
No. III Chapters 8–10 [31 May 1838]
No. IV Chapters 11–14 [30 June 1838]
No. V Chapters 15–17 [31 July 1838]
No. VI Chapters 18–20 [31 August 1838]
No. VII Chapters 21–3 [29 September 1838]
No. VIII Chapters 24–6 [31 October 1838]
No. IX Chapters 27–9 [30 November 1838]
No. X Chapters 30–3 [31 December 1838]
No. XI Chapters 34–6 [31 January 1839]
No. XII Chapters 37–9 [28 February 1839]
No. XIII Chapters 40–2 [29 March 1839]
No. XIV Chapters 43–5 [30 April 1839]
No. XV Chapters 46–8 [31 May 1839]
No. XVI Chapters 49–51 [29 June 1839]
No. XVII Chapters 52–4 [31 July 1839]
No. XVIII Chapters 55–8 [31 August 1839]
Nos XIX and XX Chapters 59–65 [30 September 1839]

2. 39B

The Life and Adventures of Nicholas Nickleby (London, 1839).

Title-page: The Life and Adventures of Nicholas Nickleby. By Charles Dickens. With illustrations by Phiz. London: Chapman and Hall, 186, Strand. MDCCCXXXIX.

Printer: Bradbury and Evans, Printers, Whitefriars.

Issued: 23 October 1839. £1 1*s.* (cloth); £1 4*s.* 6*d.* (half morocco).

Copies collated: British Library C.144.b.3 (ownership inscription dated 1840); Bodleian Dunston B 706 j.

Contents: This comprises the monthly parts without wrappers and advertisements, but with the prelims issued with Number 19/20, together with the portrait, bound at the beginning.

3. 48

The Life and Adventures of Nicholas Nickleby (London, 1848). The Cheap Edition.

Title page: The Life and Adventures of Nicholas Nickleby. By Charles Dickens. With a Frontispiece from a painting by T. Webster, Esq., R.A. Engraved by T. Williams. London: Chapman and Hall, 186, Strand. MDCCCXLVIII.

Printer: Bradbury and Evans, Whitefriars.

Issued: Published in weekly instalments of 16 pages each from October 1847 to May 1848 (in the case of *Nicholas Nickleby* numbered 32 to 63) and priced at 1½*d*. It was also issued in monthly instalments consisting of the weekly numbers stitched together and priced at 7*d*., and in one volume (*Nicholas Nickleby* on 27 May 1848), bound in wrappers for 4*s*. 6*d*. and olive green cloth for 5*s*., and in half-morocco for 7*s*. 6*d*. It was reissued several times between 1850 and 1866, and in 1865–7 at monthly intervals at 2*s*. per volume as the People's Edition, printed from stereotyped plates by Virtue and Co. for the railway bookstalls.

Copies collated: 1847–8 (weekly instalments): Bodleian Vet. A6 e. 574 1848; (bound volume): British Library 012614.a.53/2; copy in the possession of Elizabeth James; copy in the possession of Clive Hurst; 1857: V&A Forster 8vo 2399.

Contents: The edition is based on 39, probably on an early impression at least of Nos 4 and 15 (see Essay on the Text (897) and Textual Variants (954, 970)), without the illustrations and advertisements, but with a new frontispiece and Preface. The following chapter titles were slightly altered: [9] 'and of various' replaces 'and various'; [12] 'smooth' replaces 'smoothly'; [63] 'others. Tim' replaces 'others, and Tim'; a comma was introduced between 'themselves before' in [19]; a full-stop replaces the semicolon after 'occasion' in [37]; and additional words were capitalized in [43], [45], [54], [59], and [64]. A collation of the 1857 issue reveals a few corrections and a small number of new printing defects.

4. 58

The Life and Adventures of Nicholas Nickleby (London, 1858). The Library Edition.

Title-page: The Life and Adventures of Nicholas Nickleby. By Charles Dickens. In two volumes. Vol. I. [II.] London: Chapman and Hall, 193, Piccadilly; Bradbury and Evans, 11, Bouverie Street. 1858.

Half-title: Works of Charles Dickens. Library Edition. Vol. III. [IV.] Nicholas Nickleby.—Vol. I. [II.]

Printer: Bradbury and Evans, Whitefriars.

Issued: 1 March and 1 April 1858, unillustrated except for title-page vignettes, at 6*s*. per volume. (Reissued in 1861 as part of the Illustrated Library Edition with the original illustrations but lacking the frontispiece portrait, at 7*s*. 6*d*. per volume.)

Copy collated: British Library 12603.k.9.

Contents: As 48, without the frontispiece but with an engraved title page to each volume. Vol. 1 contains Chapters 1–32; Vol. 2 contains Chapters 33–65, renumbered 1–33.

5. 67

The Life and Adventures of Nicholas Nickleby (London, 1867). The Charles Dickens Edition.

Title-page: The Life and Adventures of Nicholas Nickleby. By Charles Dickens. With eight illustrations. London: Chapman and Hall, 193, Piccadilly. 1867.

Half-title: The Charles Dickens Edition.

Printer: Virtue and Co., City Road.

Issued: 1 November 1867, at 3*s*. 6*d*. The edition is known to have been reprinted in 1868, 1869, and 1870.

Copies collated: British Library 12604.dd.11/6; copy in possession of Elizabeth James; Magdalen College, Oxford 823.8 DIC 1867 (res) vol. 6.

Contents: As 58, with descriptive running headlines by Dickens on each right-hand page and slight revisions to the Preface and the text. The Prospectus made a feature of the author's 'watchfulness over his own Edition' but there are a number of typographical errors throughout.

TEXTUAL VARIANTS

This list records verbal readings in the surviving manuscript and later authorized editions which differ from those in the copy-text. It does not normally include deletions in the manuscript. It does not record typographical errors such as gaps in the type, missing, broken, or reversed letters. Nor does it record missing end-of-line hyphens, missing opening or closing speech marks, and clear mistakes such as duplicated words. It does not record variations or one-off mistakes in spelling, nor changes in upper/lower case or hyphenation which can have no implications for pronunciation or sense. It records variants in paragraphing, but not in sentence structure. Most importantly, it does not normally record changes in punctuation unless they have resulted in emendations in the present text or are of particular interest: the punctuation of *Nicholas Nickleby* is unstable, thousands of punctuation changes being introduced as the texts were transmitted from one edition to another, and it would be impractical to print them all.

In the entries the reference number is followed by the reading in the copy-text which is omitted or replaced in later editions (using an ellipsis for longer passages), a square bracket, and then the reading(s) in the manuscript or later editions, identified in each case by the standard shorter form of reference. When a word or set of words in the copy-text has been omitted later this is normally indicated after the bracket by '*om.*' and the relevant reference(s). When the editors have made an emendation the emended text appears before the bracket, followed by the references to the source and any other text(s) where the emended reading occurs, followed in turn by the form in the copy-text and the reference '39'. When the exact reading in the manuscript is likely to be useful, it appears between vertical bars | . . . | after 'MS'; in exceptional cases we offer the printed readings in the same form.

6.23	further] *om.* 48–67
7.2–5	farm; if indeed . . . of the houses.] farm, which was as small a landed estate as one would desire to see. 48–67
8.4	ever] *om.* 48–67
8.33	him: and Mr.] him. So, Mr. 48–67
11.1	Mr. Seguin gives] they give 48–67
11.29	the garment] the latter garment 48–67
12.20	till] until 48–67
12.33	visible, and that] visible; that 48–67
13.3	quite] *om.* 48–67
13.7	he] *om.* 48–67
13.11	up,"] 48–67 up" 39

13.13 then,"] 48–67 then" 39
14.17 bed; and the] bed. The 48–67
15.3–4 I had—had—" *n.p.* "Had done] I had—" *n.p.* "Done 48–67
15.39 hackney-coachman's] 48–67 hackney-coachmen's 39
16.30 arrangement] arrangements 67
18.17 bellman] bellmen 48–67
18.18 prove,] 39 *some copies* 48–67 prove 39 *some copies*
18.19 as,] 39 *some copies* as 39 *some copies* 48–67
18.23 description; and secondly] description; secondly 48–67
20.32 what] 48–67 what, 39
23.19 Nickleby,"] 48–67 Nickleby" 39
26.17 I] *I* 48–67
28.24 this may] 48–67 this, may 39
29.10 forth] *om.* 48–67
30.2 rather] *om.* 48-67
32.15 interpreted, signifieth] interpreted, often signifieth 48–67
32.23 conversation, and Nicholas] conversation. Nicholas, 48–67
33.5 ears, and what] ears. What 48–67
33.11 cold, and gloomy] cold, gloomy 48–67
33.14 this, we imagine must be] this, should be 48–67
34.5 eastwards] eastward 48–67
34.7 westwards] westward 48–67
34.16 gateway, and the] gateway. The 48–67
34.19–20 large Saracens' Heads] 48–67 large Saracen's Heads 39
34.20 is of] is decidedly of 48–67
35.23 twentys—two] twentys is two 48–67
35.25 oughts an ought] oughts is an ought 48–67
35.25 twos six] twos is six 48–67
35.30 replied] said 67
38.37 way] line 48–67
39.7 is sitting] is a sitting 48–67
39.19 so that his] so, his 48–67
39.32 affirmative, and his] affirmative; his 48–67
40.23 that] *om.* 48–67
43.12 and my] and to my 48–67
43.32 Every body] Everybody 48–67
44.9 apart, and in] apart; in 48–67
44.16 could have] could almost have 48–67
45.4 and] *om.* 48–67
51.16 till] until 48–67
51.37 Sir?] Sir! 48–67
52.18 Pshaw!] Bah! 48–67
54.2 to do to] to do, over the stones, to 48–67

54.2 on: and between] on. Between 48–67
56.3–4 was not] wasn't 48–67
56.33 every body] everybody 48–67
56.38 every body] everybody 48–67
57.14 sups] cups 58–67
58.1 earth] ground 48–67
58.22 hand] hond 67
59.2 deane] 48–67 deame 39
59.2 lad] lod 48–67
59.20 and the people] and people 48–67
60.27 gentlemen] gentleman 58–67
61.34 appeared well] appeared to be well 58–67
63.11 around] round 48–67
63.19 remaining.] 39 *some copies* 48–67 remaining 39 *some copies*
63.38 these] those 58–67
64.13 ear] ears 58–67
66.16 mother!" faltered] mother," faltered 48–67
66.32 work, and the] work; the 48–67
67.28 Alice; and the] Alice; the 48–67
68.1 affliction, and death] affliction, death 48–67
68.3 shall] will 48–67
71.29 much of pleasure] much pleasure 58–67
72.9 better. *n.p.* "But come;] better. But come! 48–67
73.32 fell] felt 48–67
74.19 company, and every] company; every 48–67
74.24 in tears] in salt tears 48–67
75.9 These] Those 48–67
75.23 me love] me, love 48–67
75.24 devil ma'am] devil, ma'am 58–67
75.30 go to——but] go——but 48–67
76.20 castle of] castle at 67
76.29 there was] there were 48–67
77.12 sighing;] sighing, 48–67
78.31 been his] been a 58–67
79.13 his stake] the stake 67
79.14 ferrule. 'Be] ferrule. *n.p.* "'Be 67
79.23 a] *om.* 48–67
79.25–6 word, and the] word; the 48–67
79.31 got] *om.* 48–67
81.17–18 enough, and about] enough. At about 48–67
82.1 obeyed, and Mr.] obeyed. Mr. 48–67
82.9 further] farther 48–67
83.19 "Here, Sir,"] 48–67 | "Here, sir," | "Here, Sir?" 39

83.38 How are] How's 48–67
85.13 God] Heaven 48–67
86.2 any way] anyway 58–67
86.18 piece] bit 48–67
87.1 "Upon] 48–67 'Upon 39
87.2 very] *om.* 48–67
87.9 death, and possibly] death; possibly 48–67
87.35 see, who] see! Who 48–67
87.38 there are] there is 48–67
88.27 effects] effect 48–67
89.1 "My] 39 *some copies* 48–67 'My 39 *some copies*
90 title HALL.] 39 *some copies* 48–67 HALL 39 *some copies*
90.18 morning."] 39 *some copies* 48–67 morning.' 39 *some copies*
90.24–5 clothes, and Squeers] clothes. Squeers, 48–67
91.2 lightness upon] lightness, on 48–67
91.25 head] hand 67
91.32 succeeded] ensued 48–67
91.39 threshing] thrashing 48–67
93.31 there] here 48–67
94.6 them] these 48–67
94.15 any thing] anything 48–67
94.16 ill-assorted] ill-sorted 67
94.33 had eat] had eaten 48–67
94.34 boys eat] boys ate 48–67
97.1 significantly] *om.* 48–67
97.20 long] *om.* 48–67
97.23 those] them 48–67
97.25 useful, and idling] useful. Idling 48–67
97.37 desk, and to eat there] desk, to eat it there 48–67
100.22 would not] wouldn't 48–67
100.30 which] this 67
101.23 led] brought 48–67
101.27 in society] *om.* 48–67
101.33 there, and at] there; at 48–67
102.7 that] this 48–67
103.3 him, and died] him; and he died 48–67
103.5 said] cried 48–67
103.6 nights?] nights! 48–67
103 title AND VARIOUS] AND OF VARIOUS 48–67
103.22 gentleman occupied] gentleman being occupied 48–67
103.30 a universal] an universal MS 48–67
104.2 quality, and from] quality; from 48–67
104.9 chair. "What] MS chair, "what *all editions*

104.12 God] Heaven 48–67

104.22 Well then,] MS Well, then, *all editions*

104.30 hearers. Neither] hearers. *n.p.* Neither 58–67

104.32 turned-up-nose] turned-up nose MS

105.20 life to witness that] life, when he witnessed that 48–67

105.21 and to see] and saw 48–67

105.37 dreamt] dreamed 48–67

106.2 mind. "Your] MS |mind "Your| mind, "your 39 mind; "your 48–67

106.11 got] MS 48–67 get 39

106.14–15 at all] MS 48–67 at all 39

106.23 was,] MS 48–67 was 39

107.28 anything] MS 48–67 any thing 39

107.29 Thank you.] MS Thank you; 39 Thank you! 48–67

108.8 As] MS as *all editions*

109.6 five] two MS

109.10 anybody] MS any body *all editions*

109.16–18 son (none . . . descent) who] MS son—(none . . . descent)—who *all editions*

109.31 that,] MS |that, <—>| that— *all editions*

111.16 thus,] MS 48–67 thus 39

111.25 rather] MS *om. all editions*

111.26 anything] MS 48–67 any thing 39

111.34 out of] in low MS

112.10–11 girls; which] MS girls; the 39 girls. These 48–67

112.29 which] that MS

113.3 awa',] MS awa,' 39–48 67 awa'. 58

113.11 time] time, MS

113.25 very] *om.* 48–67

113.35 the] and the MS

114.2 Price. "Was] MS |Price "Was| Price, "was *all editions*

114.12 not one] not a one 48–67

114.17 Nicholas. "What] MS |Nicholas "What| Nicholas; "what *all editions*

114.22 dressing beautiful] MS dressing beautifully *all editions*

114.29 fault.] *See Appendix 3 for additional text in MS*

115.13 everything] MS 48–67 every thing 39

115.35 think.] *See Appendix 3 for additional text in MS*

116.23 Weel then] MS Weel, then *all editions*

116.24 fist. "What] MS |fist "What| fist, "what *all editions*

116.26 whipster] MS whipster, *all editions*

117.5 nuptials;] MS 48–67 nuptials: 39

117.7 So that the] MS So, that the 39 So the 48–67

117.15 matter?] matter! MS
117.16 Oh! You] MS Oh! you *all editions*
117.29 people, and Miss] people. Miss 48–67
117.30–1 feelings] MS feeling *all editions*
117.37 jerk.] *See Appendix 3 for additional text in MS*
117.38 will."] will"—returned the miller's daughter. MS |will"—<said> ↑returned↓ the miller's daughter.|
117.39 words, minx] MS words. Minx 39 words, Minx 48–67
118.6 peculiarly expressive] *not in* MS
118.8 again.] MS 48–67 again, 39
118.11 tears,] MS 48–67 tears. 39
118.19 into] in 48–67
119.3–4 flesh-tint she] MS |flesh-tint <which> she| flesh-tint which she *all editions*
119.5 therein] the rein 67
119.6 patrons to] MS patrons, to *all editions*
119.23 of,"] of my dear" MS
119.28 Why,] Why my dear, MS
119.32 La, Miss La Creevy,] La Miss Creevy MS
120.26 feature] features 67
120.30 preserved] MS introduced *all editions*
121.18 great] *om.* 48–67
122.4 cried] said MS
122.20 portrait.] *See Appendix 3 for additional text in MS*
122.26 considering, with] MS considering with *all editions*
122.35 him even] MS him, even *all editions*
124.3 Ralph.] Ralph, looking at Kate to see how she received the intelligence. MS
124.4 Now,] Now MS
124.5 have] *not in* MS
125.4–5 and was warmly attached to her children, and had] MS and had *all editions*
125.30 dress-maker] dress-maker, MS
125.36 with a great] MS with great *all editions*
126.15 directly."] *See Appendix 3 for additional text in MS*
126.20 him, as] MS 48–67 him as 39
126.28 went] had gone 48–67
126.35 with, every] MS 48–67 with every 39
127.30 only] but MS
128.5 remark. "Must] MS |remark "Must| remark, "must *all editions*
128.9 Ralph. "I hope not."] MS |Ralph. <"Maybe!"> "I hope not."| Ralph. *all editions*

128.21 Attar of Roses] MS |<otto of roses> Attar of Roses| otto of roses *all editions*

128.32 upon] on 48–67

128.39 there, as] MS 48–67 there as 39

129.1 Hallo!] MS Hollo! *all editions*

129.11 you demmit] MS |you<,> demmit| you, demmit *all editions*

129.14 when, wheeling] MS 48–67 when wheeling 39

129.37 till] until 48–67

129.39 till] until 48–67

130.6 had married on] had been married for MS

130.13 per centage] percentage 58–67

130.21 "My fault] MS 48–67 'My fault 39

131.15 you!"] MS you?" *all editions*

132.7 five to seven] eight to ten MS

132.12 then] *not in* MS

132.17 though] if MS

134 title MR.] *om.* 48–67

137.39 and dark] and how dark 48–67

138.26 attic or cellar] attic and cellar 48–67

139 title SMOOTHLY] SMOOTH 48–67

141.8 anybody] nobody 48–67

141.13 yours] yourn, 48 your'n, 58–67

141.13 go in] go on in 48–67

143.2 exerted] 48–67 excited 39

144.18 I wish I was] I wish *I* was 48–67

144.38 of the] of her 48–67

146.19 of reddish] of a reddish 48–67

147.36 or to think] or think 48–67

148.1–2 Nicholas slightly bowed, and waiting] Nicholas, waiting 48–67

149.6–7 lodgement] lodging 48–67

149.25 he was] Smike was 48–67

151.12 upon his] on his 48–67

153.12 perturbation. And without] perturbation. Without 48–67

153.33 till] until 48–67

153.37 shall] should 67

154.3 very] *om.* 48–67

154.31 Nicholas, smiling.] Nicholas. 48–67

155.24 cried] laughed 48–67

155.30 Swallows's] Swallow's 58–67

158.20 reply; and Squeers] reply. Squeers 48–67

159.34 "returned] "you have returned 48–67

162.13 light, for he] light; he 48–67

162.20 on his nearer] on nearer 48–67

163.10 Weel] Well 48–67
163.22 Beatten a] Beatten the 48–67
164.15 hart] heart 48–67
164.15 Beatten a] Beatten the 48–67
164.15 it's] 58–67 its 39 it 's 48
164.17 could] might 48–67
165.17 had no] had had no 48–67
166.33 although] though 48–67
167.14–15 of its legal] of legal 48–67
167.20 got] *om.* 48–67
168.18 could say] had said 48–67
168.19 arrangement, and Mr.] arrangement. Mr. 48–67
168.21 being.] being made. 48–67
169.1 and supper] and a supper 48–67
169.2 and put] and had put 48–67
169.6 than the] than on the 48–67
169.6 he kept] he had kept 48–67
169.10–11 she had had a] she had a 48–67
169.23 the young] a young 48–67
170.4 sister] 39 *some copies (later impressions)* visiter 39 *some copies (early impressions)* visiters, 48 visitors, 58–67
The error of 'visiter' for 'sister' was noted by Dickens in a letter of ?29 June 1838, and subsequently corrected in later printings of 39. The correction was not reflected in 48, strongly suggesting that 48 was based on an early printing of 39, and perhaps that Dickens no longer objected to, or even noticed, the erroneous reading when revising for 48. The change to the plural form in 48–67 makes better sense of the error.
170.19 that] as 48–67
170.28 sitiwation, not] sitiwation, and not 48–67
171.10 was] had been 48–67
172.2–3 Mr. Lillyvick. Mr. Snewkes... Mr. Lillyvick—Miss Petowker] 48–67 Mr. Lillyvick, Mr. Snewkes... Mr. Lillyvick. Miss Petowker 39
172.10 she] 67 he 39–58
172.24 great] much 48–67
172.30 off] of 48
173.26 Which] This 48–67
174.7 "'Mother,' she] 48–67 "'Mother, 'she 39
174.9 convulsions] conwulsions 48–67
174.11 convulsions] conwulsions 48–67
174.14–15 remember that,] remember, 48–67

174.38 repeated by] repeated on them by 48–67
176.2 has] took 48–67
176.29 gets] was to get 48–67
178.6 countenance, and bore] countenance. He bore 48–67
178.12 of] *not in* MS
178.15 delight during] MS delight, during *all editions*
178.27 friend] friend's MS
179.14 hunger and thirst] hunger or thirst 48–67
179.15 Such preparations] Such simple preparations MS
179.15 make for] MS make, for *all editions*
179.28–9 taciturnity. "Both] MS |taciturnity "Both| taciturnity; "both *all editions*
180.10 malice] malice and villainy MS
180.21 hesitating] hesitatingly MS
180.26 have—] have done— 48–67
180.27 or] and MS
180.28–9 tame and passive] MS tamely and passively *all editions*
180.33 further] more 48–67
181.5 Squeers; and having] Squeers. Having 48–67
181.6 his feelings] his real feelings MS
181.11 Nicholas. Newman] Nicholas, and Newman MS
181.17 recuvvor] MS recuvver *all editions*
181.30 tortorshell] MS tortershell *all editions*
181.32 very much] very much inwardly MS
181.37 satiated] sasiated 48–67
182.6 before long] in time MS
182.19 moments' reflection] moments deep reflection MS
182.37 read it] read to 67
183.5 man. "Make] MS |man "Make| man—"make *all editions*
183.11 further thought] consideration 48–67
183.25 detention.] *See Appendix 3 for additional text in MS*
184.2 you,] you MS
184.21 dismay, and the] dismay; the 48–67
184.31 Oh, you're] Oh you're MS
184.33 cried obdurately] cried out obdurately MS
184.38 corduroy] drab 48–67
185.1 stop here, my] stop my MS
185.3 Oh, do] Oh do MS
185.11 as] and MS
185.17 shall leave] shall have to leave MS
185.32–3 are rarely sulky longer than when] are sulky only so long as MS |are <fierce> sulky only so long as|

185.37 he] *om.* 48–67
186.27 Mrs. Kenwigs;] Mrs. Kenwigs MS
186.37 *sal volatile.*] *See Appendix 3 for additional text in MS*
187.7 had] *not in* MS
188.17 any thing] anything 48–67
191.20 like that outside] like the prospect outside 48–67
194.11 although] though 48–67
195.2 you?] *you!* 48–67
195.4 post as secretary . . . gentleman to be had.] post to be had, as secretary . . . gentleman. 48–67
195.28 girl, Sir,] girl? 48–67
196.27 the morrow's] to-morrow's 48–67
196.39 hand; and as] hand. As 48–67
197.12 the narrow passage] the passage 48–67
197.25 cry] cry out MS
197.25 gentlemen] gentleman MS
197.27 gentlemen] gentleman MS
198.28 steam-boats] steam ships MS
198.32 further] farther 48–67
199.21 in the event] in event 48–67
199.35 member, and "dear Pugstyles"] member. "Dear Pugstyles" 48–67
200.9 honey—now] honey; Now MS honey; now 48–67
200.16–17 'to play the devil . . . everybody?' "] MS to play the very devil . . . everybody?" *all editions*
200.20 came . . . table,] *not in* MS
200.33 To which Mr.] To this, Mr. 48–67
200.36 DEAR PUGSTYLES] DEAR MR. PUGSTYLES 67
200.38 power] MS powers *all editions*
201.6 as I have,] *not in* MS
201.12 dear Pugstyles] dear Mr. Pugstyles 67
201.14 circumstances?] circumstances Sir? MS
201.18 God] Heaven 48–67
201.31 Gregsbury. "A] MS | Gregsbury "A | Gregsbury; "a *all editions*
202.4 you have] you've MS
202.7 those] MS 48–67 these 39
202.10 anything,] MS anything *all editions*
202.20 capacity,"] capacity, sir," 48–67
202.34 possibly,"] possibly, sir," 48–67
203.17 mean?"] mean, sir?" 48–67
203.34–5 (including . . . about my independence and good sense);] *not in* MS (including . . . about independence and good sense); 48–67

203.38 discharge of my] *om.* 48–67
204.5 duty] *not in* MS
204.14 damn] curse 48–67
204.14–15 not... privileges?] siding with the people that have got most money, MS
204.29 don't] do 48–67
204.31–2 where... affected,] *not in* MS
205.10 has] had 48–67
205.15 sum,"] sum, sir," 48–67
205.23 be,"] be, sir," 48–67
205.32 morning,"] morning, sir," 48–67
206.1 remained untasted] was untasted MS |was <not touched> ↑untasted↓|
206.15 knows. Lying] knows, and lying MS
206.20 hardly be] be hardly MS
206.27 between the assistant] between assistant 48–67
206.27 a brutal] the brutal MS
206.27–8 and the toad-eater of] and toad-eater to 48–67
207.9 and finally] and had finally 48–67
207.11 French Language as spoken by Natives] MS French language as spoken by natives *all editions*
207.18 Newman. "That's] MS |Newman "That's| Newman, "that's *all editions*
207.20 said] cried 48–67
207.36 gentlemen] gentleman MS
207.37 rather] *om.* 48–67
208.18–19 cylinder supported... and painted] cylinder, not unlike an Italian iron, supported on four crooked pegs, and painted 48–67
208.21 Mrs. Kenwigs] Mr. Kenwigs 48–67
209.32 the] *not in* MS
209.34 mournfully] *not in* MS
209.35 Lo, eh?] *not in* MS
210.3 while] and MS
210.7 regarded... lying] looked frowningly and attentively on, laying MS
210.15 towards] toward MS
212.9 workers'] worker's 48–67
212.35 came] was 48–67
213.25 have horrid] have demd horrid MS |have demd <cramp> horrid|
214.7 old] demd old MS |<that> demd old|

214.10 and crime] and a crime 48–67

214.27 it] *om.* 48–67

214.30 man] servant 48–67

214.34 his nose off his demd countenance] MS his demd nose off his countenance *all editions*

214.39 contemptuously] *om.* 48–67

215.13 could] need 48–67

215.25–6 trouble to have young people who] MS 48–67 trouble, to have young people, who 39

215.32 way;] way, MS

215.39 Madame] MS 48–67 Madam 39

216.16 anywhere] any where MS

216.30 import and meaning] intent and meaning MS |in<troduction> ↑tent and meaning↓ |

216.32 monosyllable when] MS monosyllable, when *all editions*

216.33 brain; and others] brain; others 48–67

216.34 anybody] any body MS

216.36 though] although 48–67

218.15 No, my] No my MS

218.20 any one] anyone MS

218.35 further] farther MS

219.6 was] is sometimes 48–67

219.9 their] the MS

219.14 not restrain] not quite restain 48 not quite restrain 58–67

219.18 Kate, weeping.] Kate. 48–67

219.24 "Hush—pray,"] "Hush," 48–67

220.6 wide] *om.* 48–67

220.6 riches and greatness] the two MS

220.15–16 the rich lady and the rich daughter] the lady and daughter 48–67

220.20 her:] her, MS her; 48–67

220.20 requested they] requested that they 67

220.27 the coarsest] *om.* 48–67

220.32 *un*common] uncommon MS

221.3 Why,] MS 48–67 Why 39

221.8 lottery] Lottery MS

221.8 she] it MS

221.9 she] it MS

221.14 letter] MS 39 *some copies* 48–67 latter 39 *some copies (early impressions)*

221.16 It] Poor fellow, it MS

221.18 She little] MS she little *all editions*

225.25 Kate, turning away.] Kate. 48–67

226.21 intended] intending 48–67
227.11 Fourth] Third 48–67
229.34 open, while Mr.] open; Mr. 48–67
231.38 Madame] 48–67 Madam 39
232.31 gasping, and it] gasping; it 48–67
233.6 my lord] you bad man 48–67
234.19 I have] have I 48–67
234.23 us all with] us with all 48–67
235.3 thrice, and gurgled] thrice, gurgled 48–67
235.10 But although] Nevertheless, although 48–67
235.14 Knag's] 39 *some copies* 48–67 Knag 39 *some copies*
235.29 retired] altered 48–67
237.3 enveloped] 48–67 developed 39
237.24 very] *om.* 48–67
239.7 or emigrated] or had emigrated 48–67
239.21–2 any body] anybody 67
239.24 till] until 48–67
242.7 Well, then] Then 48–67
243.5 seat, and as he did so, glanced] seat. As he did so, he glanced 48–67
243.20 "laughed consumedly."] laughed consumedly. 48–67
243.33–4 disgust and] *om.* 48–67
243.37 Lord Verisopht] Lord Frederick Verisopht 48–67
244.6 Lord Verisopht] Lord Frederick 48–67
244.11 everything] every thing 58–67
245.16 Chowser] 48–67 Chouser 39
245.24 astounded] astonished 48–67
245.26 his glass] *his* glass 48–67
246.37 now] *om.* 48–67
247.22 gone; and the] gone; the 48–67
247.22 leant back] he leaned back 48–67
247.26 Meantime] Meanwhile 58–67
247.32 started now and then when] started sometimes, when 48–67
248.8 Kate bit her lip, and looking] Kate, looking 48–67
248.21 one] a 48–67
248.22 instantly] *om.* 48–67
248.32 leant] leaned 48–67
249.12 torture] emotion 48–67
249.14 you madman] you old madman 48–67
250.33 but] save 48–67
250.35 so] *om.* 48–67
251.23 quelled by her eye, and] *om.* 48–67
251.37 wore] bore 48–67

252.3 reeled] went 48–67
252.6 west end] West End MS
252.21 anything] MS 48–67 any thing 39
252.25 hurried] trotted 48–67
253.21 confidant] MS 48–67 confident 39
253.25–28 whom—from . . . obtain—London] MS whom, from . . . obtain, London *all editions*
253.33 poor Miss] poor little Miss 48–67
253.33 Creevy] MS Creevy's *all editions*
253.34 She] The MS
Dickens has made a slip of the pen.
253.37 of] MS at *all editions*
254.14 Now,] MS 48–67 Now 39
255.3 that,] MS that *all editions*
255.10 God] Heaven 48–67
255.11 me,] MS me; *all editions*
255.27 considered——"] MS considered." *all editions*
255.34 them you] them that you 48–67
255.35 them a] them in a 48–67
255.39 will with the power.] will is with the power, *I* think. 48–67
256.6 at furthest] *om.* 48–67
256.20 recommended] recommend MS
256.26 falsehood with] falsehood along with MS
256.35 complicated] extraordinary MS
257.5 not.] MS 48–67 not, 39
257.20 furious] *om.* 48–67
257.21 burst into the centre of the] came into the 48–67
257.25–6 scowl of deadly hatred, while] scowl; while 48–67
257.29 calm; consider."] MS calm, consider—" 39–58 calm, consider——" 67
257.39 them] those I love MS
258.3 you—you, who] you—who, 48–67
258.8 blights and] MS blights, and *all editions*
258.10 that *that* man knows] that that man knows MS that he knows 48–67
258.14 he—accuse] MS 48–67 he accuse 39
258.18 wretched] *om.* 48–67
258.19 and most degrading] *om.* 48–67
258.26 this!"] this." MS
260.3 That] The 48–67
260.28 held] hold MS
260.29 now] *not in* MS

261.17 ever have strung] ever string MS
261.23 honest] *om.* 48–67
261.33 and clasping him in her arms,] *om.* 48–67
261.36 God's] Heaven's 48–67
262.19 fainted] swooned 48–67
262.27 will] shall 48–67
263.4 best."] *See Appendix 3 for additional text in MS*
263.17 even] *om.* 48–67
263.28 speak] *See Appendix 3 for additional text in MS*
264.5 get no further] say no more 48–67
264.9 now, for] now, Smike, for 48–67
264.10 give.] *See Appendix 3 for additional text in MS*
264.13 What,] What MS
265.7 interval, for the] interval. The 48–67
265.7 shrank] shrunk 48–67
267.17 demanded, and the] demanded. The 48–67
267.27 con-sarn] 39–48 con-sarn *end-of-line hyphen* 58 consarn 67
267.37 previous] previously 48–67
268.9 of] on 48–67
269.16 upon] on 48–67
269.32 too] *om.* 48–67
269.37 anythink] anything 48–67
272.2 it, however.] it. 48–67
272.17 receiving] received 58–67
274.22 except] rather than 48–67
274.35 altogether] *om.* 48–67
275.3 ever there were an Alphonse who carried] ever an Alphonse carried 48–67
276.25 "You are,] 58–67 "You are 39–48
277.18 that] this 48–67
280.25 discourse as this they] discourse, they 48–67
281.3 of] *om.* 48–67
281.11 usually] *om.* 48–67
281.12 ship, and] ship, Smike, and 48–67
282.16 it rained] it has rained 48–67
282.33–4 gentle] *om.* 48–67
283.15 remained indelibly fastened in his] remained upon his 48–67
283.29 onwards] onward 48–67
284.4 than that they had already performed] than yesterday's 48–67
284.11–12 foul and treacherous] *om.* 48–67
284.22 huge] *om.* 48–67
284.31 very] *om.* 48–67

286.21	purse] sack 48–67
289.13	very] *om.* 48–67
289.16	great] big 48–67
289.28	which] *om.* 48–67
290.2	same confidence] same degree of confidence 48–67
293.10	there] that 48–67
293.18	them] 'em 48–67
293.30	them] 'em 48–67
295.12	she, indeed?] she? 48–67
295.18	that] *om.* 48–67
295.25	that] *om.* 48–67
295.28	conversation, and Nicholas] conversation. Nicholas 48–67
295.32	set] get 48–67
296.13	prompter's] prompt 48–67
297.29	not] no 48–67
297.33–4	alone, and just] alone. Just 48–67
299.4	conversation, and deeming] conversation. Deeming 48–67
300.17	although] though 48–67
301.12	was] were 48–67
301.32	very marked] *om.* 48–67
301.35	and always] and also always 48–67
303.1	men, you are] men are 48–67
304.13	by that means] *om.* 48–67
305.39	real] regular 48–67
306.5–6	ships' provision] 48–67 ships' provi-vision *end-of-line hyphen* 39
306.29	show him where] show where 48–67
307.5	God] Heaven 48–67
309.27	it] *om.* 58–67
311.34	gold] golden 67
312.14	ones, but rather] ones; he rather 67
312.31	great] good 48–67
313.22	now] *om.* 48–67
314.34	either] *om.* 48–67
315.1	afterwards] after 48–67
315.25	and been] and had been 67
316.21	ability] utility 58–67
316.32	most] *om.* 48–67
319.38	complacency, and it] complacency. It 48–67
319.38	finished, inquired] finished, she inquired 48–67
320.32	The] At the 48–67
322.15	thoroughfares; extra] thoroughfares; and extra 48–67
324.21	till] until 48–67

326.4	that] this 48–67
326.5	severally] *om.* 48–67
326.7	inscribed] 39 *some copies* 48–67 incsribed 39 *some copies*
326.24	Nicholas, smiling.] Nicholas. 48–67
327.10	eulogium, and almost] eulogium. Almost 48–67
330.1	that] *om.* 48–67
330.2	his wife] a wife 48–67
330.3	he is] he's 48–67
331.24	woman] women 67
331.35	doubt,] 58–67 doubt; 39–48
332.22	God] Heaven 67
332.31–2	for it: for it's] for it. It's 67
337.9	everything] every thing 48
337.32–3	over and over and over] over and over 48–67
339.15	suite] suit 67
340.18	Verisopht] Frederick 67
340.38	Verisopht] Frederick 67
341.1	Verisopht] Frederick 67
341.5	Lord Verisopht] the other 67
341.18	Verisopht] Frederick 67
341.34	Verisopht] Frederick 67
343.33–4	all," replied Verisopht. "Where] all. Where 67
344.20	Verisopht] Frederick 67
348.3	Lord Verisopht] Lord Frederick Verisopht 67
352.16	sitting himself down.] seating himself. 67
354.6	Nickleby,] 48–67 Nickleby," 39
357.20	proof] proofs 58–67
358.20	Lord Verisopht] Lord Frederick Verisopht 67
358.24	Verisopht] Frederick 67
358.26	upon] on 67
360.39	Lord Verisopht] Lord Frederick Verisopht 67
361.16	Verisopht] Frederick 67
361.21	Verisopht] Frederick 67
361.25	Verisopht] Frederick 67
361.30	Verisopht] my lord 67
361.36	Verisopht] Frederick 67
362.5	with poor] with my poor 58–67
363.35	himself; passing] himself, and passing 67
364.3	Pyke] Pike 67
364.16	honour] house 67
364.26	Verisopht] Frederick Verisopht 67
365.8	Pyke] Pike 67

365.10	whole] *om.* 67
365.15	Pyke] Pike 67
365.23	turned] turn ed 39
367.23	*enfant.*'] 48–67 *enfant.* 39
367.30	"At] 58–67 "'At 39–48
368.1	"The] 58–67 "'The 39–48
368.3	Belfillaire."] 58–67 Belfillaire.'" 39–48
369.7	Verisopht] Frederick 67
369.20	Lord Verisopht] Lord Frederick Verisopht 67
369.29	quite] *om.* 67
369.30	whole] *om.* 67
370.6	Verisopht] my lord 67
370.38	twenty years] 58–67 twenty-years 39–48
371.6	Verisopht] Frederick 67
371.22	Verisopht] Frederick 67
372.23	Verisopht] Frederick 67
373.2–3	Lord Verisopht] Lord Frederick Verisopht 67
373.15	dependent] dependant 48–67
373.33	Lord Verisopht] Lord Frederick Verisopht 67
376.25–6	day; and as] day. As 67
376.32	excited] exerted 67
376.36	too."] 48–67 too.' 39
378.7	his sternest] the sternest 58–67
380.2	live,] 58–67 live 39–48
388.18	upwards] upward 67
388.26	withdrew, bowing . . . walked out.] withdrew. 67
389.24	Ralph.] 48–67 Ralph^ 39
394.24	head.] 39 *some copies* 48–67 head 39 *some copies*
397.2	Snevellicci] 48–67 Snevellici 39
398.31	"Ah! nothing] "Nothing 67
398.31	it, Sir,"] 39 *some copies* it Sir," 39 *some copies* it, sir," 48–67
399.22	of it,"] 48–67 of it, 39
399.35	Snevellicci] 48–67 Snevellici 39
402.38	Miss Squeers] 48–67 MissSqueers 39
415.1	any thing] anything 67
415.16	arranged, and Newman,] arranged. Newman, 67
416.18	every thing] every-thing *end-of-line hyphen* 48 58–67
416.21	swords,] 39 *some copies* 48–67 swords^ 39 *some copies*
416.24	dead, and churchyards] dead, churchyards 67
417.2–3	side Kingston, and cried] side of Kingston, and had cried 67
417.13	Every thing] Everything 48–67
418.31	than when he went in.] than he had gone into it. 67

418.32	any thing] anything 48–67
422.2	any thing] anything 67
422.15	bandied] 48–67 banded 39
422.39	Lord Verisopht] Lord Frederick Verisopht 67
423.39	fire—do you hear me?"] fire." 67
429.13	again,] 48–67 again. 39
431.12	the brother of] *om.* 48–67
431.26	you had had as] you had as 58–67
431.35	every thing] everything 48–67
431.39	every thing] everything 48–67
432.7–8	any thing] anything 48–67
432.9	every thing] everything 48–67
432.12	every thing] everything 58–67
437.21	these] this 48–67
440.39	was—eh?"] was!" 67
441.27	Ralph, savagely.] Ralph. 48–67
441.33	"Pshaw] 48–67 "'Pshaw 39
441.34–5	uncomfortable and private-madhouse-sort of manner] uncomfortable, private-madhouse-sort of a manner 48–58 uncomfortable, private-madhouse-sort of manner 67
443.23	Sir,] 48–67 |sir,| Sir^ 39
444.18	excellencies] excellences 48–67
444.20	and then] and he then 67
445.7–8	be expressive] be well expressive 67
445.15	that] *om.* 48–67
447.3	that's] that 48–67
447.4	which] this 48–67
447.28	quickly] *om.* 48–67
447.31	is, that he] is, he 48–67
448.5	year] years 48–67
448.17	of a way] of way 58–67
448.36	or] and 48–67
448.37	can] could 48–67
450 title	ACQUAINTANCES, AND BRIGHTER] ACQUAINTANCES. BRIGHTER 48–67
451.35	well] *om.* 48–67
453.24	now] *om.* 67
454.5–6	Pyke, that's all.] Pyke. 48–67
456.24	stop too, and Nicholas] stop too; and Nicholas 48–58 stop; Nicholas 67
456.36	it] *om.* 48–67
458.26–7	mean, eh? What d'ye mean?"] mean, eh?" 48–67

459.34	further] farther 48–67
461.6–7	for Mr. Trimmers] 48 for Mr. Linkinwater 39 from Mr. Linkinwater 58–67
461.36	mine that we] mine, that we 48–58 mine, whom 67
462.22	air, besides, two] air, two 67
462.28	And the] The 67
464.4	an't such] ain't such 67
464.39	now; but be] now—be 67
465.5	completely] *om.* 67
466.29	about] *om.* 48–67
467.3	some] *om.* 48–67
467.18	any body] anybody 48–67
467.19	there] *om.* 48–67
467.34	"whether, as] 48–67 whether, "as 39
470.5	go begging] go a begging 67
470.25	And having] Having 48–67
471.14	and] *om.* 67
472.6	any body] anybody 48–67
472.38	the flaxen] her flaxen 48–67
474.32	interfering] interposing 67
474.35	attention] attentions 67
474.36	attention] attentions 67
475.5	six and sixpence] six and six 48–67
475.7	it'll] 48 67 it 'll 39 58
475.7	home] *om.* 67
475.9	by it;] by it all; 67
476.11	those whose] those Londoners whose 67
476.18–19	and no] and has no 67
477.3	square, he keeps] square, keeps 48–67
479.17	an air] a air 67
483.24–5	complete] completed 48–67
484.38	God] Lord 67
485.35	There] They 48–67
485.36	all, and as] all. As 67
486.23	free, generous, spirited] free, generous spirited 58–67
486.25	thanking 'em] thanking of 'em 48–67
486.34	withdrew; and in] withdrew; in 48–67
489.1	Kate,"] 48–67 Kate^" 39
489.30	on, indeed I will."] on: indeed I will." 48–58 on." 67
492.27	better] good 48–67
493.13	absurd idiot] absurd old idiot 48–67
493.28	or their] or of their 67

493.29	time,] 48–67 time^ 39
494.21	I have thought] I *have* thought 48–67
494.28	he will be] he *will* be 48–67
494.38	am very easily] am easily 48–67
496.16	upon] on 48–67
496.37	and the pain] and pain 48–67
498.2–3	Lord Verisopht] Lord Frederick Verisopht 48–67
498.15	the low] his low 67
499.39	the delicate] his delicate 67
501.11	Lord Verisopht] Lord Frederick Verisopht 48–67
501.19	Cowardly, Lord Verisopht!] Cowardly! 48–67
503.1–2	downwards] downward 48–67
503.22	master, sir—] master— 48–67
505.16	and be asked no questions.] and no questions asked. 48–67
506.20	at] of 58–67
507.2	and the] and as the 67
507.20	against] again 67
507.25	a roll] a little roll 48–67
508.19	night; and taking] night; and, taking 48–58 night. Taking 67
508.21	muster] master 48–58
508.24	And what] What 48–67
508.25	sunk] sank 67
508.34	which precedes] preceding 48–67
509.8	upon the box] on the box 48–67
509.18	there] theer 67
510.32–3	summut aboot Sarah—to the Sarah Son's] something aboot Sarah—to the Sarah's Son's 48 something aboot Sarah's Son's 58–67
511.4	mun] man 48–67
511.6	Draat] Drat 48–67
511.7	wont] want 48–67
511.25–7	big one . . . little ones] big rose . . . little roses 67
512.23	directly] when 67
513.33	thot] that 48–67
514.30–1	fail; and after] fail. After 67
516.38	Thee'lt] 58–67 The'lt 39–48
516.39	bee'nt] been't 58 bean't 67
517.6	and placing] then, placing 67
517.7	out, signed to him to] out, he signed to Smike to 67
518.14	retard; and it] retard. It 48–67
519.26	very] *om.* 48–67
521.25	what one she] what prison or escape she 67

522.15	that, of course.] that. 67
522.20–1	subject; and sticking] subject; sticking 67
522.22	click, said] click, he said 67
523.8	Tim, "and] 48–67 Tim," and 39
523.11	has grown] is growing 48–67
523.18	hour and more] hour or more 48–67
523.21	"The night] 48–67 The night 39
523.28	these] those 67
527.16–17	but directly he resumed the theme, Tim relapsed into a state of most] but, directly he resumed the theme, Tim relapsed into a state of most 48–58 but, he no sooner resumed the theme, than Tim relapsed into a state of the most 67
527.19–20	nods and shrugs, which] 48–67 nods, and shrugs which 39
528.18	that] *om.* 48–67
528.32	those] these 48–67
529.18	success, and one] success: and one 48–58 success: one 67
529.35	remembered] remember 48–67
530.9	I have managed] I've managed 48–67
530.14	goodness,] *om.* 67
531.4	dead, and that] dead, that 48–67
531.7	it had required] it required 48–67
534.2	were] was 48–67
535.29	by little and little] *om.* 48–67
536.10	character, and from] character. From 48–67
536.11	were converted] they became converted 48–67
537.21	can put] can have put 48–67
537.24	before quarter-day] before the quarter-day 48–67
537.33	Kate,"] Kate?" 58–67
538.27	hurriedly] *om.* 48–67
539.2	for changing it] *om.* 48–67
540.4	God] Heaven 48–67
540.7	I'm] *I*'m 48–67
540.25	and,] *om.* 67
540.38–9	languishing, and leering] languishing, leering 48–58 languishing leering 67
541.14	any thing] anything 48–67
541.15	Nickleby, with a haughty air.] Nickleby. 48–67
542.15	which] *om.* 48–67
543.27	away, when he put] away. He then put 67
546.1	I am] I'm 58–67
553.17	vary] very 48–67
554.18	near] nigh 67

558.23 runaway boy] roonaway boy 58–67
558.25 thou'rt] thou't 67
559.7 You'll] 48–67 "You'll 39
559.26 ale, when he] ale. He 67
559.30–1 comfortable] coomfortable 67
571.28 pair] pairs 67
576.28 poor ones] poor houses 67
577.10 but there] but that there 67
580.2 to me—will you?"] to me?" 67
583.39 uttermost] utmost 58–67
586.6 some] *om.* 67
586.11 towards] toward 48–67
587.24 demder.'—] 48–67 demder.— 39
588.2 characters—hum—I] characters? I 67
589.3 else, and in] else; in 67
591.6 one] *om.* 67
591.20–1 best-humoured] 48–67 best^humoured *end-of-line space* 39
592.31 upon] on 67
593.27 bear it, by——"] bear it." 67
598.17 and] *om.* 67
599.39 day—eh?] day? 67
600.22 violence: and Squeers] violence. Squeers 67
600.28 "Now,"] 48–67 "Now" 39
601.38 but] *om.* 67
601.38 poor petty] 67 poor, petty 39–58
606.31 in short] 39 *some copies* 48–67 inshort 39 *some copies*
607.6 every thing] everything 48–67
608.27 till] until 67
609.31 have] had 67
609.34–5 him, described] him, he described 67
610.16 that] which 67
611.5 found he] 67 found, he 39–58
611.7 stanch and] *om.* 67
613.39 I am] I'm 48–67
616.31–2 stairs, and looking round saw] stairs. Looking round, he saw 67
617.18 very] *om.* 67
618.15 time two] time is two 67
619.25 upon] on 67
620.3 are!"] 39 *some copies* 48–67 are^^' 39 *some copies*
623.30 upon] on 67
624.17 his head] himself 67
624.19 expression in] expression on 67

625.1 you have] 39 *some copies* 48–67 youhave 39 *some copies*
627.19 with Madeline] with Miss Madeline 67
627.26 upon] on 67
628.12 I any] I help any 67
630.7 life—transfer] life, would transfer 67
630.9 upon] up on 58 on 67
632.6 mean time] meantime 48–67
632.36 "Do you] 39 *most copies* "No you 39 *some copies* 48–67
633.9–10 already—making . . . own—acting . . . and so] already. He is making . . . own. He is acting . . . and is so 67
633.11 the] his 67
637.32 Snevellicci] 58–67 Snevellici 39–48
646.32 laugh; and how] laugh; how 67
647.1 forgot] forgotten 67
650.13–14 "I—if I may venture to say so—oppose all change in her."] *om.* 67
651.36 is] was 67
655.23 the singular] this singular 58–67
655.38 a] *om.* 48–67
659.31 a delicious half hour] *om.* 67
660.1 away, and Kate] away. Kate 48–67
660.21–2 arm, and the door being quickly opened, had not] arm. The door being quickly opened, she had not 48–67
661.1 very] *om.* 67
661.20–1 there; to know . . . day; to feel] 48–67 there to know . . . day, to feel 39
662.26 would, was] would, there was 48–67
662.33 club-house, and half-a-mile] club-house, half-a-mile 67
662.34 was] were 48–67
662.34–5 *La Merveille*] *La Morveille* 58 other games 67
663.7–8 players, who were] players. They were 67
663.17 was, and wore] was: and wore, 48–58 was. He wore, 67
663.28–9 or fixed] or he might have been fixed 67
663.34 out this] out, which this 48–67
665.21 upon] on 67
665.33 Verisopht] Lord Frederick 67
666.15 day, will you?"] day." 67
666.18 for, hey?"] for?" 48–67
666.25 that] something 48–67
666.28 to Nickleby] to old Nickleby 48–67
666.35 inquiry, and both] inquiry. Both 48–67
667.27 of. Oh! look] of. Look 67
667.35 take, and I] take. I 48–67

667.39	reverse, and if we prolonged] reverse. If we prolonged 48 reverse. If we prolong 58–67
668.29	having thought,] *om.* 48–67
669.2	Mulberry, and this] Mulberry. This 48 Mulberry. This, 58–67
669.7	breast, and the] breast: and the 48–58 breast: the 67
669.13	Chowser] 48–67 Chouser 39
669.14	same caste, and] same caste were there, and 67
669.22	place, and they] place. They 48–67
669.28–9	indignation, and the] indignation; and the 48–58 indignation; the 67
670.19	G—,"] 58–67 G—" 39–48
670.19	replied, fiercely.] replied. 48–67
670.22	Mulberry, gnashing his teeth.] Mulberry. 48–67
670.25	upon] on 67
670.29	well] *om.* 48–67
672.6	shot; and those] shot; those 67
672.19	considerably] *om.* 48–67
672.38	brooding] breeding 48–67
673.26	shrunk] shrank 67
674.8–9	Last night seemed a week ago, and months ago were as last night.] *om.* 48–67
674.10	knew, and now] knew; now, 48–67
674.19	there, and all] there. All 48–67
674.30–1	dishevelled,—all most probably the consequences of the previous day and night.] dishevelled,—all, most probably, the consequences of the previous day and night. 48–58 dishevelled. 67
675.26	upwards] upward 67
676.8–9	voice, rattled as if 'twere] voice, rattled, as if 'twere 48–58 voice, it rattled, as if it were 67
676.12	upon] on 67
676.16	leant] leaned 67
676.19	hangings to] hangings seemed to 48–67
676.34	quantity] 48–67 quanty 39
677.18	there, and then] there. He then 48–67
677.24	I knew] *I* knew 48–67
677.25	dog!] dog of a pawnbroker! 67
678.14	upon] on 48–67
679.10	me!] *me*! 48–67 *me!* 67
679.29	I've] I have 58–67
679.31	he!—lock] he!—I'll lock 67
680.9	song, and, the] song. The 48–67
680.10	selected, replaced] selected, he replaced 48–67

680.16 upwards] upward 67
680.23 The bearer] Bearer 48–67
680.26 "A chair?" said Arthur Gride.] "—A chair?" said Arthur Gride. 48–58 "—A chair?" 67
682.27 "It's *eau-d'or*] 48–67 "Its *eau-d'or* 39
682.39 we have a] we drink a 48–67
683.27 "He was] "*He* was 48–67
684.1–2 him at all] *om.* 48–67
684.3 Brooker."] 48–67 Brooker. 39
684.22 then] *om.* 48–67
685.24 who plainly] 58–67 who, plainly 39–48
686.1 tavern, and here] tavern. Here 48–67
686.11 shrieked] cried 48–67
686.31–2 forced him down] forced the latter down 48–67
687.3 really] *om.* 58–67
687.9–10 man; and if] man. If 48–67
687.10 is one feeling] is a feeling 48–67
687.10–11 one spark] a spark 48–67
687.17 Nicholas, fiercely.] Nicholas. 48–67
688.22 monstrous] *om.* 48–67
688.35 encouragement, for the] encouragement. The 48–67
689.25 good; and perhaps] good. Perhaps 48–67
689.32 heartless] *om.* 48–67
692.27 safety, and the] safety. The 48–67
693.37 despondent, expressive] despondent, and expressive 48–67
693.37 such] *om.* 67
695.15 I] It 58–67
695.35 behaviour, and so] behaviour. So 48–67
696.10 with them] *om.* 48–67
696.33 Kenwigs'] Kenwigs's 67
697.20 perfer] prefer 58–67
697.27 himself] hisself 48–67
699.6 virtue] virtues 67
699.13 feeling] feelings 58–67
699.22 that money that] that money which 67
700.15 a] as 58
700.17 natur] nature 58–67
700.31 use] youth 58–67
701.15 which] that 48–67
701.19 view, he wandered] view, wandered 48–67
701.20 London, although perfectly] London; perfectly 48–67
701.35 down at night] down each night 48–67

701.36	race, and generation] race, generation 67
702.5	jail-door] jail-doors 58–67
702.13	injustice, and misery] injustice, misery 48–67
702.18	cause or] *om.* 48–67
702.24	by the time] when 48–67
703.3	what] how much 48–67
703.6	cold ghastly] *om.* 48–67
703.13–14	perhaps in appearance than] perhaps, than 48–67
703.26	he] Nicholas 48–67
704.3	directly] *om.* 48–67
704.25	you have thought] you *have* thought 48–67
704.34	and the sneer] *om.* 48–67
705.8	that] who 67
705.12	indignantly] *om.* 48–67
705.14	would] could 48–67
705.18	Nicholas sternly; "neither in] Nicholas; "nor in 48–67
706.17	by, and to her] by; and to her, 48–58 by; to her, 67
706.36	firmly,] *om.* 48–67
706.37	it.] mine. 67
707.3	is] be 48–67
707.5–6	by menace and intimidation] *om.* 48–67
707.15	and looked] and have looked 48–67
707.22	foul] *om.* 48–67
707.24	that] *om.* 48–67
707.24	truth;—] 48–67 truth, 39
708.12	easily, and shall] easily. I shall 48–67
708.16	come] be 48–67
708.31	their] *om.* 48–67
708.36	supplication,] 67 supplication^ *end-of-line space* 39 supplication; 48–58
709.11	again."] 48–67 |again!"| again.' 39
709.19	gone, and Nicholas] gone. Nicholas 48–67
710.4	He, he!] He, he, he! 48–67
710.9	three.] 48–67 three, 39
710.10	pound] *om.* 67
710.34–5	done—nobody else.] done. 48–67
711.28	think, and if] think. If 48–67
711.36	This, the] This lamp, the 48–67
712.1	hideous] ugly 48–67
712.10	disdainful] *om.* 48–67
712.16	thief, fellow.] thief. 48–67
712.30	This however] However 67

713.17 that] who 48–67
713.32 their hearts] their very hearts 48–67
714.2 that, to] 48–67 that to 39
714.6 accusation, and whether] accusation. Whether 48–67
714.33 fond] *om.* 48–67
714.38 anybody] any body 48–67
715.1 base] *om.* 48–67
715.35 up] *om.* 48–67
715.36 and to scold] and scold 48–67
716.21 grandmama] grandmother 48–67
717.5 my] *my* 48–67
717.26 that] one 48–67
717.28 how that last night] how, last night, 48–67
717.35 disdainfully,] *om.* 48–67
717.37 him] *him* 67
718.4 Ralph, harshly,] Ralph, 48 Ralph; 58–67
720.20 quite] *om.* 48–67
720.31 not at all uncommon] not all uncommon MS not uncommon 48–67
721.26 dressing, and when] dressing. When 48–67
721.32 sunk] sank 67
722.3–4 door, and turning . . . alone, said] door; and, turning . . . alone, said 48–58 door; turning . . . alone, he said 67
722.10 delight, and Ralph] delight. Ralph 48–67
722.26 staggered] reeled 48–67
722.27–8 rage; his eyes so . . . face so] rage: his eyes so . . . face so 48–58 rage. His eyes were so . . . face was so 67
722.39 fierce] *om.* 48–67
723.17 here—liar] here? liar 58 Here? Liar 67
723.23 We] 48–67 “We 39
723.37 tried, and I] tried. I 48–67
724.2 vile] *om.* 48–67
725.1 passionately] *om.* 48–67
725.7 and an] and, in an 48–67
725.12 violent] *om.* 48–67
725.18 dead, and his] dead; his 48–67
725.36 spoke, and Nicholas] spoke. Nicholas 48–67
726.8 them] him 48–67
726.12 that?” cried Nicholas, starting] so?” cried Nicholas, rising 48–67
726.38–9 Your day is past, and night is coming on—”] Day is past in your case, and night is coming on.” 67
728.3 warn] tell 48–67
728.17–18 violently] *om.* 48–67

728.20 great] *om.* 48–67
728.22 and] 39 *some copies* 48–67 an^ 39 *some copies*
730.17 and would] and *would* 48–67
730.30–1 right, indeed—couldn't] right, she couldn't 67
731.11 upon their] on their 48–67
731.12 commendations upon] commendations on 48–67
731.18–19 so, and without] so. Without 48–67
731.24 splendour, and all her cares were over.] splendour. 48–67
732.24 to-night?] 58–67 to-night. 39–48
733.9 but of course] *om.* 67
733.10 same, though] same. Though 67
733.37 and sometimes be moved] and, sometimes, be moved 48–58 and sometimes, would be moved 67
734.12 Nickleby, and never] Nickleby; never 48–67
734.14 never was there… generalship, or] never were there… generalship, and 48–67
734.20 schemes, and various] schemes: various 48–67
734.20–1 opposite the means which she] opposite were the means she 67
734.24 victim, and the next time they met receive] victim; the next time they met, she would receive 48–67
734.31 her to] her daughter to 48–67
735.6 upon] on 48–67
735.22 recollection upon the subject, and if] recollection on the subject. If 48–67
736.13 it's] it 48–67
736.18 upon] on 48–67
736.31 upon] on 48–67
737.8 upon] on 48–67
737.21 one thought upon] a thought upon 48–58 a thought on 67
738.12–13 really were] were really 48–67
738.14 one] a 48–67
738.16 say that, I] say, that I 48–67
738.17 upon] on 48–67
738.21 very] *om.* 48–67
738.25 a monarch his.] a monarch in preserving his. 67
738.26 done and do every] done, and what they do every 48–67
739.1 honest,] *om.* 48–67
739.19–20 convinced there] convinced that there 48–67
739.20 and resolved] and he resolved 67
739.26 assistance, and so] assistance; and so 48–58 assistance; so 67
739.31 when a boy] *om.* 48–67
740.12 and go] and will go 48–67
740.34 do not.] don't. 48–67

740.38	heaven!"] 39 *some copies* 48–67 heaven!' 39 *some copies*
741.8	for the time] *om.* 48–67
741.9	same] *om.* 48–67
741.14	stealthily and savagely] *om.* 48–67
741.30	that—that young] that young 67
742.1	constrained] *om.* 48–67
742.2–6	the livid face, the horrible expression . . . there was] the face, the expression . . . there was 48–58 his face; there was 67
742.9–10	and these evidences of the most intense and violent passions] and his face's evidence of intense and violent passion 67
742.11	them] it 67
742.18	see, and Ralph] see. Ralph 48–67
742.19	which] *om.* 67
742.29–30	Gride, writhing with pain.] Gride. 48–67
742.31	threw him off] let him go, 48–67
742.38	upon] on 67
743.12	came, and the] came. The 48–67
743.16	again] *om.* 67
743.21	and] *om.* 67
743.25	rather] *om.* 67
743.27	all, for rumours] all. Rumours 48–67
744.1	Ralph, hoarsely.] Ralph 48 Ralph. 58–67
744.10	old grim] grim old 48–67
744.15	upon] on 48–67
744.30	then] *om.* 67
745.19	Give you but] Do you but give 48–67
745.22	upon] on 48–67
745.25	upon] on 48–67
745.27	eagerly] *om.* 48–67
746.18	and abject] *om.* 67
746.23	that heap of coin which] the heap which 48–67
746.31	and] *om.* 48–67
746.32–3	said, between his set teeth:] said: 48–67
746.36	every event which is of interest to most men, had (unless it is] all the events which are of interest to most men, have (unless they are 48–67
747.19	parcel,—"how] 58–67 parcel.—"how 39–48
748.4	peremptory] 48–67 preremptory 39
749.4	in] by 67
749.24	told, and all] told; and all 48–58 told; all 67
749.29	deep] *om.* 48–67
749.39	Ralph, quietly.] Ralph. 48–67

750.1 be so;] be, 48–67
750.8–9 that account] that the account 48–67
750.17 sternly] *om.* 48–67
750.21 upon] on 48–67
751.1 have] cause to be 67
751.15–16 not occasioned] not immediately occasioned 48–67
751.20 upon] on 48–67
751.27–8 money, or even . . . applied); the] money; the 48–67
751.30 ignorant; and the] ignorant; the 67
751.32 upon] on 48–67
751.39 himself, being] himself, he being 48–67
752.1 sight, and various comments upon] sight; and various comments on 48–58 sight; various comments on 67
752.16–17 legs . . . the palms of his hands, and bit] legs, uncrossed them, scratched his head, rubbed his eye, examined the palms of his hands, bit 48–67
752.28 down] *om.* 48–67
752.36 Squeers] 48–67 Squeers, 39
753.1 doggedly.] *om.* 48–67
753.3–4 disgrace. Let me . . . must be. Let me] disgrace; let me . . . must be; let me 48–67
753.26 certainly] *om.* 67
753.31 contained, of] contained, were of 48–67
754.2 but] save 67
754.16 out] *om.* 48–67
754.22 ow-dacious] ow-dacious *end-of-line hyphen* 48 owdacious 58–67
754.31 a-call] call 58–67
754.38 bounds] bonds 48–67
755.6 and now] and who now 67
755.20 not] *not* 48–67
755.30–1 substracted, besides.] substracted. 67
756.7 What his] What this 48–67
The type is damaged in 48, so the reading is uncertain.
756.7 appeared; for, after] appeared. After 67
756.26 a hand, a heart, a highway] a and, a art, a ighway 48–67
756.30 up] *om.* 48–67
756.38 shouted] roared 48–67
757.11 and empty] and I empty 67
757.27 agues] agers 48–67
757.36 I am] I'm MS
758.19 understanding too; I'm] understanding. I'm 67
759.24 Slider—that's all."] Slider." 67

759.32	*I*] I 58–67
760.1	believe that the] believe, the 48–67
760.16	which lay] *om.* 67
760.20	to shreds, those] to shreds with, those 67
760.21	and hoped] and what I hoped 48–67
760.34	in, and them] in: and them 48–58 in. Them 67
761.5	upwards] upward 67
761.22	further and further] farther and farther 48–67
761.36	any have] any such have 67
763.35	again, and once more Frank] again. Once more, Frank 48–58 again. Once again, Frank 67
764.9–10	returned, for Newman's] returned. Newman's 48–67
765.28	so] *om.* 67
765.29	so] *om.* 67
765.34	far] *om.* 48–67
765.35	but] *om.* 48–67
766.8	up] *om.* 48–67
768.3	the] *om.* 48–67
768.4–5	shrieking] calling 48–67
768.6	cried] said 48–67
768.17	now] *om.* 48–67
768.33	in, and the people that were] in, the people who were 67
768.35	shrunk] shrank 67
769.9	ultimately] *om.* 48–67
769.13	he described] he had described 48–67
769.14	firm] *om.* 48–67
770.11	would] will 67
770.13	would] will 67
770.35	slight] light 48–67
772.25	hastily] *om.* 48–67
772.26	do you, woman?] do you? 48–67
772.37–8	stairs, and after] stairs. After 48–67
772.38	lock, entered] lock, he entered 48–67
773.9	that] whom 48–67
773.14	sneered] replied 48–67
773.21	way lies] ways lie 67
774.24	He] *He* 48–67
774.39	further] other 48–67
775.11	appeared] arrived 48–67
775.27	sarcastically] *om.* 48–67
775.39	it] that 67

776.4 hold theirs.] hold their tongues. 67
776.5 Ralph, grinning with rage;] Ralph, 48–67
776.26 whether] *om.* 48–67
777.3 down upon] on 48–67
777.39 visible, and the] visible. The 48–67
778.23 impelled] should impel 48–67
779.39–80.1 same, and in] same. In 48–67
780.8 very] *om.* 48–67
780.33 to you—eh?] to you? 67
780.38–9 degradation, and because] degradation; and because 48–58 degradation; because 67
781.3 deny that—eh?] deny that? 67
781.12 besides] *om.* 48–67
782.13–14 manner which language cannot express, the] manner, the 48–67
782.18 open the] open of the 48–67
783.13 upon] on 48–67
783.15 great] *om.* 58–67
783.15 surprise] 48–67 suprise 39
783.17 and were] and that they were 48–67
785.6–7 with the sneer of a devil,] *om.* 48–67
785.30 and this] which 48–67
786.20 the family] my family 48–67
786.24 your] *your* 48–67
786.30 great] *om.* 48–67
787.3 document; and as] document; as 48–67
787.29 Ralph, gnawing his fingers.] Ralph. 48–67
787.36 this is—a double] this is! A double 48–67
788.19 against] again 48–67
788.34 these, and the] these; the 48–67
789.12 the] his 48–67
789.36 go] come 67
790.6 closely, and seeing] closely. Seeing 48–67
790.7 excited, faltered] excited, he faltered 48–67
790.37 man, and was] man. He was 48–67
791.11 him, and muttered] him, muttering 48–67
792.1 Ralph, eagerly;] Ralph; 48–67
792.18 hollow, dejected voice] hollow voice 48–67
792.32 Brooker, and Ralph] Brooker. Ralph 48–67
793.6 fixedly] *om.* 48–67
793.38 him] the brother 67
794.5 any] *om.* 67

795.4 Smike. I paid] Smike. Year by year, I paid 48–67
795.20 reveal] recal 48–67
796.7 utter] *om.* 48–67
796.9 it] the light 48–67
796.16 pretence, and finding] pretence. Finding 48–67
796.23 that, his] that his 48–67
797.39 him?"] 48–67 him?' 39
798.5 mastery, and the] mastery; the 48–67
799.33–4 how highly I felt such disinterested love should be regarded, and] how deeply I felt such disinterested love, and 48–67
800.6 was true as] was as true as 48–67
800.26 and awakened] and has awakened 48–67
800.37 that] when 48–67
800.37 then] *om.* 48–67
801.6 shall] may 48–67
801.25 that] the 48–67
801.33 that] Kate's 48–67
802.15 up] *om.* 48–67
802.37 further] more 48–67
803.10 more unhappy] more and more unhappy 48–67
804.12 instant] time 67
804.20 any one] anyone 58–67
804.27–8 and beseech] *om.* 67
805.19 him] himself 48–67
806.7 his] Ralph's 67
806.11 respect), and full] respect): full 48–58 respect): so he was full 67
806.29 and struck] and had struck 48–67
806.30 sodden in] sodden, while alive, in 48–67
807.3 those] these 48–67
807.8 he was] the man was 67
808.4–5 for the first time] *om.* 48–67
808.14 very] *om.* 67
808.31 that] his 48–67
809.38 minutes, when] minutes. Then 67
809.39 upon] on 48–67
810.31 and marriages] and for marriages 67
811.32 hung] hanged 67
812 title OTHERS; AND TIM] OTHERS. TIM 48–67
812.2–3 absent; and Nicholas] absent; Nicholas 67
812.10 done] rendered 48–67
812.23 that] *om.* 67
812.30 I] *I* 67
813.19 upon] on 48–67

813.23	it to flight] it flight 58
814.11	upon] on 48–67
814.28	upon] on 48–67
814.33	directed, and brother] directed. Brother 48–67
816.5	than] that 48–67
816.24–5	Sir, and must] sir, you must 48–67
817.9	himself] *om.* 48–67
819.35	to.] too. 48
819.36	other, and] other! And 48–67
820.5	and put] and to put 67
820.10	manner which] manner in which 48–67
820.13	Upon] On 48–67
821.6	Then there was] Then, there was 48–58 Then, there were 67
821.21–2	aside directly they] aside, directly they 48–58 aside, as soon as they 67
823.39	female, the] female—not the lawful Madame Mantalini, but the 48 female—not the lawful Madame Mantalini, but the 58–67
826.17	through] 48–67 though 39
826.19	Grogzwig] 48–67 Grogswig 39
826.20	upon] on 48–67
826.36	mak'est] mak'st 67
827.18	"but] 48–67 ' ' but 39
827.24	Faurx] Faux 67
828.7	Cheeryble, and at] Cheeryble; at 67
828.12	sort] sart 48–67
828.22	Telle'e] Tell'ee 58–67
828.29	soom] some 58–67
829.3	mak'] make 58–67
829.16	for the rebellion] for rebellion 67
829.20	him] himself 67
829.26–7	mounted upon the] mounted on the 48–58 mounted the 67
831.4	one] a 48–67
831.7	What's] Waat's 67
832.17	believers in their opinion.] believers. 48–67
832.23	at] by 67
833.3	declined, and two] declined. Two 67
833.3–4	afterwards went] afterwards they went 67
833.29	herself and the] herself, and the 48–58 herself; the 67
833.37	upon this, as upon] on this, as on 48–67
834.10	or dishonestly] or had dishonestly 48–67
834.15	horribly] *om.* 48–67
834.16–17	as Squeers] as Mr. Squeers 48–67
834.19–20	fellow; and ultimately] fellow. Ultimately 48–67

834.20 country, was] country, he was 48–67
834.21 high, noble spirits] high spirits 48–67
834.26 was rooted] was ever rooted 58–67
836.13 upon] on 48–67
836.14 came to] came there to 67

Contents (847–50)

58 has different chapter numbers in the second volume, Vol. 1 containing Chapters 1–32, Vol. 2 containing Chapters 33–65 (numbered 1–33); 67 has no Contents list.

Ch. 9 and various] and of various 48–58
Ch. 12 smoothly] smooth 48–58
Ch. 63 others, and Tim] others. Tim 48–58

Cheap Edition Preface (1848)

853.6 this class of] private 67
853.15 that] who 67
853.15 arise] spring 67
853.22 high-handed] high-minded 67
853.26 what about] what of 67
854.2 years, to those who can afford to pay for it.] years. 67
854.11–12 about them] about Yorkshire schools 67
854.13 having won an] MS having an *all editions*
854.19 the author of the "Pickwick Papers,"] me. 58
854.20 friend here, who] friend who 67
854.23 supposititious] MS 67 suppositious 48–58
854.24 did'nt] didn't MS 58–67
854.25 tardy] *not in* MS
854.30 county] MS country *all editions*
854.31 these] the 67
854.31 most] *om.* 58
854.32 deliver any letter] MS deliver a letter *all editions*
855.11 very] *om.* 58
855.13 vary] vara 67
855.15 while] whiles MS
The repetition of the phrase at lines 19–20 has 'while' in the MS and the compositor has changed the first occurrence to match it.
855.18 if ar can] if I can MS
855.18 telle'e] MS tellee *all editions*

855.25 In] Such of this class of schoolmasters as I did see, certainly justified his good opinion; or Nature wrote a much worse hand in their cases than she usually does. But in MS | Such of the→this class … wrote a <worse> ↑much < [?] worse>↓ hand in <?her copy-books> ↑their cases↓ than she usually does. <but after we> But in |

856.26–7 I had seen occasion, I] they had given me occasion I MS | they had given me <?any ?further [?] ?at ?that ?time, I should have reprinted [?] [?]> ↑occasion I↓ | |

856.27–8 details of legal proceedings, from certain old newspapers.] details, for their better satisfaction. MS

856.29 Preface] source MS preface 67

856.38 probability. But] probability. For this reason, they have been very slightly and imperfectly sketched. But MS
At this point the MS consists of the printed 39 Preface.

875.6 hundreds upon hundreds] thousands 67

857.8 to which] which 67

857.8 has since given rise] brought down upon me 67

857.11 profit that] profit which 58 profit, that 67

857.16–17 England. *n.p.* There] England. *n.p.* The brothers are now dead. *n.p.* There 67

857.22–3 Devonshire Terrace, *May*, 1848.] *om.* 58–67

RUNNING HEADS IN THE CHARLES DICKENS EDITION

According to the prospectus for the Charles Dickens edition, published in the *Athenaeum* (4 May 1867), 600, Dickens was himself responsible for devising the descriptive running headlines: 'A descriptive headline will be attached by the author to every right-hand page.'

Chapter 1. *An Investment under Consideration.*

Chapter 2. *Mr. Ralph Nickleby at Home.*
"Promoting" a Company.
An Honorable Gentleman Moves a Resolution.

Chapter 3. *News of Death.*
Mr. Ralph Nickleby makes Miss La Creevy's Acquaintance.
Uncle and Nephew.
A Charming Opening for Nicholas.

Chapter 4. *The Saracen's Head, Snow Hill.*
Mr. Squeers Receives his Young Friends.
Mr. Squeers Enlarges his List of References.
Nicholas is Accepted to Fill the Charming Opening.

Chapter 5. *Nicholas Departs from Miss La Creevy's.*
Mr. Squeers takes Breakfast in a moral manner.
Off for Yorkshire.

Chapter 6. *The Stage-coach in a Difficulty.*
By the Fireside on the Roadside.
A Shadow falls on Nature.
One Taken and Four Left.
Another Story Volunteered.
The New Baroness Von Koëldwethout.
A Spectre Calls upon the Baron of Grogzwig.
The Spectre Takes Leave of the Baron.

Chapter 7. *Domestic Intelligence.*
Nicholas partakes of the Pleasures of the Table.
Copy of a Letter from Mr. Newman Noggs.

Chapter 8. *The young Noblemen of Dotheboys Hall.*
Mr. Squeers's Educational System.
Mr. Squeers in Conclave with the young Noblemen.
Smike.

Chapter 9. *A Family Discussion on the subject of Knuckleboy.*
Tender Confidences.
Mr. John Browdie Joins the Tea-Party.
The Green-eyed Monster Appears.
The Party Breaks Up.

Chapter 10. *Kate and her Uncle Ralph.*
Kate Provided for.
Mr. Mantalini's Winning Ways.
Kate is Engaged by Madame Mantalini.

Chapter 11. *Newman Noggs calls on the Ladies.*
Newman Noggs evinces some Sensibility.

Chapter 12. *Miss Squeers becomes reconciled to Circumstances.*
Miss Squeers in a Tender Frame of Mind.
Miss Squeers in a Raging Frame of Mind.

Chapter 13. *Time for Smike to Get Up.*
Time for Smike to be very Wide Awake.
Smike in Extremity.
Nicholas turns the Tables on Mr. Squeers.
Nicholas and Smike become fast Friends.

Chapter 14. *The Kenwigs Family.*
Mrs. Kenwigs is seen to be related to a Public Man.
The Public Man holds forth.

Chapter 15. *Two Fugitives arrive.*
A Letter from Miss Squeers.
The feelings of the Public Man are outraged.
Maternal Feelings of Mrs. Kenwigs.
Good Night.

Chapter 16. *The General Agency Office.*
The great Mr. Gregsbury, M.P.
A Deputation from Mr. Gregsbury's Constituents.
Concerning the Duties of a Secretary.
Nicholas is Rejected.
Mr. Lillyvick's Opinion of the French Language.

Chapter 17. *Madame Mantalini naturally feels Jealous.*
Madame Mantalini's First Minister.
Capricious Customers.

Chapter 18. *Miss Knag displays much Sweetness.*
Miss Knag and Mrs. Nickleby are Retrospective.
In the Height of Fashion.
Kate gives Great Offence.

Chapter 19. *The Pleasure of Miss Nickleby's Company is Requested.*
Mr. Ralph Nickleby's Private House.
Mr. Ralph Nickleby's Guests.
The Wager Decided.
An Agreeable Understanding.

Chapter 20. *Miss La Creevy as Ambassadress.*
Quite a Bill of Indictment.
Renunciation of a Reprobate.
Smike is Self-Reproachful.

Chapter 21. *In Possession.*
Remorse of Mr. Mantalini.
At Mrs. Wititterly's.
Too much Soul for any Body.

Chapter 22. *Smike and Nicholas take the Road.*
Trudging Along.
Mr. Vincent Crummles and Sons.
Mr. Crummles Discovers Smike's Mission.
Recruits for the British Drama.

Chapter 23. *Presented to Mrs. Crummles.*
Merits of the Infant Phenomenon.
The Leading Lady of the Company.
Comparative Insensibility of the Public.

Chapter 24. *Touches of Nature.*
A Melo-Dramatic Representation.
Miss Snevellicci's Lodgings.
Decline of the Drama.
Theatrical Patrons.

Chapter 25. *Another Novelty in the Bill.*
Miss Petowker Extolled to the Skies.
Miss Petowker Led to the Altar.
Mr. Crummles as Father.
Smike Rehearses.

Chapter 26. *The Cat's-Paw.*
Another Visitor announced.
A gallant Escort.

Chapter 27. *Castles in the Air.*
Mission of Messrs. Pyke and Pluck.
Mrs. Nickleby in social Request.
Introduced to Mrs. Wititterly.
Disinterested Friendship.

Chapter 28. *The pure Silver-Fork School.*
Very like a Countess.
The young Person is put down.
Kate repairs to her Uncle.
Mr. Noggs's Duster.

Chapter 29. *Favoured by Mr. Folair.*
Mr. Folair explains.
Self-Sacrifice of Mr. Lenville.

Chapter 30. *Last Appearance.*
Invited to Supper.
Miss Snevellicci's Papa is angry.
Mr. Lillyvick is put in his Place.
Good-bye to Mr. Crummles.

Chapter 31. *Master and Man.*
Mr. Noggs becomes Excited.

Chapter 32. *London at last.*
Attracted to a Coffee Room.
Face to Face with Sir Mulberry.
Run away with.

Chapter 33. *Brother and Sister re-united.*
Return to old Quarters.

Chapter 34. *In the Discount Market.*
Mr. Mantalini threatens to become a Body.
News of my Nephew.
Mr. Squeers enters into a few Details.
A few more Details.

Chapter 35. *Poor Smike again.*
A Weakness in Mrs. Nickleby's Family.
A Glorious Old Gentleman.
Another Glorious Old Gentleman.
Tim Linkinwater.
Established with Cheeryble Brothers.

Chapter 36. *Expectations of the Kenwigses.*
Petrifying Intelligence.

Chapter 37. *A City Square.*
In the Good Books of Cheeryble Brothers.
Annual Dinner.
Toast and Sentiment.
The Gentleman in the next House.
Another Vegetable Marrow.

Chapter 38. *Sir Mulberry on the Sick List.*
A Visit of Condolence.
Lord Frederick Revolts.
Smike Taken Prisoner.

Chapter 39. *A Friend in Need Arrives.*
Miss Squeers as Bridesmaid.
John Browdie goes to Bed.

Chapter 40. *Smike Makes Off.*
Smike Restored to his Friends.
Mystery.
Newman Noggs on the Watch.
Great Success of Newman Noggs.
With One Qualification.

Chapter 41. *Associations of Ideas.*
The Gentleman Next Door Appears.
And Declares his Passion.
But is Shamefully Slandered.

Chapter 42. *Renewal of Old Acquaintance.*
Touching Mr. and Miss Squeers.
Explosion of Miss Squeers.
Beginning to Spend the Evening.

Chapter 43. *The Young Gentleman Explains.*
Another Cheeryble.
Self-Invited to Tea.
The Family Tea-Party.

Chapter 44. *Gone off.*
Should auld acquaintance be forgot?
A Bargain declined.
Mr. Mantalini Poisoned.
"Thereby hangs a Tale."

Chapter 45. *Mrs. Nickleby Patronizes.*
Ralph coolly states his Case.
The Fond Father is introduced.
But is not Beloved by his Son.

Chapter 46. *Accredited to the Young Lady.*
The Young Lady's Story.
The Young Lady's Residence.
A High-minded Parent.

Chapter 47. *In the Closet.*
Going to be Married.
The Bridegroom's Scheme.
Out of the Closet.
Crafty Persuasion.

Chapter 48. *Out of Spirits.*
Prospects of the Crummleses.
A Distinguished Dramatist.
After-supper Speeches.

Chapter 49. *Home Doings.*
Something wrong with Smike.
A Pair of Legs in the Chimney.
Some Slight Incoherence.
Still, Something Wrong with Smike.

Chapter 50. *Make Your Game, Gentlemen.*
To-morrow's Intended Business.
To-night's Pleasures.
Early Morning.

Chapter 51. *A Miser at Home.*
Mrs. Sliderskew's Merits.
A Toast, in Golden Water.
Mr. Noggs might be more Explicit.

Chapter 52. *Hoping against Hope.*
Miss Kenwigs is Escorted to the Hair-Dresser's.
Mr. Lillyvick brought Low.
Reconciliation.

Chapter 53. *The Dark side of the Picture.*
Noble Independence.
He Expostulates in vain.
A change in Mrs. Sliderskew.
Gride turns upon him.

Chapter 54. *The Wedding Morning.*
Re-assuring the Bride's Father.
Family Portraits.
Madeline is Rescued.

Chapter 55. *Great Foresight of Mrs. Nickleby.*
Mrs. Nickleby's Diplomatic Relations.
Mrs. Nickleby's Disclosure.
Poor Smike's Departure.

Chapter 56. *Scarcity of Mrs. Sliderskew.*
The Usurer loses.
But resolves to Win yet.
And takes Measures accordingly.

Chapter 57. *Mr. Squeers raises his spirits.*
Mr. Squeers and Mrs. Sliderskew.
Almost successful, but not quite.

Chapter 58. *Smike's quiet Retreat.*
Smike's quiet Decline.

Chapter 59. *No Rest for the Wicked.*
Symptoms of Falling-off.
More Symptoms.
Worse and Worse.
But not the Worst Yet.

Chapter 60. *Another Rat deserts the Sinking Ship.*
Something Hidden in the Shadow.
All Brought to Light.

Chapter 61. *Regret and Sympathy.*
Self Denial.
Full Reliance on Brother Charles.

Chapter 62. *The Usurer goes Home.*
The Front Garret.

Chapter 63. *An Invitation to Dinner.*
Giving in Marriage.
A Comfortable Couple.
Mrs. Nickleby is Disgusted.

Chapter 64. *Decline and Fall of Mantalini.*
The Browdies at Home.
Dotheboy's Hall Abolished.

Chapter 65. *The Whole Summed Up.*

EMENDATION LIST

This list includes all emendations made to the copy-text, whether verbal, orthographic, or punctuational, with the exception of the normalization of chapter headings and of the spacing around inset stories, letters, and verse. The new reading comes first, followed by a parenthetical indication of the first edition in which the correction of an error was made, if it was made. Seven emendations (460.13, 516.38, 549.19, 637.29, 761.4, 814.16, 831.34) are followed by '*ed.*', which signifies that the editors have themselves emended because of some fault. On a further nine occasions (106.2, 114.2, 114.17, 116.24, 128.5, 179.28–9, 183.5, 201.31, 207.18) 'MS derived' indicates an emendation based on the manuscript but requiring editorial adjustment, in all cases the provision of a full stop where Dickens did not provide punctuation. This part of the entry terminates with a square bracket. It is followed by the reading the emendation replaces in the copy-text. The actual emendation consists of the precise change in the copy-text, but in the emendation list the editors often provide a word or phrase of context to assist readers in identifying the emendation. Gaps where characters dropped out or did not register are reported in the list by the use of the caret sign, one for each missing character, provided that a space indicates it was once present. However, defects of broken or damaged type, often affecting the ascenders of letters, have been corrected without comment where the intention is clear, e.g. 'more of' (453.14) where the broken 'f' looks like an 'r', and 'change' (703.2) where the 'h' resembles 'n'. Occasionally some explanation of the editorial thinking behind an emendation appears in a brief note. When the exact reading in the manuscript is likely to be useful, it appears between vertical bars |...| after 'MS'; in three exceptional cases (83.19, 443.23, 709.11) the same procedure is followed for printed readings.

As explained above (939) the plates in this edition have been placed in close proximity to the scenes they illustrate.

13.11	up," (48)] up"
13.13	then," (48)] then"
15.39	hackney-coachman's (48)] hackney-coachmen's
20.32	what (48)] what,
23.19	Nickleby," (48)] Nickleby"
28.24	this may (48)] this, may
34.19–20	large Saracens' Heads (48)] large Saracen's Heads
59.2	deane (48)] deame
63.19	remaining. (39 *some copies*)] remaining
83.19	"Here, Sir," (48 |"Here, sir,"|)] "Here, Sir?"

87.1 “Upon (48)] ‘Upon
89.1 “My (39 *some copies*)] ‘My
90 title HALL. (39 *some copies*)] HALL
90.18 morning.” (39 *some copies*)] morning.’
104.9 chair. “What (MS)] chair, “what
104.22 Well then, (MS)] Well, then,
106.2 mind. “Your (MS derived |mind “Your|)] mind, “your
106.11 got (MS)] get
106.15 at all, (MS)] at all
106.23 was, (MS)] was
107.28 anything (MS)] any thing
107.29 Thank you. (MS)] Thank you;
108.8 As (MS)] as
109.10 anybody (MS)] any body
109.16–18 son (none . . . descent) who (MS)] son—(none . . . descent)—who
109.31 that, (MS |that,<—>)|] that—
111.16 thus, (MS)] thus
111.25 eyes rather at (MS)] eyes at
111.26 anything (MS)] any thing
112.11 which (MS)] the
113.3 awa’, (MS)] awa,’
114.2 Price. “Was (MS derived |Price “Was|)] Price, “was
114.17 Nicholas. “What (MS derived |Nicholas “What|)] Nicholas; “what
114.22 dressing beautiful (MS)] dressing beautifully
115.13 everything (MS)] every thing
116.23 Weel then (MS)] Weel, then
116.24 fist. “What (MS derived |fist “What|)] fist, “what
116.26 whipster (MS)] whipster,
117.5 nuptials; (MS)] nuptials:
117.7 So that the (MS |So that <both> the|)] So, that the
117.16 Oh! You (MS)] Oh! you
117.30–1 feelings (MS)] feeling
117.39 words, minx (MS)] words. Minx
118.8 again. (MS)] again,
118.11 tears, (MS)] tears.
119.3–4 flesh-tint she (MS |flesh-tint <which> she|)] flesh-tint which she
119.6 patrons to (MS)] patrons, to
120.30 preserved (MS)] introduced
122.26 considering, with (MS)] considering with
122.35 him even (MS)] him, even

125.4–5 years, and was warmly attached to her children, and had no greater (MS |years, and was <as> warmly attached to her children, and had no greater|)] years, and had no greater

125.36 with a great (MS)] with great

126.20 him, as (MS)] him as

126.35 with, every (MS)] with every

128.5 remark. "Must (MS derived |remark "Must|)] remark, "must

128.9 Ralph. "I hope not." (MS)] Ralph.

128.21 Attar of Roses (MS |<otto of Roses> Attar of Roses|)] otto of roses

128.39 there, as (MS)] there as

129.1 Hallo! (MS)] Hollo!

129.11 you demmit (MS |you<,> demmit|)] you, demmit

129.14 when, wheeling (MS |<and> ↑when,↓ wheeling|)] when wheeling

130.21 "My fault (48)] 'My fault

131.15 you!" (MS)] you?"
In MS Dickens changes the question mark to an exclamation mark.

143.2 exerted (48)] excited

164.15 it's (58)] its 39
48 has 'it 's'.

170.4 sister (39 *some copies*)] visiter

172.2–3 Mr. Lillyvick. Mr. Snewkes... Mr. Lillyvick—Miss Petowker (48)] Mr. Lillyvick, Mr. Snewkes... Mr. Lillyvick. Miss Petowker

172.10 she (67)] he

174.7 "'Mother,' she (48)] "'Mother, 'she

178.15 delight during (MS)] delight, during

179.15 make for (MS)] make, for

179.28–9 taciturnity. "Both (MS derived |taciturnity "Both|)] taciturnity; "both

180.28–9 tame and passive (MS)] tamely and passively

181.17 recuvvor (MS)] recuvver

181.30 tortorshell (MS)] tortershell

183.5 man. "Make (MS derived |man "Make|)] man—"make

200.16–17 'to play the devil... everybody?'" (MS)] to play the very devil... everybody?"

200.38 power (MS)] powers

201.31 Gregsbury. "A (MS derived |Gregsbury "A|)] Gregsbury; "a

202.7 those (MS)] these

202.10 anything, (MS)] anything

207.11 French Language as spoken by Natives (MS)] French language as spoken by natives

207.18	Newman. "That's (MS derived |Newman "That's|)] Newman, "that's
214.34	his nose off his demd countenance (MS)] his demd nose off his countenance
215.25–6	trouble to have young people who (MS)] trouble, to have young people, who
215.39	Madame (MS)] Madam
216.32	monosyllable when (MS)] monosyllable, when
221.3	Why, (MS)] Why
221.14	letter (39 *some copies*)] latter
221.18	She little (MS)] she little
231.38	"Madame (48)] "Madam
235.14	Miss Knag's inmost (39 *some copies*)] Miss Knag inmost
237.3	enveloped (48)] developed
245.16	Chowser (48)] Chouser
252.21	anything (MS)] any thing
253.21	confidant (MS)] confident
253.25–8	whom—from . . . obtain—London (MS)] whom, from . . . obtain, London
253.33	Creevy (MS)] Creevy's
253.37	of (MS)] at
254.14	Now, (MS)] Now
255.3	that, (MS)] that
255.11	me, (MS)] me;
255.27	considered——" (MS)] considered."
257.5	not. (MS)] not,
257.29	calm; consider." (MS)] calm, consider—"
258.8	blights and (MS)] blights, and
258.14	he—accuse (MS)] he accuse
276.25	"You are, (58)] "You are
306.5–6	ships' provision (48)] ships' provi-vision *end-of-line hyphen*
331.35	doubt, (58)] doubt;
354.6	Nickleby, (48)] Nickleby,"
365.23	turned (48)] turn ed
367.23	*enfant.*' (48)] *enfant.*
367.30	"At (58)] "'At
368.1	"The (58)] "'The
368.3	Befillaire." (58)] Befillaire.'"
370.38	twenty years (58)] twenty-years
376.36	too." (48)] too.'
380.2	live, (58)] live
389.24	Ralph. (48)] Ralph^

394.24 head. (39 *some copies*)] head
397.2 Snevellicci (48)] Snevellici
398.31 it, Sir," (39 *some copies*)] it Sir,"
399.22 of it," (48)] of it,
399.35 Snevellicci (48)] Snevellici
402.38 Miss Squeers (48)] MissSqueers
416.21 swords, (39 *some copies*)] swords^
422.15 bandied (48)] banded
429.13 again, (48)] again.
The comma is imperfectly printed in 39.
441.33 "Pshaw (48)] "'Pshaw
443.23 Sir, (48 |sir,|)] Sir^
460.13 large-faced (*ed.*)] large-faced,
461.6–7 for Mr. Trimmers (48)] for Mr. Linkinwater
58 and 67 have 'from Mr. Linkinwater'.
467.34 "whether, as (48)] whether, "as
475.7 it'll (48)] it 'll
489.1 Kate," (48)] Kate^"
493.29 time, (48)] time^
516.38 Thee'lt (58)] The'lt
516.38 Tilly (*ed.*)] 'Tilly
523.8 Tim, "and (48)] Tim," and
523.21 "The night (48)] The night
527.19–20 nods and shrugs, which (48)] nods, and shrugs which
549.19 Tilly (*ed.*)] 'Tilly
559.7 You'll (48)] "You'll
587.24 demder.'— (48)] demder.—
591.20–1 best-humoured (48)] best^humoured
600.28 "Now," (48)] "Now"
601.38 poor petty (67)] poor, petty
606.31 in short (39 *some copies*)] inshort
611.5 found he (67)] found, he
620.3 are!" (39 *some copies*)] are^^'
625.1 you have (39 *some copies*)] youhave
632.36 "Do you (39 *most copies*)] "No you
637.29 Nicholas (*ed.*)] Nicholas,
637.32 Snevellicci (58)] Snevellici
661.20–1 there; to know . . . day; to feel (48)] there to know . . . day, to feel
669.13 Chowser (48)] Chouser
670.19 G—," (58)] G—"
676.34 quantity (48)] quanty
682.27 "It's *eau-d'or* (48)] "Its *eau-d'or*

684.3	Brooker.” (48)] Brooker.
685.24	who plainly (58)] who, plainly
707.24	truth;— (48)] truth,
708.36	supplication, (67)] supplication^ *end-of-line space* 48 and 58 have a semicolon.
709.11	again.” (48 |again!” |)] again.’
710.9	three. (48)] three,
714.2	that, to (48)] that to
723.23	We (48)] “We
728.22	and (39 *some copies*)] an^
732.24	to-night? (58)] to-night.
740.38	heaven!” (39 *some copies*)] heaven!’
747.19	parcel,—"how (58)] parcel.—"how
748.4	peremptory (48)] preremptory
752.36	Squeers (48)] Squeers,
761.4	Peg expressing (*ed.*)] Peg, expressing
783.15	surprise (48)] suprise
797.39	him?” (48)] him?’
814.16	Sir,” (*ed.*)] Sir?” 58 has a full stop, 67 an exclamation mark.
826.17	through (48)] though
826.19	Grogzwig (48)] Grogswig
827.18	“but (48)] ‘ ‘ but
831.34	’Tilda (*ed.*)] Tilda
854.13	having won an (MS)] having an
854.23	supposititious (MS)] suppositious
854.30	county (MS)] country
854.32	any letter (MS)] a letter
855.18	telle’e (MS)] tellee

END-OF-LINE HYPHENS

THE COPY-TEXT

It is safe to assume from the treatment of the manuscript fragments, the evidence of Dickens's other novels, and general practice at the time, that the printers regularized his hyphenation according to their own system. This gave the copy-text far more hyphenated words than might have been expected from the manuscript. Any inconsistencies have been accepted, even where they occur within a few lines of one another, as indicative of the fluidity of contemporary practice and the differing interpretations of individual compositors.

Most end-of-line hyphens are unambiguous: they join non-compound words split over a line end (known as soft hyphens) or create compounds which could not ordinarily be treated as single words (hard hyphens). However, there remain many end-of-line hyphens which may or may not be hard, and these ambiguous hyphens have been interpreted according to the following criteria: a mid-line example of the word in question in the copy-text; the manuscript reading where available; a closely analogous word within the text (e.g. grey-haired/grey-headed); contemporary usage (e.g. tip-top). If more than one mid-line example has been found, the dominant form is adopted. Where none of the criteria has produced a solution the hyphen is treated as hard. (The editors consulted later editions, but decided that these are largely irrelevant in an era when usage was changing so rapidly.)

The ambiguous end-of-line hyphens resolved by these processes appear in the list below in the form in which they appear in the present edition. In twelve cases ambiguous end-of-line hyphens in the copy-text happen also to be end-of-line in the present text: 'way-farers' (33.12), 'hiding-places' (257.16), 'fellow-traveller' (292.2), 'low-spirited' (301.13), 'double-knock' (318.2), 'thorough-paced' (341.10), 'counting-house' (477.24 and 526.11), coach-maker's (537.22), 'Elbow-chairs' (676.10), 'elbow-chair' (746.31), and 'brow-beating' (833.14). All these hyphens except the first, which the editors have resolved as soft, appear in the second list below ('The Present Text') to indicate that they should be regarded as hard.

7.4	street-doors	40.33	schoolmaster's
10.12	street-door	48.5	sitting-room
10.28	dark-complexioned	54.5	good-humoured
12.7	white-washed	61.13	gold-laced
12.11	smoke-dried	61.19	tip-top
34.8	coach-yard	62.31	grey-headed
35.6	fire-places	73.23	merry-making

76.4	forty-eight	321.15	good-natured
82.38	schoolmaster	327.4	fireworks
93.2	copy-books	340.5	watch-guard
99.37	business-like	355.21	store-room
101.16	self-degraded	358.34	to-night
107.36	schoolmaster's	389.1	crest-fallen
108.34	corn-factor	392.18	to-morrow
109.3	corn-factor's	395.24	coach-stand
112.6	pocket-handkerchiefs	415.25	coachman
119.20	good-natured	418.26–7	ill-fortune
119.38	waistcoats	430.12	hackney-coach
122.26	pencil-end	438.20	halfpence
130.27	horsewhipped	440.5	straightway
133.7	money-getting	442.2	coffee-house
138.27	halfpenny-worth	456.24	window-panes
139.29	hand-maiden	456.35	old-fashioned
143.3	high-minded	466.9	grape-vine
144.24	love-making	466.13	window-blind
154.18	night-jacket	471.23	saucepan
155.36	pony-chaise	471.35	bed-room
156.35	finger-ends	472.39	pocket-handkerchief
157.16	scarecrow	475.4	india-rubber
162.26	blockhead	485.37	housekeeper
170.5	back-parlour	488.29	birth-day
171.17	water-rates	490.25	likewise
173.9	overpowered	493.24	short-sighted
182.3	stage-coach	494.11	street-door
183.16	glass-full	497.26	blockhead
186.34	smelling-bottle	499.19	gaming-room
201.24	self-congratulation	509.2	north-country
213.10	egg-spoon	514.21	to-night
242.15	chimney-piece	516.14	schoolmeasther's
247.32	dining-room	517.18	bedclothes
266.27	nut-crackers	519.15	by-ways
274.20	dining-room	519.38	hackney-coach
277.37	cross-questionings	522.7	new-laid
279.6	hackney-coach	531.38	half-past
279.10	slip-shod	534.1	footsteps
296.7	saw-dust	549.9	stage-coach
303.19	to-morrow	552.29	doon-stairs
316.4	scrap-book	558.16–17	runaway
316.35	scrap-book	558.23	roonaway

565.34	good-looking
576.8	to-night
578.1	sun-burnt
597.7	tom-cats
598.6	housekeeper
599.38	a-sneezing
606.21	broken-spirited
611.34	ginger-beer
674.29	bloodshot
676.2	lantern-jawed
677.27	bottle-green
690.34	dancing-master
691.36	hair-dresser's
712.33	to-morrow
716.1	street-door
716.25	bottle-green
717.10	below-stairs
746.12	lip-service
752.13	seventy-five
752.36	street-door
758.1	serio-comic
765.27	hedge-rows
780.16	room-door
788.26	good-natured
791.32	warm-hearted
793.23	over-persuade
798.11	bed-side
802.9	blackbird
803.22	overjoyed
813.36	cross-examining
814.37	dinner-time
819.33	archway
820.14	dining-room
823.29	pipe-clayed
825.36	bedclothes
828.20	coat-sleeve
833.18	bed-chamber

THE PRESENT TEXT

All end-of-line hyphens in the present text are soft unless included in the list below. The hyphens listed here are hard, and should be retained when quoting.

7.4	street-doors
10.12	street-door
10.30	box-office
17.33	bottle-holder
23.7	elegantly-written
25.34	sister-in-law
29.19	tambour-work
30.5	life-time
32.19	stepping-stone
35.6	coffee-rooms
36.26	pocket-money
40.21	father-in-law
48.5	sitting-room
54.5	good-humoured
61.33	grey-haired
63.31	rudely-carved
73.23	merry-making
74.37	four-and-twenty
82.28	cold-looking
92.28	school-room
92.30	shooting-jacket
99.37	business-like
100.31	double-bladed
107.38	school-room
112.6	pocket-handkerchiefs
117.3	corn-factor
118.6	cut-and-thrust
119.20	good-natured
120.18	seven-and-sixpence
122.26	pencil-end
132.28	alms-houses
139.29	hand-maiden
144.17	pocket-handkerchief
152.29	stair-rail
155.36	pony-chaise
156.35	finger-ends
167.11	square-faced
170.5	back-parlour
171.17	water-rates
174.27	well-behaved
178.3	water-rate
186.34	smelling-bottle
190.25	half-past
191.24	re-arrange
195.38	matter-of-fact
198.4	thick-headed
220.13	hook-and-eye
223.6	well-behaved
228.13	twenty-second
236.29	brother-in-law
239.33	coat-sleeve
240.7	street-door
242.28	make-weight
247.32	dining-room
252.15	head-aches
257.16	hiding-places
266.27	nut-crackers
277.37	cross-questionings
279.6	hackney-coach
291.19	fire-side
292.2	fellow-traveller
295.20	port-wine
296.6	under-current
301.13	low-spirited
303.19	to-morrow
311.16	toast-and-water
315.7	Lombard-street
316.4	scrap-book
318.2	double-knock
320.8	half-a-crown
321.15	good-natured
324.32	pump-and-tub

327.32	half-dozen
332.25	fellow-creatures
334.12	field-officer
336.35	fly-driver
339.26	resting-place
341.10	thorough-paced
348.1	sweetest-tempered
354.14	brother-in-law
355.21	store-room
358.2	gold-headed
366.33	closely-written
367.19	half-playful
367.31	thoughtfully-chiselled
395.24	coach-stand
402.26	between-whiles
414.6	mother-of-pearl
416.33	half-naked
416.35	coffin-maker's
430.12	hackney-coach
442.2	coffee-house
454.16	hair-dresser
456.31	low-crowned
460.9	partitioned-off
463.34	forty-four
463.37	half-past
469.13	shirt-collar
469.24	brandy-and-water
471.35	bed-room
475.4	india-rubber
475.13	to-morrow
477.24	counting-house
480.38	seventy-six
482.25	half-past
488.29	birth-day
491.27	three-pair-of
493.17	one-and-twenty
494.11	street-door
495.34	street-door
499.19	gaming-room
503.10	hand-over-hand
508.18	up-stairs
510.24	sandwich-crumbs
514.21	to-night
515.18	re-appeared
518.7	well-remembered
526.11	counting-house
534.13	beer-barrel
537.22	coach-maker's
538.3	summer-house
549.12	tea-spoon
552.29	doon-stairs
554.13	fore-finger
565.28	good-humoured
569.30	wash-leather
571.9	self-reproach
574.9	book-keeping
591.20	best-humoured
593.1	counting-house
595.24	broad-brimmed
597.7	tom-cats
607.37	ninety-nine
619.5	old-fashioned
635.6	re-engagement
636.22	forty-four
638.20	shirt-pin
638.35	half-a-foot
642.16	Knife-swallower
644.2	to-morrow
650.4	Cock-lane
662.6	eye-glass
662.33	club-houses
676.10	Elbow-chairs
676.21	tight-locked
676.33	worm-eaten
679.4	watch-guards
681.15	to-morrow
690.34	dancing-masters
707.33	broken-hearted
711.23	half-pint
716.1	street-door
736.27	well-conducted
738.8	self-congratulation
746.31	elbow-chair
752.36	street-door

754.18	a-follering
755.15	deep-laid
765.27	hedge-rows
779.27	safety-valve
781.23	broken-down
787.37	e-r-s-Squeers
788.24	ill-natured
796.30	well-behaved
814.36	dinner-time
820.14	dining-room
833.14	brow-beating
833.18	bed-chamber

EXPLANATORY NOTES

These notes offer a comprehensive attempt to identify historical personages, places, and institutions to which Dickens refers, and the plays, songs, and popular entertainments he quotes or cites. Phrases and idioms likely to be found obscure are explained in these notes (single words are treated in the Glossary). The notes are, on the whole, brief; they offer information rather than critical comment or exposition. We call attention to those quotations or references which have eluded identification, and welcome any new information readers can provide. Wherever possible standard editions or editions that Dickens himself may have known are cited, but achieving complete consistency in this regard has not been possible. When quotations reproduce their source accurately, the reference is given without comment. The editors indicate verbal differences between the text of 1838–9 and the source from which that text derives with an introductory 'see', and a general rather than verbal indebtedness with 'compare'. Biblical references are to the Authorized (King James) version. Plays by Shakespeare are cited without authorial ascription, and references are to *The Oxford Shakespeare: the Complete Works*, 2nd edn, ed. John Jowett, William Montgomery, Gary Taylor, and Stanley Wells (Oxford, 2005). Works referred to three or more times are cited by means of an abbreviated reference, for which see 859.

The present edition owes a considerable debt to three earlier annotators of *Nicholas Nickleby*: T. W. Hill, 'Notes on *Nicholas Nickleby*', *Dickensian*, 45 (1949), 98–102, 163–6, and 46 (1950), 42–8, 99–104; the Penguin edition by Michael Slater (1978); and the Oxford World's Classics edition by Paul Schlicke (1990).

Readers wishing to examine complete sets of the novel as originally issued in numbers, with accompanying advertisements, may consult the 'Project Boz' website of Worcester Polytechnic Institute at digital.wpi.edu/collections/boz. Alternatively, they may consult the printed facsimile edition by Michael Slater (2 vols, London, 1982, and the same year in Philadelphia): originally published by the Scolar Press, Menston, Yorks., 1972–3.

5.13–15 the adventurous pair of the Fives' Court...regaling themselves in his *Book of Sports* (London, 1832), 227, Pierce Egan notes that some prisoners at the King's Bench and Fleet prisons (see notes to 611.15–16 and 729.16) attracted contributions from visitors by exhibiting their prowess in the racquets and fives (handball) courts there. Dickens's reference to 'buffetting' suggests he may also have had in mind the Fives' Court which stood in St Martin Street, N of Trafalgar Square. Although designed for racquets and 'fives' it was much better known for boxing exhibitions. It was demolished in 1826. See Lois E. Chaney, 'The Fives' Court', *Dickensian*, 81 (1985), 86–7.

5.19 between sixty and eighty pounds *per annum* roughly between £4,200 and £5,600 in modern purchasing power.

6.8 Mrs. Nickleby the character is widely held to have been based on Dickens's mother, though the degree of resemblance has been debated: see *Letters*, 1.15n.

6.12 next quarter-day in England the four quarter-days on which payments fall due are Lady Day (25 March), Midsummer Day (24 June), Michaelmas (29 September), and Christmas Day (25 December).

6.12–13 the Monument a column, 202 feet in height, designed by Sir Christopher Wren, erected in 1671–7 in Fish Street Hill to commemorate the Great Fire of London in 1666. By the time the novel was written three people had committed suicide by throwing themselves from the gallery, one in 1788 and two in 1810. After three further suicides, two in the autumn of 1839 and one in 1842, the gallery was enclosed with an iron cage.

6.13 the general post the system for sending mail between the General Post Office in London and all the post offices in the British Isles. Until the introduction of the universal penny post in 1840 the rate depended on distance, as opposed to the London District Post, which charged a flat rate of twopence from 1801 for delivery within a three-mile central zone (extended to twelve miles in 1833).

6.16 five thousand pounds roughly £350,000 in modern purchasing power.

6.18–19 christened after him, on desperate speculation named after him, in the desperate hope that the uncle would leave him a legacy.

6.21–2 born without that useful article of plate in his mouth alluding to the proverb 'He was born with a silver spoon in his mouth' (*ODEP*, 76), i.e. born into wealth and privilege.

6.25 the Royal Humane Society a voluntary body established in 1774 to publish information on how to save people from drowning, a common cause of death at the period. It promoted resuscitation and provided financial rewards, gradually replaced by medals or certificates as the norm, for anyone who performed or attempted a rescue.

6.28–9 three shillings and sixpence 17.5p. In modern purchasing power roughly £12.

6.35 Dawlish a seaside town 10 miles S of Exeter.

7.4 the size of Russell Square approximately 6 acres.

7.29 slate-pencil slates set in wooden frames were used for school exercises, being wiped for re-use thus saving expenditure on paper. Pencils for writing on them were made of softer slate or soapstone.

7.34 "two-pence for every half-penny" 0.8p for every 0.2p.

7.39 bill-discounters dealers in *bills of exchange*, which were written promises to pay a stated sum on a stated date in the future in return for goods or services rendered. Dealers might pay the value of a bill before its maturity date, with a deduction equivalent to the interest at a certain percentage for the time which it had still to run, or they might obtain cash for a bill before its maturity date, with such a deduction.

8.4 odd days refers to interest earned on loans that close on any day other than the standard day on which the lender requires interest and principal payments.

8.25 mercantile house commercial concern.

8.31 fumes of charcoal i.e. carbon monoxide.

9.1–3 impartial records...this country the Births, Deaths, and Marriages Registration Act of 1836 (6 & 7 Will. 4, c. 86) prepared the way for the civil registration on a national basis of these events in England and Wales from 1 July 1837.

9.20 Speculation is a round game a *round game* is a card game in which each player plays as an individual rather than with a partner. One such game is *speculation*, for which see note to 114.37–9.

9.39 he babbled compare the Hostess's description of Falstaff's last moments in *Henry V*, 2.3.16–17: 'a babbled of green fields'.

10.2–3 One who never deserted...children see Psalm 146.9: 'The Lord... relieveth the fatherless and widow.'

10.7–8 special pleader...notary a *special pleader* was a member of one of the legal Inns of Court, not admitted to the bar, who drafted formal statements ('pleadings') on behalf of the parties in civil cases; a *notary* is 'a person officially authorized to perform certain legal formalities, such as drawing up or certifying contracts, deeds, etc.' (*OED*).

10.12 Golden Square built as a fashionable aristocratic square NE of Piccadilly in the late 17th and early 18th centuries, it gradually came down in the world.

10.14–15 surmounting a brass model...skewer the image is heraldic: a crest *surmounts* a shield in a coat of arms.

10.30–1 the Opera Colonnade...in the season in 1816–18 John Nash (1752–1835) and George Stanley Repton (1786–1858) added a colonnade to three sides of the opera house in the Haymarket (the King's Theatre until 1837, thereafter Her Majesty's), on the site now occupied by Her Majesty's Theatre and New Zealand House. In the early 19th century the opera season normally began between late November and early January and ended in mid-June.

11.1 Mr. Seguin gives away the orders (Ralph) Arthur Seguin (1781/2–1865) was secretary, in charge of the box office, at Her Majesty's Theatre for over 50 years. He would distribute free, or reduced price, passes to the opera. By 1848 he had been succeeded by Charles Nugent.

11.5 the mournful statue a Portland stone statue of a man in Roman costume attributed to the Flemish sculptor John Van Nost (d. 1729), originally carved for Cannons, a country house in Little Stanmore, Middlesex, and moved to its present position at the centre of Golden Square in 1753. The inscription on the base maintains that it represents George II, who reigned 1727–60, but it may rather be an allegorical figure from the roof of Cannons.

11.11 **German pipes and flutes** a *German flute* is the modern transverse instrument which entirely superseded its ancient counterpart blown from the end by around the middle of the 18th century. German pipes are smoked.

11.26 **grey mixture pantaloons** tight trousers of variegated or mottled grey fabric, fastened by straps underneath the boots.

11.26–7 **Wellington boots** historically a *Wellington boot* was a high boot covering the knee in front and cut away behind.

11.31–3 **a gold repeater...the watch itself** a *repeater* is a repeating watch, a mechanical watch which sounds the hours (or even minutes) on pressing a button to activate two miniature gongs. Such watches were used before effective artificial illumination was generally available, to enable people to tell the time in the dark. The key is for winding the watch and for adjusting the time.

11.34 **a sprinkling of powder** fashionable in the eighteenth century, the general use of hair powder came to an abrupt end in 1795 when Pitt's government enacted a law (35 Geo. 3, c. 49), intended to raise revenue, requiring anyone who used powder to purchase a licence at one guinea (£1 1*s*.) a year.

12.22 **everbrowns** Dickens's jocular coinage on 'evergreens'.

12.29 **a brown study** a state of mental abstraction.

12.38 **a fixture** i.e. an artificial eye.

13.4–8 **Was that half-past twelve...regular time** Noggs's partiality for a tipple means that the public clock he would see most often would be that in his local public house.

13.4 **Noggs** the name was apparently suggested by that of a broken-down farmer, Newman Knott, whom Dickens encountered during his time with the legal firm Ellis and Blackmore in Gray's Inn in 1827–8: see Slater 2009, 27–8. It may also echo *nog*, a strong beer brewed especially in Norfolk.

13.29 **the London Tavern** a large tavern in Bishopsgate Street Within (the part of Bishopsgate within the walls of the City of London), with rooms of various sizes used for public meetings. Rebuilt in 1767–8 after a fire, it was demolished in 1876.

13.32–3 **the two o'clock delivery** the London District Post (see note to 6.13) had six daily deliveries: at 8 a.m., 10 a.m., noon, 2 p.m., 4 p.m., and 7 p.m.

13.33–4 **I shall leave the city...Charing-Cross** i.e. he will walk westwards along Fleet Street, leave the City of London and enter Westminster by passing under Temple Bar (removed in 1878), and progress along the Strand towards Charing Cross at its west end.

14.4 the tax-gatherer throughout the 19th century the taxation system was administered locally by part-time commissioners with subordinate assessors and collectors.

14.18 Crockford's a private club and gambling house established in 1828 at 50 St James's Street.

14.19 take a bottle or two of soda-water soda water has long been held to help recovery from hangovers.

14.26–7 United Metropolitan . . . Company 'One notable characteristic of the new joint-stock companies that came into existence in those years [1825–6] was their elaborate and tortuous titles. . . . The full title of the Muffin Company, and the substance of the speeches delivered at the London Tavern meeting, make it clear that Ralph and his friends intend to establish a monopoly of muffin production and distribution, excluding from the trade the simple and humble muffin men, whose livelihood they would thus jeopardise: N. Russell, '*Nicholas Nickleby* and the Commercial Crisis of 1825', *Dickensian*, 77 (1981), 144–50 (147–8).

14.29 get the shares up to a premium cause the price of shares to rise above their nominal value.

15.19 hackney cabriolet hired cab. A *cabriolet* was '[a] light two-wheeled chaise drawn by a single horse, having a large hood and usually an apron to cover the lap and legs of the occupants' (*OED*).

15.21 Bishopsgate Street Within see note to 13.29.

15.22–3 tacking . . . press of paper i.e. like boats with as many sails as possible hoisted, to increase speed.

15.25 petitioning Parliament companies seeking to establish monopolies were required to petition for Incorporation by Act of Parliament. 'This would have been a very costly process, and we may assume that the announcement was merely a clever piece of stage management, designed to send the shares rocketing to a premium': N. Russell, '*Nicholas Nickleby* and the Commercial Crisis of 1825', *Dickensian*, 77 (1981), 144–50 (147).

15.33 the great public room the great dining-room, or 'Pillar-room', of the London Tavern, measuring 40 by 33 feet, and capable of seating 355 people.

15.35 Hear! a general call to order.

15.39 a hackney-coachman's knock the coachman would knock vigorously on the door to announce his arrival.

16.8 one Irish between the Act of Union in 1801 and the establishment of the Irish Free State in 1922 the whole of Ireland was part of the United Kingdom and sent constituency representatives as MPs to the UK parliament.

16.11 a flaxen wig a wig of flaxen-coloured or white blond hair.

16.21–2 what the intentions of government were about taking up the bill what the government's plans were for taking the bill on board as government policy.

17.37 the Muffin Boys men and boys would buy muffins from bakers and sell them on the streets, usually at a halfpenny (0.2p) each, wrapped in flannel to keep them fresh and warm in the baskets.

18.17 the bellman as they traversed the streets at teatime the muffin men rang bells to advertise their presence.

18.17–18 he would prove it... at the bar of that House petitioners would present their case to the House of Commons standing at the bar, marked by a line inside the entrance to the chamber.

18.19–20 secret words and signs... right? '"Snooks" was contemporary slang denoting a practical joker; "Walker" (originally "Hookey Walker") was a Cockney slang phrase for expressing incredulity; "Ferguson, you can't come here" was a London catchphrase used in denial or derision in the early and mid-nineteenth century; "Murphy" was a generic term for Irishmen' (Slater 1978, 956).

19.4–5 he knocked the first speaker clean out of the course the image is from horse racing.

19.5 You might have heard a pin fall proverbial: *ODEP*, 363.

19.25 Fountain of justice Good God! The expression was traditionally applied to God as the ultimate source of justice, and to the sovereign as the foundation of national justice.

19.27 took the meeting proved attractive to *or* excited the meeting.

20.2–3 Commons of England in Parliament assembled the formal designation of the House of Commons used for example in Acts of Parliament until the Act of Union in 1707, here introduced as a pompous anachronism.

20.12 go the extreme animal one of several variants of the expression 'go the whole hog' (*ODEP*, 307).

20.13 propose and divide upon in committee propose and put to a vote in a parliamentary committee.

20.14–16 as patent boots... materially i.e. a fine appearance tends to prejudice people in the wearer's favour.

21.1 three guineas £3 3*s*. (£3.15), a prodigious sum for lunch. The guinea coin, worth £1 1*s*., was discontinued in 1816 but professional fees and luxury goods continued to be priced in guineas until the late 20th century.

21.7–9 As he passed Saint Paul's... dial the clock faces are on the S tower of the W front of St Paul's Cathedral. Ralph is aligning the time on his watch with that on the clock by inserting and turning his watch-key.

21.20 a sealed letter until the introduction of mass-produced envelopes in the 1840s letters consisted of a folded sheet, or sheets, sealed with wax or a wafer (black for mourning), with the address written on a space left for the purpose.

21.21 Post-mark, Strand there were two twopenny post offices on the Strand, at numbers 45 and 352.

22.8 to a nicety precisely, neatly.

23.8 card of terms list of prices.

23.13 La Creevy Miss La Creevy may be based on Dickens's witty miniature-painting aunt Janet Barrow. See William J. Carlton, 'Janet Barrow's Portrait Miniatures: an Australian Epilogue', *Dickensian*, 68 (1972), 101–3.

28.35–6 the creditors have administered the creditors have disposed of the property.

30.8 coverture *OED* defines *coverture* as '[t]he condition or position of a woman during her married life, when she is by law under the authority and protection of her husband'. The position was substantially modified by the Married Women's Property Acts of 1870 and 1882.

30.25–6 Mr. Wackford Squeers's Academy, Dotheboys Hall although Dickens indicated that Squeers is a representative figure many believe he derives in particular from William Shaw, proprietor of Bowes Academy near Greta Bridge. The advertisement only slightly parodies the genuine specimens that appeared in *The Times* in January and July each year, including those for Shaw's establishment: see 'Essay on the Text', 867–8 and V. C. Clinton-Baddeley, 'Benevolent Teachers of Youth', *Cornhill Magazine*, 169 (1957), 361–82 (360–6).

30.26–7 Greta Bridge in Yorkshire a village 12 miles W of Darlington. It was in the North Riding of Yorkshire until 1974 when it was transferred to County Durham.

30.30 the use of the globes a standard pedagogic phrase, referring to the terrestrial and celestial globes.

30.30 single stick 'fighting, fencing, or exercise with a stick provided with a guard or basket and requiring only one hand' (*OED*).

30.32 twenty guineas £21.

30.34 the Saracen's Head, Snow Hill located two or three doors down the hill from St Sepulchre's Church, the Saracen's Head inn dated back to the 12th century. It was rebuilt after the Great Fire in 1666 and demolished in 1868.

30.35 A Master of Arts the degree would be from either Oxford or Cambridge, and by the time of the novel's action it involved (as it still does) the conversion of a Bachelor of Arts degree without further study after seven years from initial matriculation.

33.15–19 the Saracen's Head... the very elements themselves for a picture of the sign of the Saracen's Head, which would be emblazoned on coaches departing from and terminating there, see B. W. Matz, *Dickensian Inns & Taverns* (London, 1922), 35.

33.24 Newgate Newgate Prison, Newgate Street, London's principal jail, medieval in origin, last rebuilt in 1780–3 and finally demolished in 1902 to make way for the Central Criminal Court.

33.29–30 four, six, or eight strong men... the world executions, often of several people simultaneously, facilitated by the use of the drop hatch operated by a lever, took place in Old Bailey Street outside Newgate between 1783 and 1868.

34.3 Smithfield the site of London's cattle market, and an abattoir, from 1638 until 1855. Up to the 17th century it had been a place of execution, and until it was suppressed as disorderly in 1855 Bartholomew Fair was held there each August.

34.4 the Compter Giltspur Street Compter, S of Smithfield, a debtors' prison from 1791 to 1855.

34.5 omnibus horses horse-drawn vehicles carrying many passengers for a fare were introduced into central London following legislation in 1831 (1 & 2 Will. 4, c. 22), breaking the hackney coach monopoly.

34.5–7 going eastwards... going westwards eastwards uphill, westwards downhill.

34.6–7 hackney cabriolets see note to 15.19.

34.10 the choice spirits of this metropolis the expression 'choice spirits' is common in literature, but Dickens is probably echoing *Julius Caesar*, 3.1.164: 'The choice and master spirits of this age' (Antony to Brutus).

34.12–13 Saint James's parish from 1685 to 1922 the fashionable civil parish of Westminster St James (or St James Piccadilly) occupied the area between Oxford Street and Pall Mall.

34.14 bell-wires a *bell-wire* connected the bell-pull beside the front door to the indoor bell.

34.17–18 the door of the hind boot the rear storage compartment of a coach had a hinged door.

34.18 the red coaches mail coaches.

34.23 the tower of Saint Sepulchre's church the Church of the Holy Sepulchre Without Newgate, Giltspur Street and Holborn Viaduct, was rebuilt after the Great Fire of 1666: the tower was altered in 1873–8.

34.30 the popular prejudice runs in favour of two see Richard Brinsley Sheridan (1751–1816), *The Rivals* (1775), 3.1.91–3: 'tho' *one* eye may be very agreeable, yet as the prejudice has always run in favour of *two*, I would not wish to affect a singularity in that article'.

35.23 took down in England one goes down from London to the provinces.

36.5 the Beggar's Petition in printed calico for a photograph of one of these objects, bought at the opening of London Bridge in 1831, see C. Van Noorden, 'The Moral Pocket Handkerchief', *Dickensian*, 6 (1910), [254], 267. The handkerchief bears a poem, 'The Beggar's Petition', by Thomas Moss, abbreviated from its original appearance, as 'The Beggar', in his anonymous *Poems on Several Occasions* (Wolverhampton, 1769), [1]–3.

36.18 mending a pen quill pens needed regular trimming with a knife. The mass production of metal pens began in 1822.

36.33–5 the Times...Advertiser the London newspapers are the *Times* (1785 to the present), *Morning Post* (1772–1937), *Morning Chronicle* (1769–1865), *Morning Herald* (1780–1869), and *Morning Advertiser* (1794 to the present).

38.4 in the oil and colour way a dealer in oil, paint, soap, and similar goods.

40.5–6 she has a little money in her own right in the early Victorian period a woman's money passed to her husband: she could exercise control of it only with her husband's permission, or if it had been placed in trust by a pre-nuptial settlement. This was no longer the case after the passage of the Married Women's Property Acts of 1870 and 1882.

40.36 That's your sort an exclamation of approval.

42.8 in the matter of fact besides in reality as well.

44.18 Porson Richard Porson (1759–1808) was a Classical scholar: in his later years his chronic alcoholism seriously affected his health, appearance, and conduct.

44.18 Doctor Johnson of Samuel Johnson (1709–84), the author and lexicographer, Pat Rogers writes: 'Almost 6 feet tall and raw-boned, Johnson towered over most of his contemporaries. His physique was as clumsy as his appearance was unprepossessing: he had a face disfigured by scrofula, and a body afflicted by involuntary convulsions. He suffered too from defective eyesight and hearing. More disconcertingly, his behaviour was marked by odd grunts and head-rolling, and despite heroic efforts at politeness, his manners and personal habits struck fastidious people as gross. A lengthening list of ailments finally made his invalid condition obvious to everyone, and often his psychological distress caused him to look still more peculiar in company' (*Oxford Dictionary of National Biography*).

45.33 bade him good morning at the time of the novel's action the 'morning' extended until dinner time in the late afternoon or early evening.

47.9 after use usefulness later on.

48.24 flats...Exeter Hall Exeter Hall in the Strand (erected in 1829–31, demolished in 1907) was regularly used for meetings by Evangelicals, punningly regarded by Dickens as *flats* (simpletons, duffers).

48.32–3 Needs must...drives alluding to the proverb 'Needs must when the devil drives' (*ODEP*, 560).

50.35 go in take his turn, like a batsman in cricket.

52.2 hackney coach four-wheeled coach for hire, drawn by two horses. The coaches were licensed and numbered, and operated from street stands and coaching inns.

52.20 get up behind for the seating arrangement for 'outside' passengers travelling on the roof of the stage coach see C. S. Stewart, *Sketches of Society in Great Britain and Ireland*, 2 vols (Philadelphia, 1834), 1.45: 'Of these outside seats there are usually twelve, except in the royal mails, in which the number is less; one by the coachman [on the box], four on the top in front, four behind, with their backs to the horses, and three, beside the guard, over the hind boot or box for luggage, articles of which are also placed in a light frame of ironwork, on the top, between the two rows of passengers in front and rear.'

54.4 **the Peacock at Islington** an inn at 11 Islington High Street, first established in 1564 (moved to this site *c.*1700, closed 1962).

54.13–14 **Three children...books as two** three children are charged two adult fares and seated accordingly.

54.25–6 **I'd take...right through** i.e. he is proposing to take them at a discount, £16.67 each instead of 20 guineas (£21).

54.35 **take down** imbibe.

54.36 **washing in** washing of their clothes is included.

56.4 **five pound five** £5 5*s*. (£5.25).

56.18 **the cloths** 'The cloths were the horse-blankets thrown over the backs of the sweating animals when they arrived at a staging-post' (Slater 1978, 958).

56.26 **going right through** going all the way to the final destination.

56.31 **Grantham** a town on the Great North Road in Lincolnshire, 110 miles N of London.

56.34 **speak as they found** proverbial: *ODEP*, 760.

57.21 **Eton Slocomb** Eaton Socon, a village on the Great North Road in Bedfordshire, 55 miles N of London: it was transferred to Cambridgeshire in 1965.

57.22 **the box** passenger sharing the box with the coachman.

57.22 **the four front outsides** four (unnamed) passengers occupying the seat behind the driver: see note to 52.20.

57.26 **a very fastidious lady** for the original of this character see Essay on the Text, 866–7.

58.2 **Stamford** a town on the Great North Road in Lincolnshire, 90 miles N of London.

58.7 **the George at Grantham** the George inn at Grantham was built in 1780. Dickens and 'Phiz' (his illustrator Hablot Knight Browne: 1815–82) stayed there on 30 January 1838 on their way to Yorkshire to investigate cheap boarding schools.

58.13 **Newark** a town on the Great North Road in Nottinghamshire, 125 miles N of London.

59.1 **while ar coot treaces** while I cut the horses' traces (straps).

60.21–2 **the "Davy" or safety-lamp** invented for the use of miners by Sir Humphry Davy (1778–1829) in 1815.

62.6 **brought out** staged.

62.28 **THE FIVE SISTERS OF YORK** the name is traditionally given to the great N window of the N transept in York Minster, the cathedral of York. Consisting of five lancets 53 feet (16.3 m) high, it dates from the 13th century and has grisaille glass, white and grey with relatively few coloured pieces (unlike the description in the story). The window was pointed out to Dickens by the verger (*Letters*, 1.376).

62.33 King Henry the Fourth Henry IV reigned 1399–1413.

63.34–6 Saint Mary's abbey...it belonged the Benedictine abbey of St Mary was founded in the second half of the 11th century and dissolved in 1539. Benedictines wear black habits.

64.6 man is but a shadow see e.g. Job 14.2: 'he [man] fleeth also as a shadow, and continueth not'.

67.11 if you list if you please.

68.19 Time passed away as a tale that is told see Psalm 90.9: 'all our days are passed away in thy wrath: we spend our years as a tale that is told'.

72.1 the waters of Lethe in Classical mythology, those about to be reincarnated drank of the waters of Lethe in the Underworld so that they forgot their previous existence.

72.15 Grogzwig the name combines *grog* (a mixture of rum and water) and *swig*.

72.16 Koëldwethout '"Cold without" was slang for a drink of spirits and cold water without sugar added' (Slater 1978, 959).

72.18 that's of course that's to be expected.

72.34 in full of in full discharge of.

73.12 Lincoln green bright green material originally made at Lincoln, subsequently the kind of green costume worn by huntsmen.

73.13 a long stage a long-distance stagecoach journey.

73.34 Nimrod Nimrod was 'the mighty hunter before the Lord': Genesis 10.9.

73.35 Gillingwater...'another fine bear' 'Gillingwater was the name of a very respectable tradesman in the perfumery line...in Bishopsgate Street Without,...who use[d] to keep young bears in the arena under the shop... Outside the shop was often to be seen the announcement—"another young bear slaughtered this day"': B. W. Matz, answering a query in *Dickensian*, 16 (1920), 222.

74.2 to a miracle marvellously well.

74.12–13 imperial pints (British) pints, each just over half a litre.

75.1–2 Till all was blue *slang* till they were all drunk.

75.10 high and palmy days see *Hamlet*, Additional Passages, A.6 (1.1.113 in other editions): 'the most high and palmy state of Rome'.

76.6–7 as fierce as a lion one of a set of proverbial comparisons including 'As bold as a lion': *ODEP*, 72.

76.7 as bold as brass proverbial: G. L. Apperson, *English Proverbs and Proverbial Phrases: A Historical Dictionary* (London and Toronto, 1929), 59.

77.4–5 what boys call 'an offer' *OED* 3a suggests that the noun *offer* in the sense of 'attempt' was becoming juvenile or regional in the middle of the 19th century.

78.21 coming over deceiving.

78.29–30 stake... run through the centre of his body traditionally suicides were buried in unconsecrated ground with a stake driven through the heart.

78.37–8 they're doing a pretty brisk business... just now since the story is probably set in the 14th or 15th century (73.4–5) the reference is presumably to the Hundred Years War (1337–1453) between the English House of Plantagenet and the French House of Valois.

79.12 see fair see that the matter is fairly handled.

81.19–20 the George and New Inn, Greta Bridge converted from a farmhouse *c.*1828 as a rival to the long-established George and Dragon, it is now Thorpe Grange.

82.25–6 put this horse up stable this horse.

82.33 Smike according to Dickens, Smike was suggested to him by an inscription on a gravestone in the churchyard at Bowes (see note to 30.25–6): 'There is an old Church near the school, and the first grave-stone I stumbled on that dreary winter afternoon was placed above the grave of a boy, eighteen long years old, who had died—suddenly, the inscription said; I suppose his heart broke—the Camel falls down "suddenly" when they heap the last load upon his back—died at that wretched place. I think his ghost put Smike into my head, upon the spot' (*Letters*, 1.481–3 (482): to Mrs S. C. Hall, 29 December 1838). The inscription actually records the age of George Ashton Taylor as 19, and this may well have suggested to Dickens that he may have stayed at the school beyond the normal leaving age as unpaid labour (Kirkpatrick, 128).

83.26 a tutor's assistant probably the immensely popular *The Tutor's Assistant: being a Compendium of Arithmetic, and a Complete Question-Book* by Francis Walkingame (1723–83), first published in 1751. It was revised by Thomas Crosby of York in 1797 and continued to be published until 1885.

83.26 Murray's grammar the standard *English Grammar* by Lindley Murray (1745–1826), first published in 1795. Murray was an American loyalist, who settled in York in 1784. His *English Grammar* went through at least 65 editions up to 1871, and was the dominant prescriptive description of English for nearly a century.

83.27 cards of terms lists of fees.

83.34 with her hair in papers with her hair in curl-papers, i.e. pieces of soft paper with which the hair is twisted up for some time, so as to give it a curl when the papers are taken out.

84.34 a Yorkshire pie an extremely large, highly decorated, raised crust pie filled with a mixture of meats or game in jelly.

85.6 skeleton suit tight-fitting boy's costume, with pantaloons buttoned over the jacket and with an extensive shirt frill.

85.26 Devil a bit absolutely nothing.

87.21–2 made on the liberal half-and-half principle...sugar the drink is half-brandy, half-water, so stiff or strong, with sugar. Squeers allows time for the sugar to dissolve.

87.26–7 the interesting legends...all the figures in the edition of *The Tutor's Assistant* (see note to 83.26) published at York in 1828 there is 'A Collection of QUESTIONS set down promiscuously, for the greater trial of the foregoing RULES' (188–96). These include such items as 'From 100 l. borrowed, take 70 l. paid, 'Twas a virgin that lent it; what's due to the maid?', the answer being £30 (192).

87.29 magnetic slumber hypnotic trance.

87.38 Brooks is full i.e. there is no more room in Brooks's bed. The name was probably taken from John Crosse Brooks: see Essay on the Text, 865–6.

88.11 whose towel to put you on whose towel to allocate to you to share.

89.6–8 at the sign of the Crown...James Street until its demolition in 1921 the Crown public house stood on the eastern corner of Silver Street (now Beak Street) and (Upper) James Street.

89.13–14 Barnard Castle...the King's Head the King's Head inn in the Market Place at Barnard Castle, Co. Durham, continued to function as a public house until it was taken over by a care home early in the 21st century.

90.4 airy nothings see *A Midsummer Night's Dream*, 5.1.16 ('airy nothing').

91.13 flower of brimstone powdered sulphur (*flower* meaning 'finest part'). Purgatives were commonly used in Victorian times, and brimstone and treacle was one of the most popular.

93.37–8 a common wooden spoon...some gigantic top the boy's game of 'chip stone' involved catching a spinning top repeatedly in a spoon: see George Forrest, *Every Boy's Book* (London, 1855), 25.

94.2 at a gasp without pausing to draw breath.

94.35–6 For what we have received...truly thankful a traditional form of grace after a meal.

96.32 the globes see note to 30.30.

98.25 with the chill on given in a constrained way.

98.35 two pound ten £2 10*s*. (£2.50).

100.21–6 Mobbs's mother-in-law...a blessing on it for the original of this character and her complaint see Essay on the Text, 866–7. *Mother-in-law* means 'stepmother', a usage becoming confined to northern dialect usage in the 19th century.

101.7 to a nicety precisely, neatly.

104.11–12 Think of who?...no grammarian strict grammatical correctness would demand 'Think of whom?'.

105.10 get up a rebellion one factor contributing to the abolition of slavery in 1833 was a series of slave revolts, the last taking place in Jamaica in 1831.

106.5–6 laying on to chastising.

106.6 as black as thunder the expression is proverbial (*ODEP*, 63), but it was not common till after 1850.

107.8 general run of legs...being crooked crooked legs were a symptom of rickets caused by lack of Vitamin D and prevalent in urban Britain in the 19th century.

108.3 a hard or a soft nib a long slit in a quill pen would result in a soft nib, a short slit in a hard version.

109.4 Dutch clock one of the German wall clocks with pendulums which were plentiful and cheap in the Victorian period.

111.2–3 "done" the friend's hair arranged the hair; put it into a fashionable style. The latter sense was new in the 19th century.

111.25–6 turned the matter off diverted attention from the matter.

112.33 John Browdie the character is generally believed to have been suggested by the attorney who advised Dickens against patronizing a Yorkshire school. See the Preface to the Cheap Edition (854–5). He was identified as Richard Barnes (1807–63) who practised in Barnard Castle between 1829 and 1847 and whose London agents were Smithson, Dunn & Minton: E. T. Jaques, 'The Original of John Browdie', *Dickensian*, 11 (1915), 296–9. Dickens's assertion that the man was old when he met him, and dead by 1848, has prompted the Pilgrim editors to conclude that he was more likely to have been John Barnes, presumably his father or other older relation, who practised until 1832 (*Letters*, 1.482n.), but Robert Kirkpatrick thinks Dickens was probably deliberately disguising his source (Kirkpatrick, 71–3). See Dickens's account of the interview in *Letters*, 1.481–3 (482–3): to Mrs S. C. Hall, 29 December 1838.

114.11 keep company be sociable (with romantic overtones).

114.36 the candle snuffed the burnt part of the wick removed.

114.37–9 speculation...go partners *speculation* is a 'round game' (see note to 9.20), 'the chief feature of which is the buying and selling of trump cards, the player who possesses the highest trump in a round winning the pool' (*OED*). Miss Squeers's point seems to be that since they are an intimate informal group they might as well make things even more intimate.

115.16 Only a dozen and eight it seems likely that Matilda has won two of the home-made tokens, one with a twelve on it and the other with an eight.

115.35 along of due to.

115.38 You'll have a bad wife...cards alluding to the proverb 'Lucky at cards, unlucky in love' (*ODEP*, 496), and echoing in particular its use in Jonathan Swift (1667–1745), *A Treatise on Polite Conversation* (1738), towards the end of the Third Conversation: 'Well, Miss, you'll have a sad Husband, you have such good Luck at Cards.'

116.24 Dang my boans and boddy the oath 'By my bones and body' is common in the 19th century.

116.25 loight an' toight the expression sounds formulaic, but it has not been found elsewhere in a relevant sense. Browdie probably means that Nicholas is of little consequence though well turned out.

116.36–7 the high state... matrimonially engaged compare the opening invitation of the marriage service in the Book of Common Prayer: 'holy Matrimony... is an honourable estate'.

117.18 which children call making a face *OED* (face, n. P2) cites a note on the use of the phrase (meaning 'grimacing') by children dating from 1890.

118.23–4 set these people by the ears put these people at variance.

119.37 the Royal Academy since 1769, the year after its foundation, the Royal Academy of Arts has mounted an annual summer exhibition of new paintings.

120.27 make it up put on a particular expression.

122.22 between you and me and the post in confidence (a post being proverbially deaf: *ODEP*, 172).

125.22 a milliner 'as Richard Altick observes, milliners' apprentices were not only overworked and badly paid, but also treated as fair game by lecherous men... ("Victorian Readers and the Sense of the Present", *Midway*, 10 (1970), 95–119).' (Schlicke, 849)

125.34 banker's book pass book issued by a bank to an account holder.

126.1–2 chip cottage bonnet close-fitting bonnet, with projecting sides, made of chip straw (thin strips of woody fibre).

126.2–3 persian lining lining of thin soft silk.

126.13 Cavendish Square originally built as a residential square N of Oxford Street over several decades after 1717.

126.25 cabinet piano tall upright piano introduced in 1807.

126.28 two pounds fifteen shillings £2.75.

128.12 provided against it made provision for it.

128.13 out-of-door worker worker living away from the workplace.

128.21 Attar of Roses otto (fragrant essence) of roses.

128.32 cheval glasses adjustable full-length mirrors in frames.

129.7 Turkish trousers baggy trousers gathered in tightly at the ankle.

129.30–1 sky parlours rooms at the tops of houses.

130.6–7 on his whiskers on the strength of his side-whiskers.

130.10 an easy independence a comfortable amount of capital which makes it unnecessary for him to earn his living.

130.13 discount... for the customers' bills see note to 7.39.

132.7 five to seven shillings 25p to 35p.

135.32–3 Gog... Magog leaders of the heathen nations in Revelation 20.8 (compare Ezekiel Chs 38 and 39). In English mythology they are warriors associated with the foundation of the City of London. They are commemorated by wooden effigies in the Guildhall provided in 1953 by David Evans (1893–1959) to replace larger figures carved in 1708 by Richard Saunders (d. 1735) which were destroyed in World War II, and which had themselves replaced effigies destroyed in the Great Fire of 1666. The Saunders statues feature prominently (with an illustration by George Cattermole) in 'Introduction to the Giant Chronicles', the first paper in 'The Clock-Case' which appeared in the first instalment of *Master Humphrey's Clock*, published on 4 April 1840 (11–12).

137.19 They went into the City i.e. they went eastwards from the Strand, at the eastern extremity of the City of Westminster, into the City of London.

138.17 some faded baize probably indicating curtains.

138.18 tent bedstead bed with arched canopy resembling a tent.

139.heading LOVE . . . RAN SMOOTHLY see *A Midsummer Night's Dream*, 1.1.134: 'The course of true love never did run smooth.'

139.13 "too far gone" too intoxicated. The inverted commas suggest that this was a new or slang phrase, but the first citation in the *OED* is dated 1616: 'far gone', *adj.*, 1b.

141.13 dress herself out deck herself up.

141.14–15 if people only saw themselves see Robert Burns, 'To a Louse, On Seeing one on a Lady's Bonnet at Church' (1786), 43–4: 'O wad some Pow'r the giftie gie us | *To see oursels as others see us!*'

141.25 laying herself out exhibiting herself.

141.28 'Tilda's friends 'Tilda's family, relations.

141.31 take copy by follow the example of; imitate.

141.38 take pattern by follow the example of; imitate.

142.12 far gone committed.

142.13–14 very glad to be off with Miss Price, and on with Miss Squeers compare the proverbial 'It is best to be off with the old love before you are on with the new': *ODEP*, 586.

143.29 to be put up to be included in the banns of marriage to be read in the parish church on three successive Sundays demanding that anyone with any objection in law to the proposed union should declare it.

143.32 gall and honey the expression is found in e.g. Edmund Spenser, *The Faerie Queene* (1590–6), 4.10.1.2.

145.12 the holy state of matrimony a common expression, slightly varied from the marriage service vows in the Book of Common Prayer: 'the holy estate of Matrimony'.

148.7 "found" in provided with.

150.31–2 The world is before me see the description of Adam and Eve leaving Eden at the end of John Milton, *Paradise Lost* (1667, rev. 1674), 12.646–7: 'The world was all before them, where to choose | Their place of rest.'

154.38 take pattern by follow the example of; imitate.
156.28 fifteen shillings 75p.
157.34 ten or twelve shillings 50p or 60p.
162.13 four shillings 20p.
163.39 Where there's a will there's a way proverbial: *ODEP*, 891.
164.31 Boroughbridge a small town on the Great North Road, 16 miles NW of York. It is some 30 miles SE of Greta Bridge.
165.17 than he looked for than he expected.
166.26 porter pots pewter mugs with handles, from which porter (dark ale) was drunk. Porter could be taken home from public houses in pots, or delivered by potboys.
166.28 a thought a very little.
166.37 a calculating boy mathematical prodigies were exhibited as curiosities throughout the 19th century. (Schlicke, 850)
167.3 flush of plentifully supplied with. This example is cited in the *OED.*
168.23 the wife and olive branches see Psalm 128.3: 'Thy wife shall be as a fruitful vine by the sides of thine house: thy children like olive plants round about thy table.'
168.24 turner in ivory fashioner of ivory objects on a lathe.
168.28 collected a water-rate until 1852 London water rates were calculated by each of eight principal companies (with wide variations), on the basis of an estimated consumption arrived at by counting e.g. rooms or chimneys.
168.37–8 the church of England as by law established a standard legal formula.
169.3 made upon a juvenile principle in a style appropriate for a young person.
169.24–5 the two-pair back the rear flat on the second floor (up two *pairs* or flights of stairs).
169.37 "went on" acted.
170.8–9 a round game see note to 9.20.
171.7 ***lignum vitæ*** a hard brownish-green wood.
171.37 kept house in Mr. Lillyvick's parish resided in the parish for the collection of whose water rates Mr Lillyvick was responsible.
172.3–4 the Theatre Royal Drury Lane the Theatre Royal dates from 1663, but the present building was constructed in 1811–12, with external additions in 1820 and 1831. With Covent Garden it was one of the two patent theatres licensed for drama.
172.11 speculation see note to 114.37–9.
172.14–15 all should be fish . . . net alluding to the proverb 'All is fish that comes to net' (*ODEP*, 264–5).
172.15–16 was by no means scrupulous in appropriating the property was not deterred by any scruples from taking possession of the property.
172.27 plucked up took heart; recovered vigour.

175.11–12 **the Blood-Drinker's Burial** the work is imaginary, but it represents the penny serials or popular recitations which Dickens loved as a child. He himself mentioned the cheap magazine *The Terrific Register*: 'there was an illustration to every number, in which there was always a pool of blood, and at least one body' (Slater 2009, 26).

175.28 **had the soles of her shoes chalked** to stop them slipping when dancing.

175.33 **out at the Opera** on stage at the opera house in the Haymarket (see note to 10.30–1).

178.14 **aperient medicine** a laxative.

186.37 ***sal volatile*** an aromatic solution of ammonium carbonate used as a restorative in fainting fits.

187.13 **two-pair back** see note to 169.24–5.

187.15–16 **a strange cat had... sucked the baby's breath** there is a persistent, though unfounded, belief that a cat will kill a baby by sucking its breath away.

187.34 **all out** completely finished.

190.6–7 **when Lords break off door-knockers... other people's money** complaints about unruly and boorish aristocratic behaviour in London are common in the 18th and 19th centuries: see e.g. Charles Mackay, 'Ancient and Modern Mohocks', *Bentley's Miscellany*, 6 (1839), 357–66.

191.1 **look after** seek.

191.8 **the leads** the roof (covered with strips or sheets of lead).

191.10 **the parlour lodger** the lodger occupying the best room in the house.

191.22 **familiarity breeds contempt** proverbial: *ODEP*, 243.

192.28 **servants-of-all-work** servants hired to perform the entire range of cleaning, cooking, and caring for children.

193.3 **shepherd's-plaid boots** boots made of a cloth with a black and white tartan pattern.

193.5–6 **Russell Place, Russell Square** until 1867 Russell Place was the name given to the portion of Fitzroy Street S of Fitzroy Square between the present Maple St and Howland St. It is nearly half a mile W of Russell Square, but that is the location here added to distinguish it from the Russell Place formerly in Covent Garden.

193.6 **tea and sugar found** tea and sugar included.

193.11 **Finsbury** a middle-class residential area N of the City, developed from the last quarter of the 18th century.

193.17–18 **the Little Bethel Congregation** a dissenting assembly, adopting the name that Jacob gave to the place where he had a dream of a ladder with angels moving up and down between heaven and earth (Genesis 28.10–19).

193.27–32 **the Observance question... dressing herself** The Lord's Day Observance Society, founded in 1831, campaigned for the banning of all but religious activities, and others deemed to be duties of necessity and mercy, on Sundays. The cooking of meals was included on the list of prohibited activities, following Exodus 16.23.

195.12 Mr. Gregsbury David Chandler suggests that Gregsbury is, at least in part, based on the Radical MP Joseph Hume (1777–1855). Among the features they have in common are failure to fulfil the expectations of their electorate, relentless provoking of divisions in the Commons, and opposition to copyright legislation ('Dickens's Mr Gregsbury, Joseph Hume and Radical Politics', *Dickensian*, 99 (2003), 201–10).

195.13 Manchester Buildings a double row of private houses principally occupied by bachelor Members of Parliament, on the site NW of Westminster Bridge now occupied by Portcullis House.

196.20 general postmen see note to 6.13.

196.21 in quest of franks until the introduction of the penny post in 1840 Members of both Houses of Parliament could endorse letters (and indeed blank sheets) for anyone they chose to enable them to be sent free of charge.

196.22 Complete Letter-writers departed *The Complete Letter-Writer* was first published in 1755 and went through numerous editions.

196.25–6 the water which washes the Buildings' feet the Thames, before the Victoria Embankment was constructed in 1864–70.

196.28–9 a grinding of organs... boxes of music barrel organs operated by turning a crank; and clockwork musical boxes which could play up to three minutes of music, operatic overtures being particularly popular.

197.2 making up to approaching.

198.29–31 balloons... any other nation the most spectacular developments in English ballooning in the period are associated with Charles Green (1785–1870). Between 1821 and 1835 he made 200 ascents and travelled some 6,000 miles in his balloons filled with the newly available coal gas which was cheaper and more efficient than hydrogen. The high point of his career involved the *Royal Vauxhall* (renamed the *Great Nassau*), in which he flew from Vauxhall Gardens in London to Nassau in Germany in 1836. Dickens introduced a race between two balloons in 'Vauxhall-Gardens by Day', published in the *Morning Chronicle* on 26 October 1836 as one of the *Sketches by Boz*, and on 21 March 1837 the second edition of the second series bore on its title page a vignette of Dickens and Cruikshank making such an ascent: *Sketches by Boz*, ed. Paul Schlicke with David Hewitt (Oxford, 2020), 460–4, 558–9, [704].

200.9 milk and honey Joshua 5.6.

200.14 move for returns demand detailed information from ministers, which would often involve their staff in considerable labour.

203.24–5 might be made a point of... lying on the table a petition could be debated at any of its four stages: when brought up, received, lying upon the table, and printed. See Josef Redlich, *The Procedure of the House of Commons*, 3 vols (London, 1908), 1.76.

204.4 come out acquit myself.

204.4–5 timber duty questions for an example of such a question see Anthony Landers, *The Shipowners' Complaint, and Appeal to the United Kingdom* (London, 1828), arguing that the difference between the duty payable on timber imported on British and foreign ships should be increased to encourage merchants to use the former.

204.6–9 the disastrous effects of a return to cash payments...bank notes from the Bullion Report in 1810, which recommended that paper currency should only be issued when backed up by sufficient reserves of bullion, until the late 1830s, there was much debating of the relationship between paper currency and specie, including the part played in determining it by the widespread practice of exporting bullion: see Henry Dunning Macleod, *The Theory and Practice of Banking*, 2 vols (London, 1855–6), Vol. 2, Chs 9 and 10.

204.10 Do you take me? Do you follow me?

204.17–29 any preposterous bill...don't you see? the Copyright Act of 1710 (8 Anne, c. 21) established copyright for a period of 14 years from publication, with the possibility of a 14-year extension. Dickens was one of those who advocated better provision for authors. On 25 April 1838 his friend Thomas Noon Talfourd (1795–1854) unsuccessfully introduced in the House of Commons the second reading of a Bill which would have extended copyright to 60 years from the author's death. David Chandler suggests that Dickens is imitating the successful attack on the Bill in the House of Commons on 25 April 1838 by John Hume's successor in the debate, the solicitor-general Sir Robert Rolfe (1790–1868: for Hume see note to 195.12). In support of his argument Rolfe mockingly twisted Talfourd's citation of Wordsworth as representative of a class of authors who stood to benefit, claiming that Talfourd 'had shown, that the illustrious Wordsworth, in the obscurity in which he voluntarily remained, was careless of present benefit, satisfied that posterity would do him justice. Why, that showed, not only that the existing protection was sufficient, but that it did not require any protection whatever to induce great writers to instruct and amuse the public with their lucubrations.' See David Chandler, 'Dickens on Wordsworth: *Nicholas Nickleby* and the Copyright Question', *English Language Notes*, 41 (2003), 62–9 (64). Eventually in 1842 a new Copyright Act (5 & 6 Vict., c. 45) extended the period of copyright to 42 years from publication, or the life of the author plus seven years, whichever was longer.

204.27 take with the house be favourably received by the House of Commons.

204.35 live in lodgings, and are not voters lodgers (mostly single young men) were excluded from the franchise until the Second Reform Act of 1867.

205.7 fifteen shillings 75p.

205.7–8 find yourself provide for your own needs.

207.11–12 five shillings . . . realm 25p. The phrase 'in the current coin of the realm' was standard in legal enactments.

207.14 take it out in grammar have lessons in grammar to the value of the extra shilling.

208.15–16 on their form of audience sitting on a bench as if giving a formal hearing.

208.16 porter's chair high-backed chair with arched hood, designed to protect porters sitting at a door from draughts.

208.19 Italian iron cylindrical iron with rounded end, made hollow for the reception of the heater, used for fluting or crimping lace, frills, etc. (*OED*).

209.21 the last war the Napoleonic wars (1803–15).

210.12–13 the city i.e. the City of London.

210.16–17 the poor worm the silkworm.

212.17–18 rout seats small chairs for use at parties.

212.27 in an easy manner informally.

214.15 the park Hyde Park.

216.38–9 you may trust them as far as you can see them, and no farther proverbial: *ODEP*, 843.

221.7–8 the ten thousand pounds prize in the lottery a state lottery ran from 1694 until 1826. In the final years the top prize was most frequently £20,000.

221.11 Westminster School an independent school tracing its history back to the early 14th century.

222.12–16 A thief in fustian . . . poetry and adventure the so-called Newgate novel was a popular genre of the 1830s and included Edward Bulwer-Lytton's *Paul Clifford* (1830) and William Harrison Ainsworth's *Rookwood*, which featured Dick Turpin. It was attacked by Thackeray for its unrealistic glamorizing of criminals in 'Horæ Catnachianæ. A Dissertation on Ballads, with a few unnecessary remarks on Jonathan Wild, Jon Sheppard, Paul Clifford, and — Fagin, Esqrs', *Fraser's Magazine*, 19 (April 1839), 407–24.

222.17 the one great cardinal virtue strictly speaking, charity—or love—is not one of the *cardinal* (natural) virtues (prudence, justice, temperance, and courage), but a theological virtue along with faith and hope: according to 1 Corinthians 13.13 it is greater than either of the latter. In Dickens's time the term 'cardinal' began to be applied by some writers to all seven virtues.

223.2 taking her weary way homewards compare the third line of Thomas Gray, *Elegy Written in a Country Churchyard* (1751): 'The ploughman homeward plods his weary way'.

223.33–4 as the man said about the blind horse . . . respect it the sentiment has not been found elsewhere. It was perhaps suggested by the proverb

'The blind horse is the hardiest', or 'Nothing so bold as a blind Mare' (*ODEP*, 67).

225.23 Heaven suits the back to the burden proverbial: *ODEP*, 312.

225.28 Saint Anthony's fire erysipelas, a skin disease resulting in heat and redness.

226.1 cooling ... her heels proverbial: *ODEP*, 143.

226.3–4 doing the last new carriage customer at second-hand i.e. imitating the most recent affluent customer.

226.37 out at interest lent or invested so as to obtain interest.

227.9–11 Old Boar ... George the Fourth fictional public houses. George IV reigned 1820–30.

228.9 circulating library library with books circulating among subscribers.

228.22 snuffed himself took snuff.

229.27 call yourself out of your name call yourself anything other than what you are.

229.31 nine shillings 45p.

230.20 post octavo measuring approximately 8 by 5 inches (20 by 13 cm). Post was a sheet of paper measuring 19½ by 15¾ inches (49.5 by 40 cm.). A book printed on such sheets, which were folded to produce eight leaves, was called post octavo. Novels were commonly published in three volumes in this kind of format.

230.36 any other fire than St. Anthony's see note to 225.28.

233.34 vinegar and hartshorn liquids whose pungent smell was used to assist recovery after fainting. *Hartshorn* was a mixture of ammonia and water, the ammonia being made originally from the antlers of deer; it was used medicinally and as a detergent.

236.16 a committee of ways and means alluding to a committee of the House of Commons (between 1641 and 1967) concerned with raising government revenue.

239.6 Rats and mice, and such small gear see *King Lear* (folio text), 3.4.130: 'mice and rats and such small deer'.

242.11 upon town in London.

242.36–7 reckoned without his host alluding to the proverb 'He that reckons without his host must reckon again' (*ODEP*, 667). To 'reckon without one's host' means 'to calculate one's bill or score without consulting one's host or landlord; to come to conclusions without taking into consideration some important circumstance of the case' (*OED*).

243.16 tack it on to the other five-and-twenty i.e. increase the interest payable on the loans by Ralph Nickleby to 27.5%.

243.19 a pleasant oath regarding Mr. Nickleby's limbs *probably* damn your legs.

243.20 "laughed consumedly" George Farquhar (1678–1707), *The Beaux' Stratagem* (1707), 3.1.67–8: 'I believe they talk'd of me, for they laugh'd consumedly.'

243.26–7 fair play's a jewel proverbial: *ODEP*, 239–40.

244.23–4 toads in ordinary sycophants occupying official positions (compare 'chaplain-in-ordinary' etc.).

245.9 discounting dinner see notes to 7.39 and 243.16. Lord Frederick jocularly observes that it is fine if a dinner as splendid as this results in him having to pay Ralph an increased rate of interest.

245.17 the Militia an emergency force whose primary role was home defence but which could be called on to supplement the regular army in service abroad.

245.39 make love to pay amorous addresses to.

246.20 favours the mahogany so much keeps looking down at the table.

247.29 the gentlemen would take coffee at table the normal practice was for the women to move to the drawing room after dessert, leaving the men to their port until it was time for the men to follow the women for the concluding tea or coffee.

248.14 crush hat top hat which can be folded by means of an internal spring.

251.9 wronged you in thought, or word, or deed see the general confession in the Book of Common Prayer's Communion Service, where sins are acknowledged as being committed '[b]y thought, word, and deed'.

251.32 the light from a neighbouring lamp this would be a gas lamp (producing a weak illumination before the invention of the gas mantle towards the end of the 19th century), either part of the municipal grid or installed by an affluent householder.

254.32 I need look I must look.

255.8–9 cast his duplicity and malice in his throat a violent form of 'make him swallow his words', i.e. retract them, probably derived from accusations of treason in Shakespeare. Compare *Richard II*, 1.1.44: 'With a foul traitor's name stuff I thy throat.'

256.23–4 hold up his hand at the Old Bailey plead guilty at the Old Bailey Sessions House (rebuilt in 1774, becoming the Central Criminal Court in 1834), adjoining Newgate Prison.

257.2 my bounden duty see the introduction to the Sanctus in the Communion Service in the Book of Common Prayer: 'our bounden duty'.

257.34 Or bronze *bronze* had the figurative sense 'impudence'.

260.32 the loftiest gallows in all Europe traditionally a particularly prominent or notorious offender would be hanged on a gallows of unusual height. See Esther 5.14 and 7.9–10 for the monstrously high instrument of Haman's execution.

261.25 the Workhouse until the Poor Law Amendment Act of 1834 (4 & 5 Will. 4, c. 76) the main responsibility for providing workhouses for the destitute lay with individual parishes.

261.25 the Refuge for the Destitute a refuge catering for destitute women was founded in Lambeth in 1805 and moved to Hackney Road in 1811, surviving until 1902.

261.25–6 the Magdalen Hospital an institution for penitent prostitutes, situated at the S end of Blackfriars Road from 1772 to 1868.

267.15 a tendency to horseflesh i.e. a fondness for buying expensive horses.

268.11 above stairs upstairs.

268.13–14 if it's made a favour on if it's treated as involving the granting of a favour.

269.4 writ of execution warrant authorizing the seizure of the goods or person of a debtor in default of payment.

269.28–9 four and ninepence ha'penny 24p.

271.1 along of because of.

272.11–12 skirt pocket pocket in the lower part of a coat.

273.31 Mrs. Wititterly inspirations for Mr and Mrs Wititterly were Thomas Haynes Bayly (1797–1839), song-writer and dramatist, and his wife: *Letters*, 1.225n.

273.32 Cadogan Place a development of fashionable terraced houses originally built during the first decade of the 19th century.

273.35 Belgrave Square construction of this large fashionable square began in 1826 and continued until the 1840s.

273.35 Chelsea a large village with market gardens and nurseries, Chelsea began to be built up at the end of the 18th century.

273.35 Sloane Street originally a fashionable residential street, it was built in 1780 and substantially rebuilt in 1860–90.

273.37 Brompton until the second half of the 19th century Brompton was sparsely built up and dominated by market gardens and nurseries.

273.38 the New Road begun in 1756, the New Road (divided and renamed in 1857 as Marylebone Road, Euston Road, and Pentonville Road) had many fashionable houses by the end of the 1820s.

273.39–74.1 Grosvenor Place a fashionable residential street on the W side of the royal palace gardens, mostly constructed in 1805–10.

274.9 the Siamese twins Chang and Eng Bunker (1811–74) were joined at the waist by a tubular band of tissue. They were exhibited as a curiosity at the Egyptian Hall, Piccadilly in 1829.

274.13–14 his head floured... powder see note to 11.34.

278.16–17 Saint George's Hanover Square St George's, built in 1720–5 in George Street (St George Street from 1938) running S from the square, was popular for fashionable weddings.

278.19–20 the two-pair back... the three-pair front the rear flat on the second floor... the front flat on the third floor (up two/three flights of stairs).

278.heading MR. VINCENT CRUMMLES for Crummles and his theatrical company see Essay on the Text, 869–70.

278.27–8 in possession, reversion, remainder, or expectancy four conditions of estates, as defined in exhaustive detail in Sir William Blackstone's *Commentaries on the Laws of England* (1765–9), Bk 2, Ch. 11.

279.10 the chilly cry of the poor sweep the 1834 Chimney Sweepers Act (4 & 5 Will. 4, c. 35), designed to regulate and protect chimney sweeps, forbade them (section 14) from soliciting for business by crying in the streets (as in William Blake's 'London' in *Songs of Experience* of 1794: 'the Chimney-sweepers cry | Every blackning Church appalls').

279.11–12 the official watcher of the night during the 18th century London parishes increasingly employed official paid night watchmen rather than relying on burgesses undertaking the duty. The function was assumed by the Metropolitan Police on their foundation in 1829, though the City of London was excluded, establishing its own police force in 1832: this took over watch duties from the ward authorities in 1838.

279.15–16 ineffectual knocking at the doors of heavy sleepers knockers-up would, in return for a small payment, wake their clients by knocking on their doors with a short heavy stick, or on their windows with a long cane.

280.11 Kingston Kingston upon Thames, a town 10 miles SW of central London.

280.38 Portsmouth the principal naval port in the United Kingdom.

280.38 Port Royal a sea-port in Jamaica.

281.14–15 Where there's a will, there's a way proverbial: *ODEP*, 891.

281.17–18 it shall go hard but without doubt.

281.21 Godalming a town 30 miles SW of central London.

284.9 the Devil's Punch Bowl a deep hollow skirted by the Portsmouth road just before Hindhead, 8 miles SW of Godalming.

284.10–12 the inscription upon the stone...by night the inscription reads: 'Erected in detestation of a barbarous murder committed here on an unknown sailor on Sep. 24th, 1786, by Edwd. Lonegan, Michl. Casey, & James Marshall, who were all taken the same day and hung in chains near this place.'

286.16 how they are a going of it what a performance they are putting on.

286.26–7 what is called in play-bills a terrific combat the expression 'terrific combat' frequently appears in the elaborate theatrical advertisements produced in the 19th century.

286.38 pot companion drinking partner.

288.3 knock under yield.

290.26–7 well up in done up as.

290.28 three rounds i.e. of applause.

290.29–30 the practicable door...O. P. a usable door, real rather than a simulation, slid on stage as part of the scenery by means of *grooves*, on the actors' right-hand side facing the audience (Opposite Prompt, the prompter sitting on their left side).

290.34 the heavy children children in serious or tragic pieces.

291.1 sharp set hungry.

292.7–8 melting the sealing-wax...his little finger sealing-wax was applied to the stem of clay pipes to avoid chafing the smoker's lips, with the danger of cancer.

292.12 new rum new rum was cheap but considered unhealthy, partly because of contamination by lead from the vessels used in its preparation. See e.g. William Nicholson, *A Journal of Natural Philosophy, Chemistry, and the Arts*, 33 (1812), 311.

292.22 they as plentiful there...streets the impact on Portsmouth of the reduction of naval strength from 100,000 to 33,000 when the Napoleonic wars ended in 1815 would still have been apparent at the time of the novel's action a decade later. Throughout the 19th century oysters were a staple diet, not a luxury.

293.1 goes on takes the stage.

293.1 Timour the Tartar horses play a prominent part in *Timour the Tartar. A Grand Romantic Melo-drama in Two Acts, First Performed at the Theatre Royal, Covent Garden, May 1, 1811* by M. G. ('Monk') Lewis (1775–1818). The Advertisement notes 'the favour with which the Horses were received by the Public'.

293.2 bring you out exhibit you on the stage.

293.7 touch-and-go farce superficial farce, demanding little attention from the audience: 'There is an art in writing for the Theatre, technically called *touch and go*, which is indispensible when we consider the small quantum of patience, which so motley an assemblage as a London audience can be expected to afford': [James and Horatio (Horace) Smith], *Rejected Addresses: or The New Theatrum Poetarum* (London, 1812), xi.

293.9 the lamps the stage-lights.

293.13 capital bills excellent advertising.

294.21 a four-wheeled phaeton a *phaeton* was a light four-wheeled open carriage with one or two seats facing forwards, usually drawn by a pair of horses.

295.13–14 ate apple-pie at a circus...nightcap for a parallel, perhaps a source, see Ruth Manning-Sanders, *The English Circus* (London, 1952), 52: the clown John Ducrow (d. 1834) 'had a way with animals, and two little ponies helped him in his fun-making. There is a print of these two, gravely seated on their haunches before two little tables. One wears a matronly bonnet, the other a gentlemanly hat; both have napkins tied under their chins; the matron sedately drinks a dish of tea, the gentleman solemnly laps his supper.'

295.15 took the low comedy entirely completely dominated the low comedy (slapstick) department.

295.18 jobbed out let out; hired out.

295.30 the drawbridge at Portsmouth until the demolition of the fortifications in 1875 Portsmouth was approached by a drawbridge across the moat at Landport Gate N of the High Street.

296.9–10 the Portsmouth Theatre established in 1761 it was situated on the High Street of Old Portsmouth until its demolition in 1854.

296.13 the prompter's side the side to the actors' left, as they face the audience.

297.14–16 the Indian Savage and the Maiden... ballet interlude a ballet interlude was a short ballet given between longer dramatic pieces. This example is apparently imaginary. It was realized by J. H. Horncastle in *The Savage and the Maiden or Crummles and his Daughter in One Act*, produced at the Grecian Saloon on 29 and 31 May 1844 (British Library Add. MS 42975, ff. 785–96 (ff. 785r, 795r–796r): Lord Chamberlain's Plays, Vol. 111 (May to June 1844)).

297.30 sound as a church the phrase is proverbial.

298.11 the infant phenomenon see Essay on the Text, 869–70.

298.34–5 the memory of the oldest inhabitant a stock phrase indicating that an event was exceptional.

298.36–7 put upon an unlimited allowance... growing tall see e.g. William Buchan, *Domestic Medicine*, 17th edn (London, 1800), 99: 'Intoxication is peculiarly hurtful to young persons. It heats their blood, impairs their strength, and obstructs their growth.'

299.18 Mr. Folair the name may derive from that of an actor called Billy Floyer, who played comic roles for many years at Portsmouth: see Paul Schlicke, *Dickens and Popular Entertainment* (London, 1985), 57.

299.35–6 put up in the best business given the most prominent parts.

299.39 fifteen and sixpence 15*s*. 6*d*. (77.5p).

300.1–2 the Highland Fling this vigorous Scottish dance requires delicate balance and precision.

300.2–3 put up in it given that act to perform.

300.9 come it act, perform.

300.11 chalk applied to prevent slipping on the stage.

300.11 dancing in fetters a performance elaboration: see e.g. *Sketches by Boz*, ed. Paul Schlicke with David Hewitt (Oxford, 2020), 34.73–4, and an illustration reproduced in J. S. Bratton, 'Dancing a Hornpipe in Fetters', *Folk Music Journal*, 6 (1990), 65–82 (77).

300.31 Do the honours make the introductions.

301.3 a part of twelve lengths i.e. a part of 504 lines, a *length* being 42 lines.

301.30 lantern jaws long thin jaws, giving a hollow appearance to the cheek.

301.35 a medley dance a dance involving a mixture of styles.

301.36 benefit performance from which the financial proceeds (or a portion thereof) went to a member of the company, who was allowed to choose the programme or, as in Miss Snevellicci's case, to invite patrons to 'bespeak' the programme. See St Vincent Troubridge, *The Benefit System in the British Theatre* (Society for Theatre Research, 1967). (Schlicke, 854)

302.6 "in character" in costume.

303.16 retired up moved to the back of the stage.

303.19 the Mortal Struggle no such work has been identified.

303.20 Intrigue *Intrigue: A Comic Interlude, in One Act*, by John Poole (1785/6–1872), was first performed at the Theatre Royal, Drury Lane in 1814.

303.20–1 Ways and Means *Ways and Means; or, A Trip to Dover: A Comedy*, by George Colman the Younger (1762–1836), was first performed at the Theatre Royal, Haymarket in 1788.

304.18 turn-up bedstead bed frame which is hinged to lift off the floor onto a wall to create space in a room.

304.35 Saint Thomas's Street a road parallel to the High Street in Old Portsmouth.

305.29 the Fairy Porcupine no such work has been identified.

305.30–1 four pound twelve £4 12*s*. (£4.60).

305.33 was trust was on credit.

306.16–17 play up to the infant act in such a way as to support the infant prodigy.

306.23 Rover the hero of *Wild Oats; or, The Strolling Gentlemen. A Comedy, in Five Acts*, by John O'Keeffe (1747–1833), first performed at the Theatre Royal, Covent Garden in 1791.

306.24 Cassio in *Othello*.

306.24 Jeremy Diddler a character in *Raising the Wind, A Farce*, by James Kenney (1780–1849), first performed at the Theatre Royal, Covent Garden in 1803.

306.25–6 Here they are, cues and all the individual actors would not have complete scripts but cue-scripts, booklets with their speeches accompanied by short cues.

306.37–8 up three pair of stairs i.e. on the third floor (up three flights).

306.39 the Common Hard now simply 'The Hard', it was originally constructed in 1720 as a landing place for small boats.

308.5 House, house, house! the interjection 'house!' was used to summon the landlord or waiter at a public house.

309.15 that's a sure card that's certain to hit the target.

309.27 ***pas de deux*** dance for two.

310.10–11 close in with a picture end with a tableau.

310.18 go on go on stage.

312.28 dark lantern lantern with a slide for concealing the light.

313.7 desperate fellows to shout terribly keen on shouting.

313.18 work up progress.

315.7–8 Lombard-street between High Street and St Thomas's Street.

315.11 getting up preparing for use.

317.29 a few words of course a brief unremarkable exchange.

318.14 post octavo see note to 230.20.

318.14–18 the character of the Nurse's deceased husband...report him see *Romeo and Juliet*, 1.3.42.

318.29–30 his right fore-finger... Sterne see the 1760 portrait of the novelist Laurence Sterne (1713–68) by Sir Joshua Reynolds (1723–92), now in the National Portrait Gallery, London (NPG 5019).

318.36 high and palmy days see note to 75.10.

319.15 the unities Renaissance interpretations of Aristotle's *Poetics* demanded unity of time (limiting the supposed time of a play to the time taken to act it, or to a single day), place (use of one scene throughout), and action (concentration on the development of a single plot). They had a particular influence on 17th-century French neoclassical drama.

320.8–9 two-and-sixpence for half-a-crown smaller coins of the same total value in exchange for a half-crown coin (12.5p).

322.25 Fifteen shillings 75p.

324.33 blue fire 'a blue light (typically produced by igniting a mixture containing sulphur) formerly used on the stage to create an unearthly or ghostly atmosphere, or to convey the effect of supernatural happenings' (*OED*).

325.9 thirty shillings £1.50.

325.30 the Theatre Royal, Drury Lane see note to 172.3–4.

326.13 'The Blood Drinker' see note to 175.11–12.

326.38 Helen Macgregor Rob Roy's wife in *Rob Roy Macgregor; or, Auld lang syne! A Musical Drama*, by Isaac Pocock (1782–1835), based on the novel *Rob Roy* published anonymously by Walter Scott in 1818. It was first performed at the Theatre Royal, Covent Garden the same year.

326.39 the skipping-rope hornpipe the advertisement for the clown Grimaldi's farewell appearance at Sadlers Wells theatre on 17 March 1828 included 'Mrs. Searle's skipping-rope dance': it is included in a publication edited and rewritten by Dickens, *Memoirs of Joseph Grimaldi. Edited by "Boz."*, 2 vols (London, 1838), 2.222.

327.12 the General Post see note to 6.13.

328.13 below stairs downstairs.

329.8–9 collect... the water-rate see note to 168.28.

329.30 turned on derived.

330.14 I shall draw her salary see note to 40.5–6.

330.29–30 got out a commission of lunacy obtained 'a commission issued by a court, authorizing an inquiry as to the soundness of a person's mind' (*OED*).

331.3 at breakfast-time at the time of the novel's action it was common to celebrate a wedding with a wedding-breakfast given after the marriage ceremony.

333.15 ***sal volatile*** see note to 186.37.

334.21 "made up" although commonplace now, Dickens's intransitive use of the term was new in 1838–9, hence the quotation marks.

334.22–3 a brown George a wig resembling a loaf known as a 'Brown George', of coarse brown bread.

336.24 passed their words promised.

336.37 Ryde the town on the Isle of Wight where the Portsmouth ferry arrives.

337.5 travelling bridesmaid it was normal practice in the period for a bridesmaid to accompany the bride on her honeymoon.

337.28 'Who calls so loud?' *Romeo and Juliet*, 5.1.57 (the Apothecary's first utterance).

339.18 Sir Mulberry Hawk the character may be based on Baron de Ros (1792–1839), a worldly man of fashionable society known for mentoring and swindling gullible young men and seducing women: see A. B. Crowder, 'A Source for Dickens's Sir Mulberry', *Papers on Language and Literature*, 12 (1976), 103–9.

340.39 You take me you follow my drift.

346.14 the stamp office people by an Act of 1831 (1 & 2 Will. 4, c. 22) the collection of the duties on hackney carriages was placed under the Commissioner of Stamps. The Act does not include the provisions which Mrs Nickleby imagines it does; but a Bill of 1835, 'For the better Regulation of Cabriolets and other Hackney Carriages', provides for a fine of up to twenty shillings for 'any broken window, door or step' (section 61, or 53 as amended by committee).

346.22 the Corn Laws between 1815 and 1846 the controversial Corn Laws imposed protective tariffs on imported grain.

346.37 the Old Bailey see note to 256.23–4.

347.3–6 All down Newgate Street... a mile Spigwiffin's Wharf is apparently imaginary. The distance involved is indeed a good mile.

350.5 St. George's, Hanover Square see note to 278.16–17.

350.6 the Bishop of Llandaff Llandaff is a diocese in S Wales (Sir Mulberry being Welsh, albeit from 'North Wales').

350.22 half-a-dozen of the annuals gift books which were fashionable Christmas presents between the 1820s and the 1850s. They contained miscellaneous short prose and verse pieces and 'embellishments' (engravings). Contemporaneous portraits were not the norm, but two publications featuring society portraits accompanied by matching prose or verse descriptions were *Heath's Book of Beauty* (1833–49) and *The English Annual* (1834–8).

354.26 have me out challenge me to a duel.

357.38 the Royal Academy the activities of the Royal Academy of Arts (see note to 119.37) included the teaching of drawing from life models.

358.30 wine in; truth out proverbial: *ODEP*, 895.

361.28 that dear little dull house he was born in Shakespeare's birthplace in Stratford-upon-Avon became a place of pilgrimage in the 18th century. Dickens was involved in its purchase in 1847 when it was threatened with exportation to America.

362.5 a post-chaise '[a] horse-drawn, usually four-wheeled carriage (in Britain usually having a closed body, the driver or postilion riding on one of the horses) used for carrying mail and passengers, esp. in the 18th and early 19th centuries' (*OED*).

362.10–13 Shakespeare's tomb... two tassels Shakespeare is buried in Holy Trinity Church, Stratford-upon-Avon. On the wall beside his tomb is a bust. The only resemblance to Mrs Nickleby's description is the 'lay-down collar': there are two tassels, but they are attached to a cushion rather than the collar. The monument was painted white in 1793 and the colours were not restored till 1861.

362.19 an Italian image boy one of the boys who carried boards on their heads with plaster figures for sale as ornaments: their cry was 'Buy my images!' See William Hone, *The Every-Day Book*, 2 vols (London, 1826–7), 2.310–14.

366.34 closely-crossed closely written vertically over the normal horizontal writing. This was a common way of maximizing the content of a letter when postage was payable (by the recipient) by the sheet.

367.11 "The Lady Flabella" the work appears to be imaginary. For 'three volumes' see note to 230.20.

367.21 salon de danse *French* ballroom.

367.22–3 Chérizette... mon enfant *French* Cherizette, my dear, please give me some eau-de-Cologne, my child.

367.26 mouchoir *French* handkerchief.

367.39 billet *French* letter.

368.2 *envelope* the word is italicized because it is of French origin, and because envelopes were not in general use at the time of the novel's action (see note to 21.20): they attracted an additional charge and were normally used only by the wealthy for sending invitations etc.

371.39–72.1 took the new medicine... Kensington Gravel Pits at the time of the novel's action there was no effective statutory regulation of medicines. Kensington Gravel Pits was a residential area N of Kensington Gardens.

376.35–6 Honesty is the best policy proverbial: *ODEP*, 380.

380.8 Guy Faux a straw effigy of Guy Fawkes (1570–1606), to be burned on a bonfire on 5 November in commemoration of the failure of his plot to blow up the Houses of Parliament in 1605.

383.14 Newmarket coat close-fitting tailcoat for men, cut away at the front and originally worn for riding (*OED*).

385.5 right down absolutely.

385.6 honour bright word of honour!

385.18 second business subordinate parts.

385.26–7 play Tybalt with a real sword see *Romeo and Juliet*, 3.1.

385.36 eight or ten shillings 40p or 50p.

386.2 shown the white feather proverbial: *ODEP*, 885.

386.3–4 sworn the peace against him sworn that he was in bodily fear from him, so that he would be bound over to keep the peace.

386.22 with a very high hand very imperiously.

387.31–2 if it were to be done at all...at once see *Macbeth*, 1.7.1–2: 'If it were done when 'tis done, then 'twere well | It were done quickly' (Macbeth in soliloquy, contemplating the murder of King Duncan).

393.12 in an attitude adopting a theatrical pose.

393.20 hornpipes by the later 18th century hornpipes commonly featured between the acts of plays and at their close: see George S. Emmerson, 'The Hornpipe', *Folk Music Journal*, 2 (1970), 12–34 (17).

393.21 the legitimate drama according to Schlicke, 856, the Licensing Act of 1737 had given Drury Lane and Covent Garden exclusive right to stage spoken drama, a privilege extended in the 18th century to other theatres (all of them outside London, except the Theatre Royal, Haymarket). The law, designed in theory to ensure the purity of dramatic art, in fact forced the great majority of theatres to develop alternative forms of entertainment; but by the time the novelist and MP Edward Bulwer-Lytton (1803–73) chaired a Select Committee on the theatres in 1832 the distinction between 'legitimate' and 'illegitimate' drama had eroded beyond recognition, and the monopoly was finally abolished in 1843. See Dewey Ganzel, 'Patent Wrongs and Patent Theatres: Drama and the Law in the Early Nineteenth Century', *PMLA*, 76 (1961), 384–96.

393.28 notes of admiration exclamation marks.

395.21–2 more knave than fool *King Lear* (folio text), 1.4.294 (Goneril to the Fool).

398.14 the Coburg the Royal Coburg Theatre opened in 1818 in Waterloo Road. In 1833 it was renamed the Victoria Theatre, leading to its popular designation 'The Old Vic'.

398.21–2 that bourne...returns see *Hamlet*, 3.1.80–2: 'something after death, | The undiscovered country from whose bourn | No traveller returns' (Hamlet, in soliloquy).

401.8 One good turn deserves another proverbial: *ODEP*, 325.

405.13 the one pair front the front room on the first floor (up one flight of stairs).

409.22 mending a pen see note to 36.18.

410.5 offer to go look as if you are going.

410.15 Broad Street a street on the eastern perimeter of the City ward of the same name, in the financial district N of the Bank of England and Stock Exchange.

412.25 on the high ropes elated, disdainful.

412.28 in state with dignity.

413.2 false hound a common imprecation: e.g. *Coriolanus*, 5.6.113.

413.7 Mr. Canning the Tory politician George Canning (1770–1827) was twice Foreign Secretary, and Prime Minister briefly in the last year of his life.

414.9 half-quartern loaf one weighing two pounds (0.9 kg).

414.17 Heart alive! an oath expressing emphatic assertion.

416.1 touched up struck lightly or sharply.

416.26 the fantastic groups of the old Dutch painter see the set of 41 wood engravings representing the Dance of Death by the German painter Hans Holbein the Younger (1497/8–1543), published anonymously in Lyons in 1538 and frequently reprinted. In the 19th century *Dutch* could still mean 'German' as well as 'Netherlandish'.

416.36–7 funeral hatchment... mansion a wooden tablet bearing the coat of arms of a deceased person would be attached to the front of that person's house.

416.38–9 repletion and starvation laid them down together compare Isaiah 11.7: 'the cow and the bear shall feed; their young ones shall lie down together'.

417.2 Kingston see note to 280.11.

417.36 Finding her from home finding she was not at home.

424.21 French clock clock in the elaborate style of the French 18th century.

430.13 Whitechapel an eastern suburb of London.

431.14 a bag wig a wig fashionable in the 18th century, the back-hair of which was enclosed in an ornamental bag (*OED*).

431.15 a black watch-pocket a *watch-pocket* is *either* a small pocket in a garment for carrying a watch *or* a pocket or pouch at the head of a bed, to hold a person's watch at night (*OED*).

432.6 the straw straw was scattered on the coach floor for heat insulation.

432.10–11 a bye place an out of the way spot.

432.15–16 Ill news travels fast proverbial: *ODEP*, 400.

434.3 blue convulsions a fit rendering the skin's colour blue or leaden.

434.8 as deaf as a... post proverbial: *ODEP*, 172.

434.16 mint sauce *slang* money.

435.16 Two months, and four the bills are credit notes payable in two months and four months respectively. Nickleby will take them over from Mantalini, paying him £50 for the bills which will produce £75 when they fall due.

436.6 Tom Tidler's ground a children's game in which a player stands behind a line demarcating 'Tom Tidler's ground'. The other players run over, calling out, 'Here we are on Tom Tidler's ground, picking up gold and silver.' The last to be caught becomes the new Tom Tidler (also spelt 'Tiddler').

436.12 **popolorum tibby** *mock Latin* 'populorum tibi'. Mantalini's pet name probably incorporates *tibby*, 'a female cat' (*OED*, under 'Tib-cat'), with an echo of *poppet*, 'darling, pet'.

438.20 **change for a sovereign in halfpence** 480 halfpennies, weighing some 10 pounds (4.5 kg).

438.22 **I will put a note in the twopenny-post** Dickens has adopted part of a speech from his abortive farce *The Lamplighter* composed in November and December 1838, where Tom Grig recalls his lamplighter uncle's suicide after being refused compensation when the advent of gas lighting made him redundant: 'At last, he went and hung himself on a lamp iron, in St. Martin's Lane, that he'd always been very fond of; and as he was a remarkably good husband, and had never any secrets from his wife, he put a note into the twopenny post as he went along to tell the widder where the body was' (Charles Dickens, *The Lamplighter: A Farce* (London, 1879), 11). For the twopenny post see note to 6.13.

440.25 **bring grist to my mill** proverbial: *ODEP*, 339.

441.33 **It is but manner** it's just a way of speaking.

441.39 **a tip-top sawyer** a top person. Mantalini is combining 'tip-top' with 'top-sawyer', a skilled timber man, and by extension the best person in any profession.

443.19 **Wellington boots** see note to 11.26–7.

444.14 **To see... pen-knife** for the source of this operation see 'Essay on the Text', 865–6.

444.24–5 **Vinegar and brown paper** the traditional remedy for minor injuries, as in the nursery rhyme 'Jack and Jill went up the hill', where Jack's head is patched 'With vinegar and brown paper': Opie, 224 (No. 254).

446.26 **high feeding** luxurious diet.

446.36–7 **a penny, a halfpenny, and two farthings** adding up to 2*d.* or 0.8p.

447.13 **Devil a bit** not at all.

448.7 **five pound five** £5. 5*s.* (£5.25).

448.29 **cry quits with** declare ourselves even with.

451.33–4 **In the churchyard we are all alike** compare the proverb 'We shall lie all alike in our graves': *ODEP*, 459.

454.20–1 **was it a bear... hair-dresser's?** see note to 73.35.

454.35–6 **the Grimbles... the North Riding** the name may have been suggested by Crimble Hall in Lancashire or Grimblethorpe Hall in Lincolnshire.

455.6 **Taunton Vale** the area round Taunton in Somerset.

456.34–5 **not one of your stiff starched apoplectic cravats... neckcloth** in the 18th century men's cravats were neckcloths of lawn, muslin, or silk, folded round the neck, the ends tied in a knot or bow in front. The 19th century preferred a starched version, often supported on a stiffener.

See C. Willett Cunnington, Phillis Cunnington, and Charles Beard, *A Dictionary of English Costume* (London, 1960), 55.

457.19–20 so many little lights...mouth and eyes *lights* here is an extension of the sense recorded by *OED* (1h): 'a gleam or sparkle in the eye, expressive of animated feeling or the like' .

457.23 in the fact in the act.

459.37 the Bank the Bank of England, on Threadneedle Street.

460.2–3 Cheeryble, Brothers see Essay on the Text, 870–1.

460.5 German-merchants merchants trading with Germany.

460.13–14 a powdered head see note to 11.34.

460.22 the East India Docks the East India Company's docks at Blackwall, E of the Isle of Dogs, opened in 1806.

462.10 plums from Fortune's choicest pudding perhaps echoing the nursery rhyme 'Little Jack Horner': Opie, 234–7 (No. 262).

463.38 Foreign Post nights on Tuesdays and Fridays at the time of the novel's action letters with foreign destinations were accepted until half past midnight at the General Post Office, St Martin's-le-Grand.

465.25 Bow a village formerly on the outskirts of London, N of the Isle of Dogs.

470.38 the sign of the Britannia over in the Holloway road there were several Britannia taverns in the 1820s, but the only one in the general direction of Holloway Road leading to Highgate was over a mile S at 83 Camden High Street.

471.4 a deal a good deal.

474.18 the Fondling the Foundling Hospital, established in 1741 for the reception of abandoned children. A building was erected in Guilford Street beginning the following year: it was largely demolished in 1926, but the charity continues to exist and the Foundling Museum is housed in a building occupying part of the original site.

475.5 six and sixpence 6*s*. 6*d*. (32.5p).

476.12 Grosvenor Square and Hanover Square Grosvenor Square, Mayfair, is the second largest in London, originally consisting of large residences built *c*.1725–31. The similar Hanover Square, in the area bounded by Oxford Street and Regent Street, was laid out *c*.1715.

476.13 Fitzroy Square the square, designed by Robert Adam (1728–92), was begun in 1793 but not completed until 1835.

476.14 the Squares of Russell and Euston Russell Square, one of the largest in London (see note to 7.4), was laid out in the first decade of the 19th century; Euston Square, built in the second decade, was for over a century twice its present size.

476.17–18 The City square the square is imaginary.

477.8 ticket-porter man licensed to carry goods at prescribed rates, usually wearing a white apron and displaying his ticket of authority as a badge.

477.27 the fabled goodness... Horse Guards the clock in the Horse Guards building in Whitehall, constructed in 1750–9, was considered the most accurate in London until 1859 when 'Big Ben' in the Clock Tower of the new Houses of Parliament started operating.

477.33 wafers small disks of flour mixed with gum, which when moistened were often used for sealing letters before the general adoption of envelopes in the 1840s.

477.33 pounce-box box with a perforated lid used to sprinkle powder to prevent ink from spreading.

477.33 fire-box tinder box containing fire stone, fire steel, and tinder, used to make a flame for melting sealing wax. Matches were a novelty at the end of the 1820s.

479.9 ledger and day-book a *ledger* is organized on a debtor-and-creditor basis, or by subdivisions of the trade; a *day book* records transactions on a daily basis.

480.37–8 the cities of London and Westminster the commercial City of London to the E, and the residential and administrative Westminster to the W.

482.17 make one join us.

483.3–4 the full extent of which... foresee compare *A Midsummer Night's Dream*, 4.1.208–11 ('The eye of man hath not heard, the ear of man hath not seen... what my dream was'), where Bottom is mangling 1 Corinthians 2.9: 'Eye hath not seen, nor ear heard... the things which God hath prepared for them that love him.'

483.13–14 had taken the air... hackney-coach i.e. had hung on to the back of the coach.

483.14 Camberwell a semi-rural residential area formerly on the southern outskirts of London.

483.15 Punches... the Stilts Punch and Judy, and acrobats on stilts.

483.17–18 went upon his way rejoicing see Acts 8.39, where the eunuch baptized by Philip 'went on his way rejoicing'.

483.34–5 For these and all other blessings... truly thankful the conventional grace before a meal.

485.1–2 they eat with their knives i.e. with knife and fingers, not using knife and fork in the manner customary in polite circles.

485.4 nearly out nearly finished.

485.8 the double-diamond a high-quality tawny port wine produced by Dixon, Morgan & Co.

486.18 no time like the present proverbial: *ODEP*, 824.

486.18–19 no two birds in the hand... bush compare the proverb 'A bird in the hand is worth two in the bush': *ODEP*, 59.

486.35 a round game see note to 9.20.

487.8 five-and-twenty shillings £1.25.

487.15–16 a shilling over and above his fare the London Hackney Carriage Act of 1831 (1 & 2 Will. 4, c. 22) required hackney coaches to be licensed and numbered (sections 2–23); schedules B and C fixed fares at one shilling (£0.05) for up to a mile, and sixpence (£0.02½) for every half-mile thereafter, or a shilling for up to thirty minutes and sixpence for every quarter hour thereafter.

488.17–18 sticking it... like a blue-coat boy pupils at Christ's Hospital, founded in Newgate Street in 1553 by Edward VI as a charity school, wore a small round black cap until its use was discontinued in 1858; the distinctive long blue coat remains in use.

488.24–5 the Oxford nightcaps... strength and goodness Dickens probably has in mind (but Mrs Nickleby certainly does not) [Richard Cook], *Oxford Night Caps. Being a Collection of Receipts for Making Various Beverages Used in the University* (Oxford, 1827).

490.7 The Prince Regent... legs George IV, Prince Regent from 1811 until he succeeded his father George III in 1820, was indeed proud of his legs, but he was notoriously prone to obesity as well as personal vanity: see Christopher Hibbert, *George IV* (Harmondsworth, 1976), especially 370, 674.

490.8 Daniel Lambert by the time of his death Daniel Lambert (1770–1809) weighed 52¾ stone (739 pounds, 336kg), his legs resembling pillows.

490.9 Miss Biffin in spite of being born without arms or legs, Sarah Biffin (1784–1850) became a distinguished miniaturist.

491.27–28 three-pair-of stairs room on the third floor (up three flights).

492.20 a musical glass one of a set of glasses filled with different amounts of water to sound with different pitches when their rims are rubbed or struck.

494.11–12 street-door scraper a fixed metal bar for scraping dirt off boots and shoes before entering a house.

495.32 the omnibus arrived there were no fixed stops: the omnibus could be hailed and boarded at any point.

495.35 ten-pennyworth of halfpence 20 halfpennies, worth just over 4p in all.

498.35–6 lay their ruin between us regard us as responsible for their ruin.

502.24–5 Ludgate Hill... Newgate Ludgate Hill leads up from Fleet Street to St Paul's Cathedral. For Newgate Prison see note to 33.24.

505.10 Didn't I catch hold of his leg, neither, father? I caught hold of his leg, didn't I, father? Didn't I?

505.30 I could hang you up outside of the Old Bailey public executions took place outside Newgate Prison, adjoining the Old Bailey (see note to 256.23–4), from 1783 until 1868, when they began to be carried out inside the prison building.

505.32–4 it's a hanging matter... from a dwelling-house corpses of executed criminals were available for medical dissection until the practice was prohibited in an Act for Regulating Schools of Anatomy of 1832 (2 & 3 Will. 4, c. 75 section 16): the Act gave the medical profession access to unclaimed or donated bodies.

505.36 eight-and-twenty shillings £1.40.

505.37 seven-and-six 7*s.* 6*d.* (37.5p).

506.24 the check string a string held by the driver by which a passenger signalled to him to stop.

506.33–4 I'll summons you for having a broken winder see note to 346.14.

506.37 sons (*in law*) stepsons.

507.1 Somers Town a residential area between St Pancras and Hampstead Road.

507.33 cottoned to took to.

507.35 milk of human kindness *Macbeth*, 1.5.16.

509.6 the Post-office the General Post Office, St Martin's-le-Grand, completed in 1829 and demolished in 1912, was an imposing neoclassical building by Sir Robert Smirke (1780–1867). The coach terminus is probably the nearby Bull and Mouth, Aldersgate Street, demolished in 1830.

509.23 dooble-latthers until the introduction of the penny post in 1840 letters consisting of two pages were charged twice as much as those with only one.

509.29 Dang my bootuns dash my buttons! An exclamation of surprise.

512.31 stond threat stand treat, pay for.

513.3 charges it on adds a charge for it to the bill.

513.36–7 The schoolmeasther agin all England i.e. Browdie would wager on the schoolmaster being capable of taking on the whole of England.

514.17–18 taken three outsides booked seats for three outside passengers.

516.13 coot awa' cut away; be off with you.

522.8 Leadenhall market a general market off Gracechurch Street, S of Leadenhall Street.

523.21–2 The night will not be long coming... earth compare the words of Jesus at John 9.4: 'I must work the works of him that sent me, while it is day: the night cometh, when no man can work.'

527.36 Out of sight, out of mind proverbial: *ODEP*, 602.

528.20 as times go as things are nowadays; according to current standards.

532.33 the Edgeware-road the main North Road starting at Marble Arch.

537.8 made gravy 'a gravy artificially compounded, as opposed to one consisting only of the juices obtained during cooking' (*OED* made *adj.* 3a).

539.17 went out to Botany Bay was transported to one of the penal colonies in Australia. Botany Bay itself, in New South Wales, was intended to be the first of these colonies in 1785, but the site proved too unhealthy and the colony was instead established at Sydney Cove, now the city of Sydney. However, the name continued in general use. The practice of transportation—for life, as an alternative to capital punishment, or for a specified number of years—was ended in stages during the 1850s and 1860s.

541.22 **killed with brimstone** before taking the honey from hives the bees would be killed by burning long matches with linen rags dipped in sulphur.

541.22 **Barbary** the countries along the N coast of Africa.

541.24–5 **the statue at Charing Cross** the equestrian bronze of Charles I by Hubert le Sueur (born *c.*1580, died between 1658 and 1668), cast in 1633 and erected on its present site in 1675.

541.25 **the Stock Exchange** in 1802 the Stock Exchange moved into a new building accessed by Capel Court, Bartholomew Lane, and replaced in 1853–4.

541.26 **the Pump from Aldgate** until the 1860s the Aldgate Pump stood in Aldgate High Street a few yards E of its present location at the junction with Leadenhall Street and Fenchurch Street.

542.3–5 **in the absence of the planet Venus...between us** i.e. the old gentleman maintains that unlike soldiers he is not lecherous. For the Horse Guards see note to 477.27.

543.4 **the Commissioners of Paving** there were many such bodies responsible for maintaining roads in different areas of London.

543.5 **the Lord Mayor** the head and chief magistrate of the City of London.

543.5–6 **Court of Common Council** the principal governing body of the City of London.

543.21 **the fourteen binn** a case in a wine-cellar designated by this number.

543.21–2 **a bar of iron...to keep the thunder off** this is probably a transfer of the popular belief that thunder causes milk to curdle.

543.36 **the East India Company** the company's headquarters, East India House, in Leadenhall Street, rebuilt in 1726, enlarged in 1799, and demolished in 1862.

544.7 **the Royal Exchange** the main trading centre of the City, Threadneedle Street and Cornhill, rebuilt in 1667–9 after the Great Fire, and replaced after another fire in 1838.

544.15 **the Lord Chancellor** the highest judicial functionary in England and Wales.

544.38 **Gog and Magog** see note to 135.32–3. They are invoked in an oath reported in Ch. 24 of Walter Scott's novel *The Bride of Lammermoor* (published anonymously in 1819), ed. J. H. Alexander, Edinburgh Edition of the Waverley Novels, 7a (Edinburgh, 1993), 197.

546.35 **Tartary** a popular name for the Mongol Empire which reached the height of its power in Asia and Eastern Europe in the 13th century.

547.16–20 **making love to...making love** courting...paying amorous attention.

548.27–8 there's... method in *his* madness alluding to Polonius on Hamlet: 'Though this be madness, yet there is method in't': *Hamlet*, 2.2.207–8.

549.32 Stars and garthers an expression of astonishment deriving from distinctive accoutrements of nobility (see note to 566.26).

550.8 for wa'at we're aboot to receive see notes to 94.35–6 and 483.34–5.

550.10 play such a knife and fork eat so heartily.

551.12–13 mak' oop tiv'ee make advances to you.

553.20–1 along o' owing to; because of.

553.33–4 coming Yorkshire over us cheating us. Proverbial: *ODEP*, 926.

556.2 dra' it mild tone it down; don't exaggerate. The metaphor derives from the actions of a careful publican pulling a pint of ale.

557.4–5 listeners are never to hear any good of themselves proverbial: *ODEP*, 468.

559.33 Dash ma' wig! goodness me!

560.8–9 the holy state of matrimony see note to 145.12.

560.9–10 the two friends... than one because, according to the marriage service in the Book of Common Prayer, 'by Matrimony' they have been 'made one', becoming 'one flesh'.

562.14 a round game see note to 9.20.

563.7 come off returned from; finished.

566.24–5 made a virtue of necessity proverbial: *ODEP*, 861–2.

566.26 the order of the Garter the Most Noble Order of the Garter is the highest order of English chivalry, founded by Edward III in the 14th century.

566.36 making love to paying court to.

567.21 books of precedent collections of established legal procedures founded on precedent.

572.38–9 two cardinal virtues—faith and hope see note to 222.17.

574.4 a floating balance a varying balance of readily available cash.

574.7–9 lay up treasure... treasure in this see Matthew 6.19–21: 'Lay not up for yourselves treasures upon earth... But lay up for yourselves treasures in heaven... For where your treasure is, there will your heart be also.'

574.10 certain autobiographies Dickens is probably thinking of some of the many spiritual autobiographies by Puritan writers in the 17th century.

574.12 the recording Angel the angel charged with keeping a record of each individual's life in preparation for the Last Judgement, originally found in Laurence Sterne, *The Life and Opinions of Tristram Shandy, Gentleman* (1760–67), Bk 6, Ch. 8.

574.20–1 scriptural admonition... "know thyself" the admonition is Classical rather than biblical; it is particularly associated with the philosopher Socrates who lived in the fifth century BC.

575.26 What is even money...this *even money* denotes odds in betting that offer the gambler the chance of winning as much as they have staked. The sentence might be differently interpreted as Ralph expressing surprise, dismay, and frustration at the realization that not even money can prevail against Nicholas now.

575.26 Devil's luck uncommonly good luck.

577.14 Pimlico a residential district near the Thames SW of Westminster.

577.15 Saint James's Park a royal park E of Buckingham Palace, opened to the public by Charles II (King of England 1660–85).

579.10 the daily bread of the Lord's Prayer referring to one of the petitions in the prayer which Jesus taught his disciples: 'Give us this day our daily bread' (Matthew 6.11; compare Luke 11.3).

580.12 made submission yielded; gave in.

580.22 had I? hadn't I?

580.38 was sent away a convict for seven years see note to 539.17.

581.35 look sharply after keep a close eye on.

582.10–11 intervals of the hard labour that vagabonds are put to the Vagrancy Act of 1824 (5 Geo. 4, c. 83, section 10) provided that a rogue or vagabond could be sentenced to detention with hard labour for up to a year.

582.23 leaving Golden Square on his right in other words he proceeds up Regent Street, or streets adjacent, towards Cavendish Square.

585.29 prussic acid hydrogen cyanide, a rapid-action poison, available from chemists.

585.39–86.1 separation, I'll have one in law a process before church courts. Litigants of either sex could petition for separation on the grounds of cruelty and adultery. Women who obtained a *divortium a mensa et thoro* (separation from bed and board) could live apart from their husbands. Madame Mantalini would have petitioned the Consistory Court of the Bishop of London.

586.13–14 A married woman has no property see note to 40.5–6.

588.1 sets the wind that way so soon? compare the proverb 'Is the wind in that corner?' (*ODEP*, 893).

588.1–2 Half knave and half fool compare the proverb 'More knave than fool' (*ODEP*, 543).

590.2 a glazed hat a waterproof hat. The hat could be made of any material, and be any shape, but was waterproofed with a mixture of resin, pitch, and other ingredients. One of the industries of east London was hat glazing.

590.15–16 the Saracen with Two Necks a combination of the names of two coaching inns, the Saracen's Head (see note to 30.34) and the Swan with Two Necks in Lad Lane (since 1845 part of Gresham Street).

590.19 a double knock as used by, for example, a postman.

590.23 put it upon that ground argue on that basis.

591.18–19 the statues of the Twelve Apostles . . . Saint Paul's cathedral there are indeed statues of the twelve disciples on the upper part of the façade, but Mark, Luke, and Paul appear with them.

591.37 a note of admiration an exclamation mark.

593.21 put up stir up.

597.2 cutting away running away; making off.

597.7–8 rabbits and tom-cats . . . sometimes devour their offspring the practice is attested, though it is more common with female than male cats.

599.27 a minor under the age of 21.

604.36–7 before you could say 'Jack Robinson' proverbial: *ODEP*, 40.

606.1–2 Like the famous parrot . . . a word in a fable attributed to Aesop a thoughtful parrot is capable of uttering only one sentence: 'I think the more.' See *Select Fables of Esop & Other Fabulists*, [ed. Robert Dodsley], (London, 1761), 120.

608.1 blackleg . . . groom (gambling) swindler . . . assistant. See 'Midway', *Fraser's Magazine*, 26 (July 1842), 514–26 (524).

611.15–16 "the rules" . . . Prison from 1755 to 1880 the King's Bench Prison (Queen's Bench from 1840) was located at the E end of Borough Street, Southwark. Its relaxed regime included provision for prisoners to buy the right to lodge within the 'Rules', three square miles surrounding the prison.

611.16–17 the obelisk in Saint George's Fields the obelisk at St George's Circus, some 600 yards W of the site of the King's Bench Prison, was erected in 1771 in honour of the Lord Mayor of the City of London at the time. St George's Fields, the area around the Circus, was comprehensively built over from 1810 onwards.

611.29 the furniture of their pockets their financial resources.

611.34 spring vans ones fitted with spring suspension.

612.11–12 turpentining . . . a tent-bedstead the application of turpentine was to discourage fleas.

613.7–8 there is one broad sky . . . heaven beyond it compare Samuel Taylor Coleridge, 'Christabel' (written 1797–1800, published 1816), line 331: 'For the blue sky bends over all!'

618.2–3 The penny . . . the crown in the reigns of George IV (1820–30) and William IV (1830–7) the crown (5*s*. or 25p) was slightly larger than the penny (0.4p), 39 mm as against 34 mm, and substantially heavier (28.3 or 27.5 gm as against 18.8 gm).

618.13–14 it can't want more by this time the business must be completed by now.

619.9 some large gold seals precious metal seals bearing various devices were attached to the watch-chain by ornamented 'fobs': they could be used to stamp sealing wax on letters, but they were often largely decorative.

619.11 his grey hair was gathered behind a fashion of the 1790s.

620.30 a wilful man, as the Scotch say 'A wilful man will have his way': *ODEP*, 890. The proverb is first found in this form in Walter Scott, *Waverley* (published anonymously in 1814: Edinburgh Edition of the Waverley Novels 1, ed. P. D. Garside (Edinburgh, 2007), 150) and occurs several times in his subsequent novels.

620.32 Time is money proverbial: *ODEP*, 823–4.

624.11 you would have no finger in such a pie as this alluding to the proverb 'To have a finger in the pie' (*ODEP*, 258).

625.2–4 an edged-tool...the proverb alluding to the proverb 'Children and fools must not play with edged tools' (*ODEP*, 120).

625.12 detaining creditor a creditor to whom a person in prison for debt owes money.

625.15 four and threepence 4*s*. 3*d*. or 21p.

625.17 a detainer a legal writ authorizing the sheriff to detain a person already in his custody.

625.28–9 Practice makes perfect proverbial: *ODEP*, 856.

625.31–2 just t'other side the water on the near Continent, the European mainland.

626.8–9 five shillings...six and eightpence—ten shillings 25p, 33.3p, 50p.

627.5 a brown study a state of mental abstraction.

627.25 deaf as an adder proverbial, deriving from Psalm 58.4: *ODEP*, 172.

628.26 from home out of the house.

628.32 men must live *I Henry IV*, 2.2.88: 'Young men must live' (Falstaff).

629.7 Matches are made in Heaven proverbial: *ODEP*, 514 ('Marriages are made in heaven').

629.21 beat about the bush proverbial: *ODEP*, 36.

634.17 the mistake of a figure an error in calculation.

634.33 Minor Theatre one without a royal patent (see note to 393.21).

635.21 a castanet pas seul a solo dance to castanet accompaniment.

640.13–14 sustained the vice were on the vice-chair's left and right, as though they were heraldic supporters.

640.26 some of them faster than they had come out William Gibbs Thomas Moncrieff (1794–1857) had dramatized *Pickwick Papers* as *Sam Weller; or, the Pickwickians* in July 1837 before Dickens had completed the serialized novel. When on 20 May 1839 his version of *Nicholas Nickleby* opened at the Strand Theatre as *Nicholas Nickleby and Poor Smike; or, The Victim of the Yorkshire School*, Dickens was particularly annoyed because it anticipated the revelation that Ralph is Smike's father (Slater 2009, 134). In November 1838 Dickens gave his reasons for objecting to the dramatization of his works while still in progress: 'My general objection to the adaptation of any unfinished work of mine simply is, that being badly done and worse acted it tends to vulgarize the characters, to destroy or weaken in the minds of those who see them the impressions I have endeavoured to create, and consequently to lessen the after-interest in their progress' (*Letters*, 1.463: to Frederick Yates, [?29 November 1838]. Dickens goes on to make an exception of Yates's version of *Nicholas Nickleby*: 'No such objection can exist for a moment where the thing is so admirably done in every respect as you have done it in this instance').

641.3 **Richard Turpin, Tom King, and Jerry Abershaw** three celebrated highwaymen: Richard ('Dick') Turpin (1705–39), his partner Tom (really Matthew) King (*c.*1712–1737), and Jerry Abershawe (1773–95). The first two were romanticized in the novel *Rookwood* (1834) by Harrison Ainsworth (1805–82).

641.8–14 **Shakspeare dramatised stories... in general circulation** almost all of Shakespeare's plays draw on sources familiar in his time: for notable examples, see the headnotes to *Romeo and Juliet*, *Hamlet*, and *The History of King Lear* (The Quarto Text) in *The Oxford Shakespeare*.

642.4 **Men must live** see note to 628.32.

642.7 **put it upon that ground** argue on that basis.

644.2 **had a word** had a disagreement; quarrelled.

645.2 **opened upon him** been disclosed to him; appeared to him.

645.22 **a dread disease** consumption, i.e. tuberculosis.

648.31 **the Halfway House** this establishment was situated on the main road from London to Colchester ¾ mile W of Bow.

649.32 **the Thirsty Woman of Tutbury** Ann Moore (b. 1761), 'the fasting woman of Tutbury' in Staffordshire, took to her bed in 1807 and claimed to be able to survive without food or drink, but she was exposed as a fraud in 1813. See *A Statement of Facts, Relative to the Supposed Abstinence of Ann Moore, of Tutbury, Staffordshire: and a Narrative of the Circumstances which led to the Recent Detection Of the Imposture: To Which is Subjoined an Appendix, Containing Medical and other Papers, illustrative of the Statement: compiled and published at the request of the Committee, formed for the investigation of the case, by the Rev. Legh Richmond, A. M. Rector of Turvey, Bedfordshire* (Burton-on-Trent, 1813).

649.32 **the Cock-lane Ghost** at the age of 11 or so Elizabeth Parsons (1749–1807) acted the part of the ghost of the deceased partner of her father's lodger William Kent in an attempt to blackmail him by suggesting that he had murdered her. The local parish priest, Stephen Aldrich (*c.*1707–69), Rector of Clerkenwell, headed the investigation which exposed the deception in spite of Elizabeth's persistence in the fraud. Those with Methodist sympathies were believed to be particularly liable to believe in the ghost's reality.

650.6 **Train up a Ghost—child, I mean** see Proverbs 22.6: 'Train up a child in the way he should go: and when he is old, he will not depart from it.'

652.33–4 **the once popular air... I adore** a popular song set by Henry Rowley Bishop (1786–1855): the author of the words is unknown. The next two lines are 'Shall I never again hear her voice | Nor see her loved form any more?', and the last of the four stanzas ends 'Death now is my only desire— | I give myself up to despair'. See J. W. T. Ley, 'Sentimental Songs in Dickens', *Dickensian*, 28 (1932), 313–21 (315).

655.2 a pig-faced lady belief in pig-faced women was commonplace in the early 19th century, leading fair showmen to exhibit as such shaven bears dressed in women's clothing.

656.31 bottled lightning the phrase is used of strong drink found in the dressing room of a theatre in 'The Stage', a poem originally published pseudonymously by Frances Reynardson (1693/4–1725) in 1713 and anthologized in *Bell's Classical Arrangement of Fugitive Poetry*, 15 vols (London, 1789–92), Vol. 1 (1789), 86–105 (99):

> Hard-by a quart of bottled lightning lies,
> A bowl of double use, and monstrous size;
> Now rolls it high, and rumbles in its speed,
> Now drowns the weaker crack of mustard-seed.
> So the true thunder, all array'd in smoak,
> Launch'd from the skies now rives the knotted oak,
> And sometimes, nought the drunkard's prayers avail,
> Ah! sometimes condescends to sour ale.

657.16 gas and gaiters this nonsensical expression is a Dickens coinage. In later usage the expression 'All is gas and gaiters' came to mean 'All is well'.

657.23 Cormoran and Blunderbore Cornish giants defeated by the hero in the story of 'Jack the Giant-Killer'.

657.26–7 Mrs. Rowland... Kalydor advertisements in the monthly numbers of *Nicholas Nickleby* assert that the use of Rowland's Kalydor, 'the only efficient protector of the skin', will result in 'the Neck, Hands, and Arms, assuming and retaining the Radiant Whiteness so much admired, and so unequivocal a mark of attention to the niceties of the TOILET, and the graces of personal attraction' (Part 13: Chapters 40–2).

657.28 the three Graces in Greek mythology, the three Charities, goddesses who personify loveliness and grace.

657.28 the nine Muses in Greek mythology, goddesses associated with the different arts.

658.19–20 Puss... Brindle six common names for cats.

661.4 The little race-course at Hampton a racecourse which normally operated in June at Molesey Hurst, Surrey, on the S bank of the Thames 16 miles SW of the centre of London, from 1814 to 1887.

661.29 God send that would that.

662.4 pea and thimble table in the game *thimblerig* a dupe was invited to guess under which of three thimbles there was a pea and bet on their choice: the sharper used sleight of hand to ensure that he chose wrong.

662.8 flash notes counterfeit banknotes.

662.17–18 Ring the Bull a game in which participants throw or swing a ring on to a hook fixed on a wall or a target (*OED*).

662.32–4 the Stranger's club-house...to play *in* 'before 1840 no gate-money was charged at race courses and race organizers raised money by letting ground space for gambling marquees and refreshment tents' (Schlicke, 861). The club-houses here are probably comic. A London club would have a strangers' room for visitors; the Athenæum, established in 1824, to which Dickens was elected at the age of 26, disapproved of the gambling widely practised in London clubs; the Hampton is named after the racecourse itself; and the Saint James's is named after the area round St James's Street and Square where gambling 'hells' were concentrated.

662.34 rouge-et-noir the phrase usually designated a card game, but what is involved here (663.38–665.3) is a variety of roulette in which stakes are placed on the colours red and black: the croupier calls it 'rouge a noir'. On 5 November 1859 the periodical edited by Dickens *All the Year Round* was to carry (2.35–7) an article entitled 'Moloch's Chapel of Ease' with a depiction of a gambling saloon in terms of a religious rite. In one room the service book is entitled 'Rouge et Noir', and the expression appears in the index to the bound volume of the periodical. The article provides little information on the detailed conduct of the game.

662.34 French hazard a game, played with dice, in which the players staked against the bank, as distinguished from English, or chicken, hazard, in which they played against each other (from *OED*).

662.34–5 La Merveille *French* the marvel. The game has not been located elsewhere. It was changed to 'other games' in the Charles Dickens Edition.

665.25–6 a Newmarket coat see note to 383.14.

665.34 pulled down weakened, depressed.

673.4 Twickenham area on the N bank of the Thames about 11 miles W of the City.

673.7 Petersham to Ham House on the other side of the river opposite Twickenham, and S of Richmond, the adjoining manors of Ham and Petersham were a royal estate. Ham House was built in the early 17th century, passing into the ownership of the Earls of Dysart, and in the 20th century it was transferred to the National Trust. Two of the three avenues of trees leading to the house are still in place.

675.6–7 We must leave this place immediately although illegal, duelling was not uncommon in the 1820s, but killing your man could be treated as murder.

676.2 lantern-jawed see note to 301.30.

676.27–9 Ta—ran—tan—too...lucky the song has not been found elsewhere. Throwing an old shoe after a newly-married bride for luck is still a current custom in some places.

677.26 Lord Mallowford a fictional character.

677.27 the post-obits fell in a *post-obit* is '[a] bond given by a borrower, securing to the lender a sum of money to be paid on the death of a specified person from whom the borrower expects to inherit' (*OED*). To *fall in* is to become due.

682.27 eau-d'or alcoholic drink including oranges, lemons, and gold leaf.

683.19 a committee of ways and means see note to 236.16.

683.25 necessity has no law proverbial: *ODEP*, 557–8.

688.31–2 Don't leave a stone unturned proverbial: *ODEP*, 453.

690.21 the Eel-pie Island at Twickenham an islet in the River Thames 11 miles SE of the centre of London.

691.1 italian-ironing see note to 208.19.

693.39–695.1 water cut off for non-payment of the rate see note to 168.28.

695.8–9 The plug of life...mud is left compare *Macbeth*, 2.3.94–5: 'The wine of life is drawn, and the mere lees | Is left this vault to brag of.'

697.21–2 Peter, or Alexander, or Pompey, or Diorgeenes names of great men: Peter the Great, Emperor of Russia 1682–1725; Alexander the Great, King of Macedon 336–323 BC; Pompey the Great (106–48 BC), Julius Caesar's rival; and Diogenes of Synope (4th century BC), the founder of the Cynic philosophical system.

698.19 hartshorn...vinegar see note to 233.34.

698.28–9 yesterday was a week a week ago yesterday.

698.29 a half-pay captain a captain on half-pay in retirement, or while not in actual service.

700.7 a crown bowl of punch a bowl containing punch to the value of a crown (5*s*. or 25p).

707.20–1 opens upon you becomes apparent to you.

710.12–13 per contra *Latin* on the other side of the account.

710.14–15 Faint heart never won fair lady proverbial: *ODEP*, 238.

715.29 open upon attack.

716.19–20 the canons of the church for such cases made and provided the Church of England's Table of Kindred and Affinity prohibits marriage with a grandparent. The expression 'for such cases made and provided' is a standard phrase, though more common in America than Britain.

717.27–8 according to appointment as arranged.

720.34–5 upholding of faith above works compare James 2.20: 'faith without works is dead'.

724.27 shaving paper paper for wiping the lather from razors.

729.15–16 a chancery ward a ward of court, not permitted to marry without the court's permission.

729.16 the Fleet prison a prison of medieval origin in Farringdon Road, closed in 1842.

729.22 forbidding people's banns *literally* raising objections to proposed marriages announced by *banns* read on three consecutive Sundays in the parish churches of the relevant parties.

730.14 rushlight shades tin cylinders pierced with holes to allow light to shine through. The shades, used as nightlights, were designed to hold a *rushlight*: a low-powered candle made by dipping the pith of a rush in tallow.

730.15 like Christians as if they were human.

733.3–4 appetite was the best clock in the world see the proverb 'The belly is the truest clock' (*ODEP*, 45).

734.27 bounden duty see note to 257.2.

738.24 hewer of wood and drawer of water see Joshua 9.21, 27.

738.39 break out reveal abruptly.

745.30 Newgate Newgate Prison: see note to 33.24.

746.22 cent. per cent. a hundred per cent.

747.22–3 it's a ill wind as blows no good to nobody proverbial: *ODEP*, 401.

747.25–7 if a boy repines... the scripter see Proverbs 13.24: 'He that spareth his rod hateth his son: but he that loveth him chasteneth him betimes.' Compare the familiar formulation 'Spare the rod and spoil the child': *ODEP*, 759.

753.9 Lambeth the borough on the opposite side of the Thames to Westminster.

754.1 dirty commonly used by Dickens when describing a street to indicate the presence of ordure.

754.12 snuff the candle see note to 114.36.

754.24 in for a penny... in for a pound proverbial: *ODEP*, 402.

756.21 Slider an abbreviated form derived from Sliderskew.

758.4–5 twenty pound ten £20 10*s*. (£20.50).

763.7 an engrossing hand legal handwriting.

763.18–19 they're all M. P's., so it's of no use to anybody Members of Parliament were immune from arrest for debt, a sanction largely abolished in 1870.

763.30 the camel and the needle's eye see Matthew 19.24: 'It is easier for a camel to go through the eye of a needle, than for a rich man to enter into the kingdom of God.'

764.29–30 he whose sands of life... dwindling rapidly away see *3 Henry VI*, 1.4.26 ('The sands are numbered that makes up my life'), and *Pericles*, 22.1 ('Now our sands are almost run').

775.25 I saw him through the window-blind the blind would be *either* a louvre blind, with wooden slats, *or* a blind made of wire gauze on a frame like a modern insect screen.

783.11 at fault baffled.

783.35 took counsel together see Psalm 2.2: 'the rulers take counsel together'.

786.18 in blow in bloom.

786.18 Norval the hero of the tragedy *Douglas* (1756) by John Home (1722–1808).

786.37–8 resurrected and dissected until the Anatomy Act of 1832 (see note to 505.32–4) criminals known as 'resurrection men' provided dead bodies disinterred from churchyards for the purposes of medical dissection, the supply of executed criminals being insufficient for the demand.

787.36–7 a cobbler's weapon i.e. an *awl* (a small tool used to punch holes in leather).

789.8 like the beasts in the fable 'A lion worn out with years lay stretched upon the ground, utterly helpless, and drawing his last breath. A Boar came up, and to satisfy an ancient grudge, drove at him with his tusks. Next a Bull, determined to be revenged on an old enemy, gored him with his horns. Upon this an Ass, seeing that the old Lion could then be treated with impunity, thought that he would show his spite also, and came and threw his heels in the Lion's face. Whereupon the dying beast exclaimed: "The insults of the powerful were bad enough, but those I could have managed to bear; but to be spurned by so base a creature as thou—the disgrace of nature, is to die a double death."' (Thomas James, *Æsop's Fables* (London, 1852), 133.)

794.4 breaking failing in health.

798.32 never is a long day proverbial: *ODEP*, 562.

799.5 my bounden duty see note to 257.2.

800.6 true as steel proverbial: *ODEP*, 840.

804.27–8 pray and beseech you from the opening exhortations of the Orders for Morning and Evening Prayer in the Book of Common Prayer.

807.3 dear departed brothers and sisters see 'The Order for the Burial of the Dead' in the Book of Common Prayer: 'the soul of our dear *brother* here departed'.

807.6–7 he had been one of a jury . . . cut his throat in England a coroner holds inquests into unexpected deaths, summoning a jury at their discretion.

808.29–30 the stripling . . . his head the younger man who eloped with Ralph's wife: see 794.9–13.

810.30 iron tongue *A Midsummer Night's Dream*, 5.1.356: 'The iron tongue of midnight hath told twelve'; also *King John*, 3.3.38.

810.31–2 marriages that are made in hell compare the proverb 'Marriages are made in heaven': *ODEP*, 514.

810.32 the dead whose shoes are worn already compare the proverb: 'He goes long barefoot that waits for dead men's shoes' (*ODEP*, 171).

810.35 No bell or book for me compare the proverbial 'Bell, book, and candle': *ODEP*, 44.

816.11 make love to court.

817.29 sow his wild oats proverbial: *ODEP*, 889.

822.27 go westward the more fashionable shops of London were then, as now, in the West End, whereas the Saracen's Head, Snow Hill, was in the City.

823.1–2 that labyrinth of streets which lies between Seven Dials and Soho the Seven Dials district N of Trafalgar Square was notoriously squalid in Dickens's time.

823.21–2 old horse in a demnition mill a horse, walking in a continuous circle, was used to power a mill as an alternative to wind, water, or steam.

823.26 a coarse red coat with a little tail a *coatee*, or tight-fitting uniform coat or jacket, waist length at the front with short tails behind. It began to replace the long tail coat at the end of the 18th century, and was superseded by the tunic in the mid-19th century.

825.14 two pound fourteen £2 14*s*. (£2.70).

825.20–1 he has gone to the demnition bow-wows alluding to the proverb 'Go to the dogs': *ODEP*, 308.

825.31 turn me up fold me up (in the turn-up bed which folds up into a cabinet when not in use).

827.23–4 the pooder plot wa'... the Guy Faurx line see note to 380.8.

827.35 Yorkshire pie see note to 84.34.

833.30 a twelfth cake a large frosted cake for Twelfth Night festivities on 6 January, a favourite occasion for Dickens: it was the day on which his eldest son Charley was born in 1837.

834.7 swept at last into the coffers of the state Ralph having died intestate, and his next of kin choosing not to enter a claim, his estate passes to the state.

834.16 went beyond the seas was transported as a criminal.

834.18–19 courted and caressed a standard phrase, best known from its use in Walter Scott, *The Lay of the Last Minstrel* (1805), Introduction, line 15. The word *caressed* has the sense 'made much of'.

1839 PREFACE

843.1–17 It has afforded...*so* like him see Essay on the Text, 867.

843.7 learned in the law see *2 Henry IV*, 1.2.135–36: 'my learned counsel in the laws'.

844.17 trials at law see Essay on the Text, 867.

845.8–9 The Brothers Cheeryble see Essay on the Text, 870–1.

845.21–846.6 The author of a periodical performance... the tenderness of a friend see the last number of *The Lounger* by Henry Mackenzie (1745–1831), No. 101 (6 January 1787), 324.

845.26–7 Horace's rule... study see Quintus Horatius Flaccus (65–8 BC), *Ars poetica* (The Art of Poetry), 388–9: 'nonumque prematur in annum, |

membranis intus positis' (let it [your composition] not see the light for nine years, keeping it at home).

846.10 on the first of next month *Nicholas Nickleby* appeared on the last Saturday of each month from 31 March 1838 to 30 September 1839.

1848 PREFACE

853.2 the completed 'Pickwick Papers' published in monthly parts from April 1836 to November 1837, omitting June, and in one volume on 17 November 1837; the first number of *Nicholas Nickleby* appeared on 31 March 1838.

853.12–13 the butcher, the baker, the candlestick maker the trio are taken from the nursery rhyme 'Rub-a-dub-dub, | Three men in a tub': Opie, 376 (No. 460).

854.5 Rochester Castle the Dickens family lived in Chatham from 1817 to 1822. Rochester Castle, originally built in the 12th century but now a ruin, was within easy walking distance.

854.5–6 PARTRIDGE, STRAP, TOM PIPES, AND SANCHO PANZA characters in novels Dickens enjoyed as a boy: Partridge in *Tom Jones, a Foundling* (1749) by Henry Fielding (1707–54); Strap from *The Adventures of Roderick Random* (1748) by Tobias Smollett (1721–71); Tom Pipes from *The Adventures of Peregrine Pickle* (1751), also by Smollett; and Sancho Panza from *Don Quixote de la Mancha* (1605–15) by Cervantes (Miguel de Cervantes Saavedra, 1547–1616), which had been translated into English several times by the early 19th century.

854.8–10 a suppurated abscess...pen-knife there is some uncertainty about this incident. The boy apparently in question later asserted that the wound was self-inflicted: see 'Essay on the Text', 865. The expression 'guide, philosopher, and friend' is from Alexander Pope, *An Essay on Man* (1733–4), 4.389.

854.19 the 'Pickwick Papers' see note to 853.2.

854.19–32 a professional friend...my travelling companion...a certain town see Essay on the Text, 866.

857.13–14 combined patronage of all the Lord Chancellors royal patronage was exercised through the office of the Lord Chancellor (see note to 544.15).

857.14–15 the accession of the House of Brunswick Georg Ludwig of the House of Hanover, a branch of the House of Brunswick, came to the British throne as George I in 1714 by right of his late mother Sophia's descent from James VI of Scots and I of England.

857.22 DEVONSHIRE TERRACE Dickens lived at 1 Devonshire Terrace, S of Regent's Park, from December 1839 to November 1851.

GLOSSARY

This selective glossary defines single words, phrases being treated in the Explanatory Notes. It covers archaic terms and occurrences of familiar words in senses that are likely to be strange to the modern reader. Dialect words and spellings representing regional pronunciation are included when they may be found obscure: for the most part, Dickens's dialect speech will present few problems when it is heard either by reading aloud or in the head. At times a more expansive discussion of a word than can be accommodated within a glossary is required, and in such cases the most economical and effective way of expanding a definition is to refer the reader to the appropriate explanatory note. Up to four references for each usage are noted; where a word is used more frequently only the first occurrence is noted, with the rest covered by 'etc.'.

abroad outdoors, out of the house 11.25, 519.11, 771.3; bewildered, confused 58.30; around 578.34
accommodation convenience 172.35
address skill, adroitness, ability 231.25 etc.
adjust settle 278.21, 362.26, 670.30, 794.12
adjustment settling 103.22
admiration for 393.28 and 591.37 see note to 393.28
admire wonder 685.29
advise confer 489.8, 506.15, 587.37
after-piece additional entertainment (usually comic) after the main play 315.2
airy *dialect* area, court below pavement level giving access to basement 229.30
apothecary pharmaceutical chemist 9.30 etc.
appointments furniture, table furniture 244.39
apron leather covering for the legs in an open carriage 157.21, 425.12
aptitude readiness 355.35
ar *dialect* I 59.1
area court below pavement level giving access to basement 73.17 etc.
awful fearfully impressive 131.9 etc.
a-winking dozing off 755.9
bandbox, band-box box of cardboard or very thin chip covered with paper for hats etc. 397.3 etc.

bate reduce 713.27
bean't, beant *dialect* isn't, aren't 113.3 etc.
beard confront boldly or insolently 449.35, 705.30
beggar wretched fellow 159.38
behoof benefit 57.28
bellman for 18.17 and 18.18 see note to 18.17
benefit for 301.36 etc. see note to 301.36
bespeak *noun* benefit performance 308 title etc. (see note to 301.36)
bespeak *verb* give evidence of 212.18 etc.; book in advance 108.39, 715.15; choose 313.15
bestowed situated 379.26
bill-discounter for 7.39 see note
bishop sweet mulled wine 486.37, 486.37
black flake of soot 12.23
blacking boot-polish 208.20
blacking-bottle bottle containing (or for) boot polish 167.10, 522.17
blacklead graphite polish for cleaning cast-iron grates, stoves, etc. 194.22
blackleg (gambling) swindler 608.1
blade gallant, good fellow 73.24, 717.29
blaze *noun* conspicuous brilliance 173.25, 296.18
blaze *verb* be brilliantly conspicuous 630.9
blooming in the prime of youth 310.22
blunderbuss short gun with a large bore 478.24, 478.26
board table 73.27 etc.
bobbish in good health and spirits 755.9
bone steal 758.14, 758.14
booked provided with books 30.27, 36.26, 42.3, 787.33
book-muslin fine muslin (folded like a book when sold by the piece) 170.3
bottle-holder supporter 17.33
box compartment 35.5 etc.; passenger sharing box seat with coach driver 57.22, 59.26; driver's box seat at front of coach 61.13, 137.18, 503.28, 509.8
box-passenger passenger sharing box seat with coach driver 61.15
break fail in health 794.4
brick-field piece of ground where bricks are made 12.16
broad unrefined, unrestrained 295.20, 295.20
broker second-hand dealer 191.17, 271.9, 278.29, 611.34
bronze impudence 257.34
buck young fellow 246.34, 397.31
buff buff-coloured, light brownish yellow 297.11
bumper cup or glass filled to the brim 73.38, 316.23

cabriolet for 15.19 etc. see note to 15.19
cambric fine white linen 367.26
camlet light fabric 408.3
cap-riband cap ribbon 583.4
caressed made much of 834.19
carmine red or crimson pigment obtained from the cochineal insect 120.19
carse *dialect* because 58.26
cartel written challenge 384.9
case-bottle square bottle with short narrow neck designed to fit in a case 196.30
cast add 463.34
catamaran difficult woman 711.10
cattle horses 415.31
chaff-biscuit coarse biscuit made of the husks of peas and beans 292.12
chamber bedroom 138.19
chariot light four-wheeled carriage with only back seats 57.30 etc.
cheval-glass, cheval glass full-length mirror hung on frame 128.32, 231.28, 268.26
chick-a-biddy term of endearment usually applied to a young child 825.8
chit *contemptuous* girl 148.8, 234.4, 548.27, 717.3
circuit route regularly followed by an itinerant entertainer 295.9, 406.1
closely-crossed see note to 366.34
cob short-legged stout horse 156.28
'cod a softened version of 'A God!' or 'By God!' 113.20, 164.15, 517.1
cognovit acknowledgement by defendant that plaintiff's case is just 763.39
combination conspiracy, trade union 18.16
comfortable sustaining, refreshing 502.13, 502.14, 559.30
comforter long woollen scarf 383.13, 384.32
compass attain 7.16, 713.13, 746.17
compassionate pity 142.37, 265.20, 478.4
composition mixture 94.31; settlement by mutual arrangement 626.17
con pore over, peruse, read 150.6, 301.8
condition social standing 166.19, 492.34, 529.2
conjure entreat 634.18, 699.15
connection commercial contacts 38.19; circle of clients 690.25
consequential self-important 104.23
considerate prudent 56.7, 56.8
consideration social consequence 168.25
consumption tuberculosis 739.34
coorch *dialect* coach 58.27, 558.28
coot *dialect* cut 59.1, 516.10, 516.13, 831.23

coral toy given to teething infants 226.39
cordial invigorating, stimulating 136.2
cords corduroy trousers 162.22
corn pickle 74.24
cornelian (made of) red quartz 511.32
corn-factor corn-merchant 108.34 etc.
correspondent business connection 528.23
corse corpse 388.11
counting-house office 460.10 etc.
coverture for 30.8 and 267.12 see note to 30.8
crock smear with soot or grime 555.8
cross-grained difficult to deal with, refractory 121.7
crotchet whimsical fancy, peculiar notion 685.23
crown (coin worth) 5 shillings (25p) 548.1, 618.3, 664.5, 700.7
curricle light two-wheeled carriage drawn by two horses abreast 628.15
cut *ballet* make a coupé, replacing one foot with the other 297.8
cyphering-book elementary arithmetic exercise-book 479.2
dang *euphemism* damn 58.23 etc.
deal fir or pine wood 167.6
demnition damned, damnably 212.35 etc.
detainer see note to 625.17
develop reveal 222.22, 235.9, 373.36; unfurl 322.17
dimity (made of) stout cotton fabric, woven with raised stripes or fancy figures 83.33
ding *euphemism* damn 549.39 etc.
dinnot *dialect* don't 551.18 etc.; do you not 553.27
direction name of addressee and address 56.36 etc.
discount for 130.13 etc. see note to 7.39
diurnal daily 10.18
dom *dialect* damn 58.27 etc.
dooble-latther letter consisting of two sheets 509.23
doting deranged, senile 492.29, 493.10, 682.13
double-lock (use) a lock operated by two turns of the key 413.11, 716.4
drab *adj.* dull light-brown or yellowish-brown 456.31, 663.18
drab *noun* slut 724.29
drabs breeches of drab coloured cloth 171.6
draggled befouled with wet and mud 194.21
dram-shop shop selling liquor in small quantities 690.15
dray low cart without sides used by brewers 496.9
dress *perhaps* cook 193.31
drink toast 420.18 etc.
duodecimo small book with each leaf one twelfth of a sheet 316.5
eau-d'or see note to 682.27

ecod, 'Ecod a softened version of 'A God' or 'By God' 113.15 etc.
edition version 789.38
eel-pot pot used to catch eels 196.30
Egad a softened version of 'A God' or 'By God' 422.4, 456.3
eighteenpence, eighteen-pence 7.5p 99.35 etc.
embarrassed in financial difficulties 6.9
emptiness lack of thorough consideration or proper thought 250.10
enclosure letter 704.10
eneaf *dialect* enough 58.25 etc.
erysipelas St Anthony's fire (see note to 225.28) 575.8
escheat confiscate and hand over 188.28
essay try 235.8, 340.24, 605.14
everbrown see note to 12.22
expectant person expecting to inherit 810.31
express special messenger 183.27
extras items beyond the curriculum 29.9
eye-glass monocle 662.6
fag drudge 781.20
fain obliged 164.11 etc.
fairy child *or* seductive young woman 212.39
fanlight fan-shaped window over a door 34.32
farthing (coin worth) ¼ of an old penny (0.1p) 403.24 etc.
father-in-law stepfather 39.39, 40.21, 40.25, 40.32
favor, favour ribbon, cockade 719.7, 758.32
fiddle nonsense 9.12
field-officer army officer ranked above a captain and below a general 334.12
figure imagine 646.31
file rascal 754.30
find provide 148.7, 193.6
flaming brightly shining 582.26, 638.20
flash swaggering 242.23; counterfeit 662.8
flighty guided by fancy rather than reason 548.23, 609.23, 647.7, 659.8
flint skinflint, miser 547.31
floor-clothed with a floor covered in oil-cloth 192.18
flourish talk big 204.16; make a conspicuous display 662.29
flue fluff 267.34
flush see note to 167.3
fly one-horse covered carriage 333.10, 334.4
fly-driver driver of a one-horse covered carriage 336.35
fob small pocket in a waistband 22.7
folding-door, folding-doors double door, door with two leaves 212.20, 214.23, 498.4
fortification science of constructing defensive works 30.31

fourteenpence 5.8p 467.2
frank for 196.21 and 203.35 see note to 196.21
fright grotesque-looking person 232.5, 234.32, 813.15
front band or bands of false hair (or set of false curls) worn over the forehead 234.33
fumigation perfume 267.32
fustian (made of) thick twilled cotton cloth with short pile or nap 92.30
gadzooks *euphemistic exclamation of surprise* (God's ?hooks) 309.31
gaiters cloth or leather covering for ankle (and lower leg) 39.18 etc.
gallant courteously attentive to a lady 651.1, 718.23
gallantry courteous attention to ladies 49.13 etc.
gammon *slang* nonsense, humbug 199.3, 199.4
gammoning humbugging 200.25
gang *dialect* go 59.3 etc.
genial pleasantly warm 12.12
genius supernatural spirit 11.5 etc.
gewgaw trifle 70.16
ghostly priestly 228.24
giddy incapable of serious thought or steady attention 66.6, 282.3, 396.29
'gin *dialect* if 509.21
give propose the health of (a person) 643.14
glass coach window 503.27
glee-singer singer of English part-song for three or more voices 11.14
go *noun* turn of events 90.16 etc.
go *verb* be successful 313.17
golden of inestimable utility 7.34
gravy gravy-boat 236.30
grazier one who grazes cattle for market 456.32
grievous sorrowful 19.3, 20.18, 628.7
griping grasping, avaricious 619.22, 701.31
groom assistant 608.1
grub toil 204.18, 754.32
guinea for 21.1 etc. see note to 21.1
gull dupe 246.5, 344.26, 668.36
habiliments *grandiloquent* clothes 393.24, 535.31
hack for hire 156.28
hackney for hire 15.19 etc.
hackney-coach, hackney coach for 52.2. etc. see note to 52.2
hair-chain ready-made braid made out of hair 679.5
half-and-half mixture of ale and porter 355.31
half-boot boot reaching half-way to knee or considerably above ankle 35.10
half-a-crown, half-crown coin worth 2*s.* 6*d.* or 12.5p 320.8 etc.
halfpenny, half-penny 0.2p 7.34 etc.

ha'porth, halfpenny-worth halfpenny worth (0.2p) 52.16, 138.27
hartshorn solution of ammonia used as smelling salts 233.28, 233.34, 698.19
heeltap fag-end of a bottle 420.18
heyday exclamation denoting surprise or wonder 121.20, 144.28
hipped morbidly depressed 80.38
hobbledehoy stripling 43.21
hobby hobby-horse 76.3
hock white German wine from Hochheim on the Main 74.13
hold bet 246.3
holden held 15.24, 639.16
hot-bed bed of soil in glass frame heated by fermenting manure 490.18
hunks surly old person, miser 450.8
hyseters *dialect* oysters 474.36
ideal imaginary 301.26
ill-conditioned badly-disposed 5.8
ill-favoured with an unpleasing aspect 26.13, 295.7, 577.39, 780.6
imp attendant spirit 397.34
incompatibility incapacity 24.30
inexpressibles *euphemism* trousers 288.26
inlet entrance 297.5
inside inside passenger in a coach 57.22, 61.25
instrument formal legal document 627.34, 750.24, 815.29, 816.3
intelligence channels of information 350.20
interfere interpose 474.32
intiv *dialect* into 113.16
italian-ironing see note to 691.1
jade hussy, minx 420.26, 776.5
Jezebel wicked woman 776.1
journeyman assistant 491.26 etc.
kennel gutter 166.8, 500.33
knee-smalls knee-breeches 301.36
knowing smartly dressed 664.35
laissez-aller *French* unconstrained 853.23
lantern-jawed for 676.2 see note to 301.30
latther *dialect* letter 516.39
Lawk *euphemistic interjection* Lord 510.31
leader introductory comment 203.36
learn *verb* teach 106.25
learn *adjective dialect* lean 113.20
length 42 lines of a script 301.3
lion celebrated person, chief person in the room 169.36, 185.29, 185.32
liquorish lecherous 621.11

longest-headed shrewdest 129.34
lure bait, trap 120.22
magnum double bottle containing 2 quarts (*c*.2.25 litres) 420.19, 424.25, 485.8, 485.14
main essential point, chief part 329.29
mantie-making *dialect* manteau-making (cloak-making) 267.27
mermaid siren, seducer, prostitute 555.18
mignionette plant with fragrant yellowish-white flowers 464.1, 522.9
mind hear 688.29
mob-cap indoor bonnet 192.22
monosyllabic curt 200.26
mortification subjection of the body to austere living or severe discipline 39.19, 70.17
mother-in-law stepmother 100.21, 313.32
motion suggestion 92.2
mummery extravagant costume or behaviour, meaningless show 662.28
mun *dialect* man 58.25 etc.
mustachio'd with moustaches 11.7
mustachios, moustachios moustaches, moustache 73.11, 74.33, 208.2, 208.3
myrmidon law enforcement officer 599.29
nap smooth pile 385.11
neither see note to 505.10
nice scrupulous, punctilious 580.15, 580.19, 702.35
ninepence approximately 3.5p 188.27, 269.28, 269.32
notary see note to 10.8
Ods-bobs *mild oath* (God's body) 515.29
offer *noun* attempt 77.5, 77.8 (see note to 77.4–5)
offer *verb* presume 410.5
oil-cloth linoleum 612.9
omnibus for 34.5 etc. see note to 34.5
opine think, suppose 11.21, 514.38; declare 87.30
oppose face, sit opposite 305.18
orchestra orchestra pit 296.15
order free or reduced-price pass to a theatrical performance 11.1
orthography correct spelling 30.29
ottoman low upholstered seat without back or arms 248.3, 613.32
ought nought, zero 35.25, 35.25
out-and-outer beyond the norm 547.31
outrageous furious 148.39
outside outside coach passenger 57.22, 57.28, 59.25; outside coach place 514.18
over-night before nightfall 280.9

over-persuade bring over by persuasion 793.23
pass *noun* bad state of affairs 500.10; point 531.8
pass *verb* give 336.24, 708.6
passenger passer-by 127.17, 137.15, 687.2
pathetics pathetic sentiments 19.4
patten *either* thick-soled shoe *or* overshoe 192.30
pease-pudding dish of dried peas usually with various other ingredients cooked to a pulp 292.12
pembroke-table small table with drop-leaf on each side 305.19
pending during 16.30 etc.
penny 0.4p 9.16 etc.
perpendicular very steep 23.16, 25.36
personate act 334.20, 381.25
pew-opener officer showing worshippers to seats in box pews 334.28
phaeton see note to 294.21
physick dose with medicine 94.21
picture tableau 288.1, 310.11
pink *noun* embodiment 499.38
pink *verb* pierce 385.27, 385.34
pipe large cask 485.28
pipe-clay whiten with white clay 823.29
piquet game with 32 cards for two players 497.2
pluck swindle, rob 662.4
plume pride 120.21, 362.29
pocket-pistol pocket spirit flask 618.7, 628.20
pollis *dialect* police 515.38
pomatum ointment 693.14
pony-chair light carriage drawn by a pony 765.12
portionless without a dowry 738.33
post-chaise for 362.5, 362.6, 362.7, and 362.9 see note to 362.5
postern back or side entrance 64.10, 68.12, 69.12
post-obit see note to 677.27
pot-boy boy or young man who serves drinks or collects glasses in a pub 203.31
powder rush 517.2
premise state, say by way of introduction 484.3, 624.33
presentation (right to) nominate a person to a vacancy 132.28, 763.22
presently at once 50.24, 212.22, 229.12
pressure impression 239.3
principal person engaged in a fight or duel, main participant 5.10 etc.; master 460.18; head of establishment 693.8
proper own 208.5
proud-stomached arrogant 154.25

quarter-day for 6.12 and 537.24 see note to 6.12
quizzical open to mockery 488.18
quondam former 118.10
rasper harsh unpleasant person 754.31
rate berate 716.17
ready-reckoner book or table listing common numerical calculations (especially those used in commerce) 7.33
rebel rebellion 828.31
recover get over 243.21, 353.31, 405.23
recruited restored 321.32, 535.23
reference referee 38.36, 40.34, 276.6, 787.10
register-office office where a register is kept 524.20, 564.37, 565.2, 566.5
rejoiced delighted 197.38 etc.
relict widow 536.39
repeater for 11.31 and 13.16 see note to 11.31–3
requisition demand 200.30
Rest[1] reserve fund 857.15
rest[2] device attached to breastplate to support butt-end of lance or spear when charging 207.34
resurrect disinter 786.37
re-telegraph signal again 86.28
reticule small handbag 57.34 etc.
revolve consider 6.11, 252.10, 566.1, 609.11
riband ribbon 168.30, 770.26, 813.21
rip dreadful fellow 547.39
road railway track 198.28
rook person living by their wits and gulling others 500.9
room *dialect* rum, odd 827.30
Roosher *dialect* Russia 561.38
roué libertine, playboy 500.9
round *adj.* brisk 624.11
round *noun* rung 853.17
rubbishing worthless, rubbishy 555.30
rubicund red (as a result of over-indulgence in alcohol) 12.39
Ruler debtor residing in the 'Rules' 612.10
rusticate live in seclusion 666.9
rusty faded, worn, shabby 10.20, 383.12
salt salt-cellar 236.30
salutation kiss, kissing 231.31
salute kiss 640.5, 821.17
saving frugal, niggardly 168.1
'scape-gallows one who has escaped the gallows though deserving it 582.7
scene stage 324.4

score bill 642.9
scout dismiss 581.27
seriatim in turn 190.31
set-out display 299.23
shake-down makeshift bed 84.23
shilling 5p 6.28 etc.
shop place of business 54.34, 92.35
shorts knee-breeches 184.38, 655.20
shrub drink of citrus juice, sugar, and rum 690.22
signalise distinguish 189.36, 245.2
signify matter 173.14, 821.34
sike *dialect* such 600.10, 827.13, 828.31
silly feeble- or simple-minded 85.39, 260.3
single-hearted straightforward, honest, sincere, simple-hearted 394.20
sixpence (coin worth) 2.5p 6.29 etc.
sixpenny containing items priced at 2.5p 207.28
sixpen'orth amount costing 2.5p 353.20
slate-pencil see note to 7.29
sloppy to contain rinsings 129.26
slopseller dealer in cheap ready-made clothing 406.17
small-clothes breeches 535 title etc.
small-plaited, small plaited closely braided 11.27, 488.8
smalls breeches 316.3, 490.5
smifligate *slang* handle roughly 358.9
smifligation *slang* rough handling 358.12, 358.15
snuff *noun* partly consumed candlewick 361.11
snuff *verb* for 114.36, 228.21, 736.10, and 754.12 see note to 114.36
snuff-colour brownish colour 677.4
snuff-coloured brownish 334.23, 677.3
snuffer instrument for snuffing candles (see note to 114.36) 399.11
sovereign gold coin worth £1 164.8 etc.
spark *depreciatory* smart young man 715.26
speculation for 9.20, 114.37, and 172.11 see note to 114.37
spencer short double-breasted overcoat 11.25 etc.; close-fitting jacket or bodice 297.7, 511.20, 511.28
squab cushion 126.27
stage-box proscenium box 311.4
stagnation-blooded cold-blooded 754.36
stand act as 626.18
stay satisfy 558.8; stem 592.17
steam-packet steamboat 478.22
stick indifferent actor 395.13
stir-about porridge 97.35

stirrup-cup parting glass 75.18
stop stay, reside 113.16 etc.
stuff nonsense 91.31
summat *dialect* something 116.21
superscription name of addressee and address 327.13, 432.28, 527.25
support occupy a position by the side of (a person) 640.12
sustain occupy a position by the side of (a person) 640.13
tact skill 244.27, 271.9, 752.1
taking receptive, appreciative 305.36
tambour-work embroidery 29.19
tamper enter into secret dealings 183.7 etc.
tapster barman 61.31
tea take tea 111.23, 514.21, 549.35
telegraph signal 385.3, 393.33
tell make an impression, have an effect 289.23; count 435.36, 581.34, 746.22
tellee, tell'ee, telle'e *dialect* I tell you 116.30 etc.
terms charges 23.8 etc.
terrific terrifying 610.2, 610.3, 725.8
thee *dialect* thy 163.22, 513.37, 549.37, 827.2
thorough-paced thoroughly accomplished 341.10
tidy good 415.25, 828.12; *ironical* pretty good 553.20
tiv *dialect* to 59.2
tiv'ee *dialect* to you 551.13
tiv'un *dialect* to him 828.31
toad sycophant 244.23
toad-eater attendant of a charlatan, sycophant 206.28
toast-and-water, toast and water drink made by immersing toast in boiling water and straining it 57.15, 311.16
toilet style of dressing 383.18; washing dressing and/or arranging the hair 139.25 etc.
toils net(s), snare(s) 688.27, 725.14
tops top-boots, high boots with tops of white, light-coloured, or brown leather or the like 85.11
town-made originating from the town 503.29
train retinue 68.27 etc.
transparency translucent screen lit from behind 393.13
treaces *dialect* traces, straps 59.1
trench encroach 191.3
trepan trap, ensnare 594.36
trim state 427.8
Turk *depreciatory* cruel rigorous tyrannical person 533.18
twopence 1p 446.32
twopenn'orth tuppence worth (0.8p) 50.1, 50.4

twopenny-post for 438.22 see note to 6.13
type pattern 461.23, 574.17
'un *dialect* one 59.10 etc.; him 113.31 etc.; you 163.11
unhand let go of 248.31
unliquidated *nonce usage* unalloyed 556.4
unsuited not accommodated 306.34
usher assistant schoolmaster 92.28 etc.
vagabond good-for-nothing, dreadful fellow 249.15 etc.
valise suitcase 162.8
varieties miscellaneous articles 636.4
vere *dialect* where 268.6, 510.29
vice vice-chairman 640.14
vindicate defend against interference 492.33
vittles victuals, food 50.15 etc.
wa' *dialect* way 509.21 etc.
waiter salver, small tray 212.17
walk parting 692.18
wall-eyed squinting 58.26
wash-leather soft leather 569.30
watch-guard chain used to secure a pocket watch when being worn 10.29, 340.5, 679.4
way-bill list of passengers and goods 53.19
weasen, weazen wizened, withered, shrivelled 677.30, 807.16
Wellington-boot, Wellington boot for 11.26, 443.19, and 505.36 see note to 11.26–7
wen cystic tumour 590.11, 590.11
whipster insignificant person 116.26, 450.10
whoam *dialect* home 59.3 etc.
wight creature 568.13
wink tear 74.36
without outside 477.19
wor *dialect* was 514.9
worsteds stockings made of woollen fabric 546.21, 655.21
wrapper shawl, mantle 318.27
yan *dialect* one 164.6, 516.2, 831.22
zooks (compare **gadzooks**) *exclamation of surprise* 394.30

INDEX OF BRIDGES, BUILDINGS, PLACES, AND STREETS

The numbers (but not the letters) in bold run on from map to map: 1–6 refer to the general map of London, 7–11 to that of the West End, 12–16 to that of the City, and 17–19 to the general map of England. References to the Explanatory Notes are indicated by an added 'n'. In a few cases where there are many references to a place only the first is given, followed by 'etc.'.

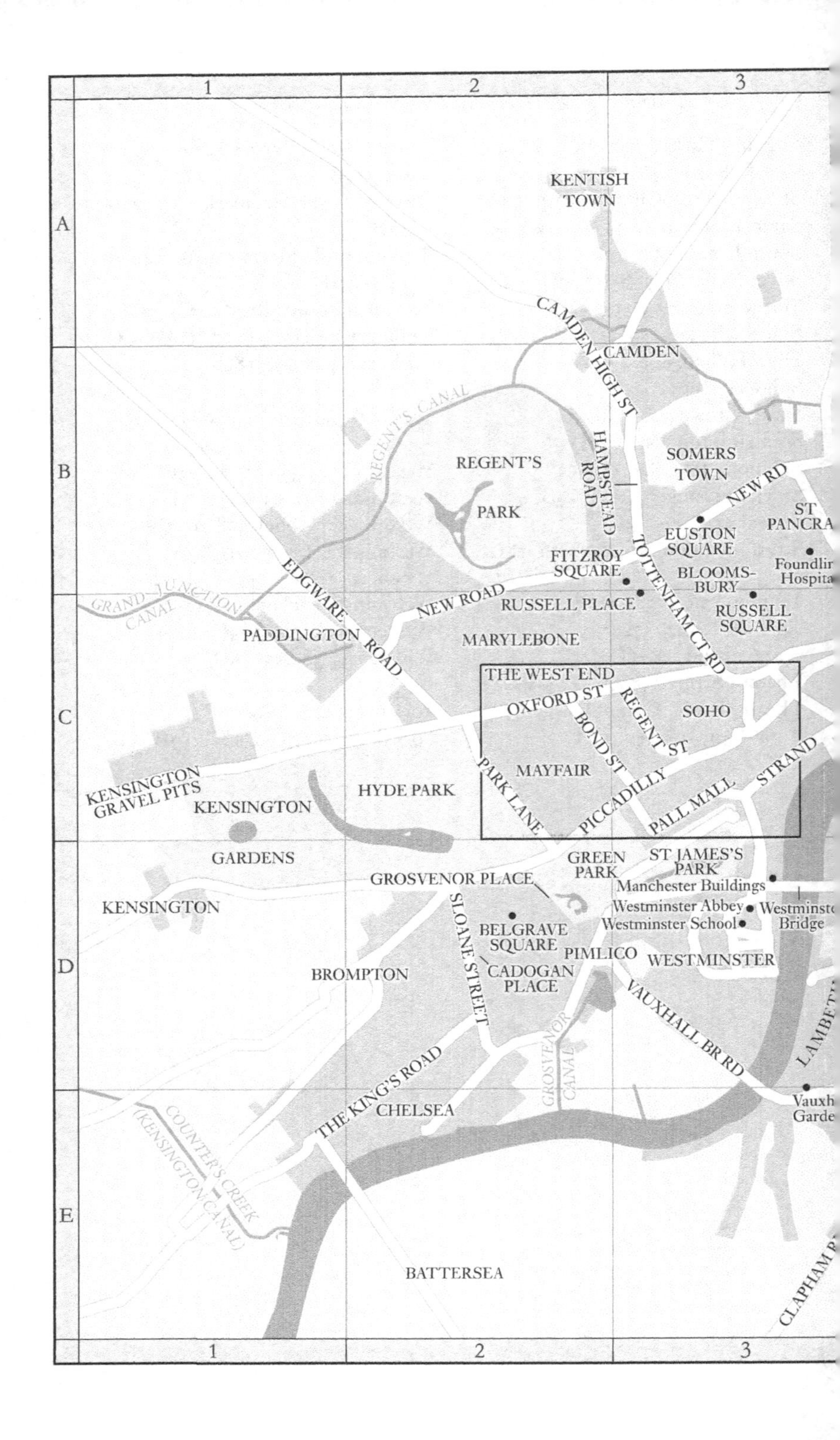
1
2
3
A
B
C
D
E
KENTISH TOWN
CAMDEN
CAMDEN HIGH ST
REGENT'S CANAL
REGENT'S PARK
HAMPSTEAD ROAD
SOMERS TOWN
NEW RD
ST PANCRA
EUSTON SQUARE
Foundlir Hospita
FITZROY SQUARE
TOTTENHAM CT RD
BLOOMS-BURY
EDGWARE ROAD
GRAND JUNCTION CANAL
NEW ROAD
RUSSELL PLACE
RUSSELL SQUARE
PADDINGTON
MARYLEBONE
THE WEST END
OXFORD ST
REGENT ST
SOHO
BOND ST
KENSINGTON GRAVEL PITS
PARK LANE
MAYFAIR
HYDE PARK
PICCADILLY
PALL MALL
STRAND
KENSINGTON
GARDENS
GREEN PARK
ST JAMES'S PARK
GROSVENOR PLACE
Manchester Buildings
KENSINGTON
SLOANE STREET
Westminster Abbey
Westminste Bridge
Westminster School
BELGRAVE SQUARE
PIMLICO
WESTMINSTER
BROMPTON
CADOGAN PLACE
VAUXHALL BR RD
GROSVENOR CANAL
LAMBETH
THE KING'S ROAD
CHELSEA
Vauxh Garde
COUNTER'S CREEK (KENSINGTON CANAL)
BATTERSEA
CLAPHAM

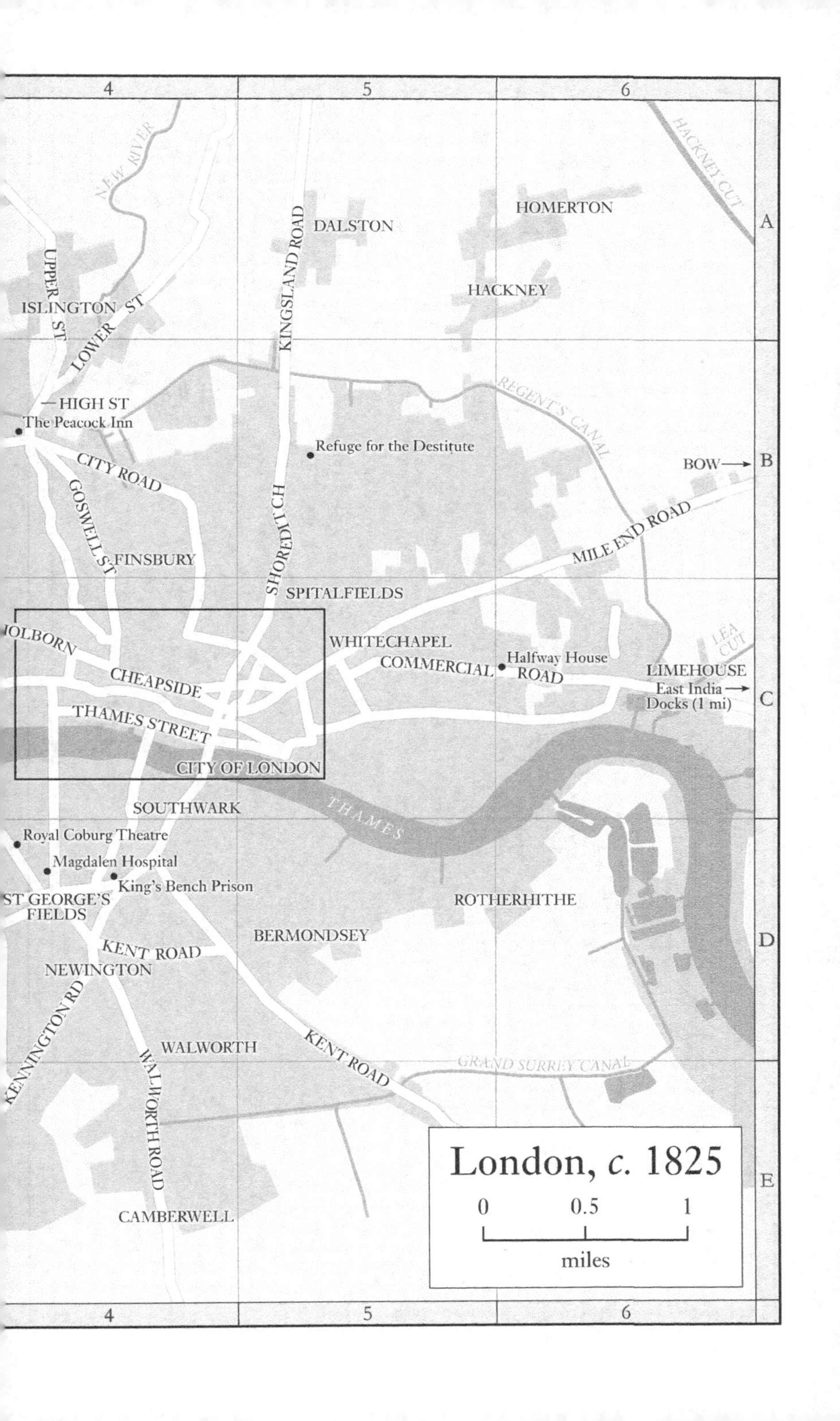
London, c. 1825
0
0.5
1
miles
4
5
6
A
B
C
D
E
NEW RIVER
HACKNEY CUT
HOMERTON
DALSTON
KINGSLAND ROAD
HACKNEY
UPPER ST
ISLINGTON
LOWER ST
HIGH ST
The Peacock Inn
REGENT'S CANAL
Refuge for the Destitute
BOW
CITY ROAD
GOSWELL ST
SHOREDITCH
MILE END ROAD
FINSBURY
SPITALFIELDS
HOLBORN
WHITECHAPEL
LEA CUT
CHEAPSIDE
COMMERCIAL ROAD
Halfway House
LIMEHOUSE
East India Docks (1 mi)
THAMES STREET
CITY OF LONDON
SOUTHWARK
THAMES
Royal Coburg Theatre
Magdalen Hospital
King's Bench Prison
ST GEORGE'S FIELDS
ROTHERHITHE
BERMONDSEY
KENT ROAD
NEWINGTON
KENNINGTON RD
WALWORTH
KENT ROAD
GRAND SURREY CANAL
WALWORTH ROAD
CAMBERWELL

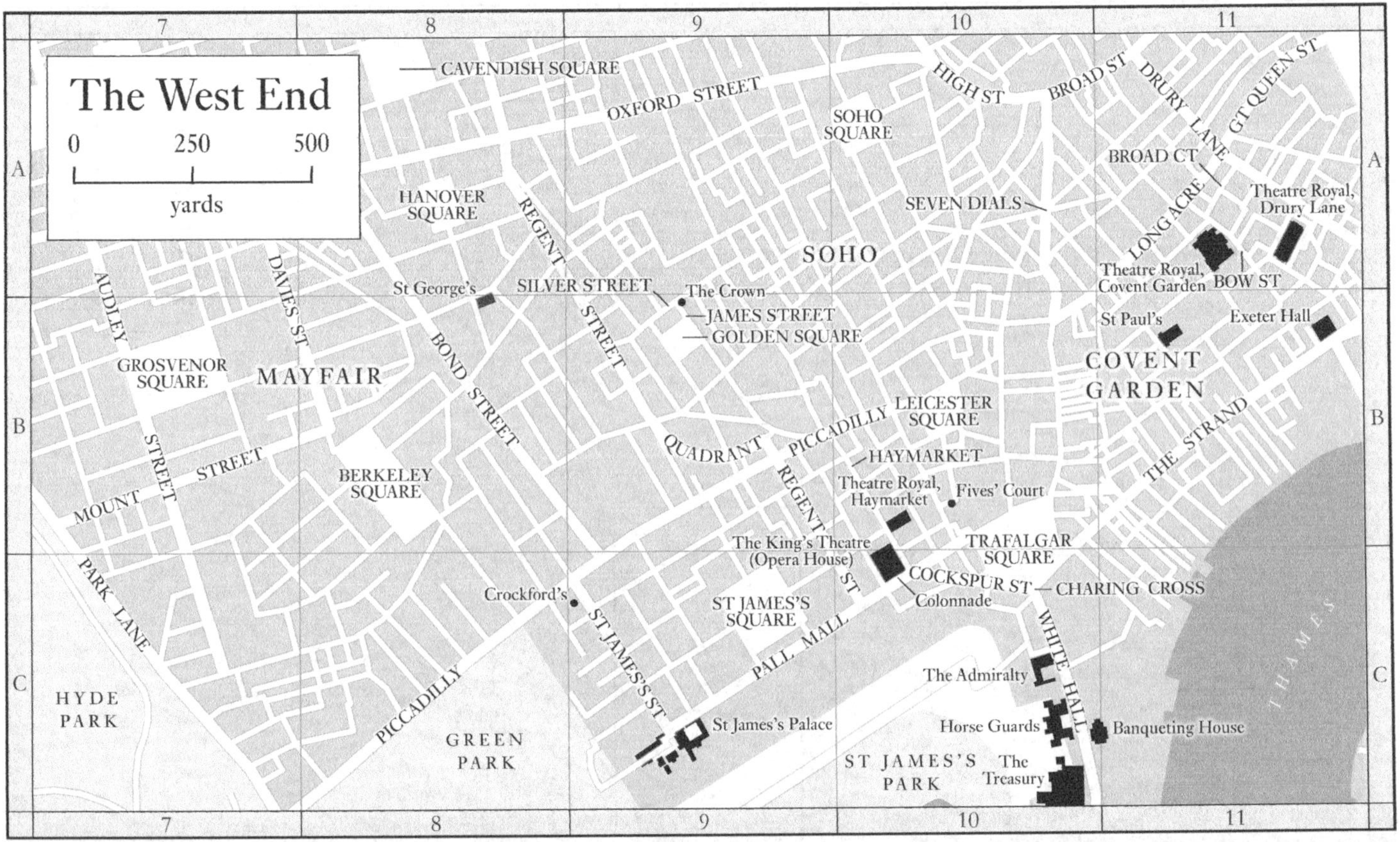

The West End

0
250
500
yards
7
8
9
10
11
A
B
C
CAVENDISH SQUARE
OXFORD STREET
HIGH ST
BROAD ST
DRURY LANE
GT QUEEN ST
SOHO SQUARE
BROAD CT
SEVEN DIALS
LONG ACRE
Theatre Royal, Drury Lane
HANOVER SQUARE
REGENT STREET
SOHO
Theatre Royal, Covent Garden
BOW ST
St George's
SILVER STREET
The Crown
JAMES STREET
GOLDEN SQUARE
St Paul's
Exeter Hall
AUDLEY STREET
DAVIES ST
GROSVENOR SQUARE
MAYFAIR
BOND STREET
COVENT GARDEN
LEICESTER SQUARE
PICCADILLY
QUADRANT
HAYMARKET
THE STRAND
BERKELEY SQUARE
MOUNT STREET
Theatre Royal, Haymarket
Fives' Court
REGENT ST
TRAFALGAR SQUARE
The King's Theatre (Opera House)
COCKSPUR ST
CHARING CROSS
Colonnade
PARK LANE
Crockford's
ST JAMES'S ST
ST JAMES'S SQUARE
PALL MALL
WHITE HALL
The Admiralty
THAMES
HYDE PARK
PICCADILLY
GREEN PARK
St James's Palace
Horse Guards
Banqueting House
ST JAMES'S PARK
The Treasury

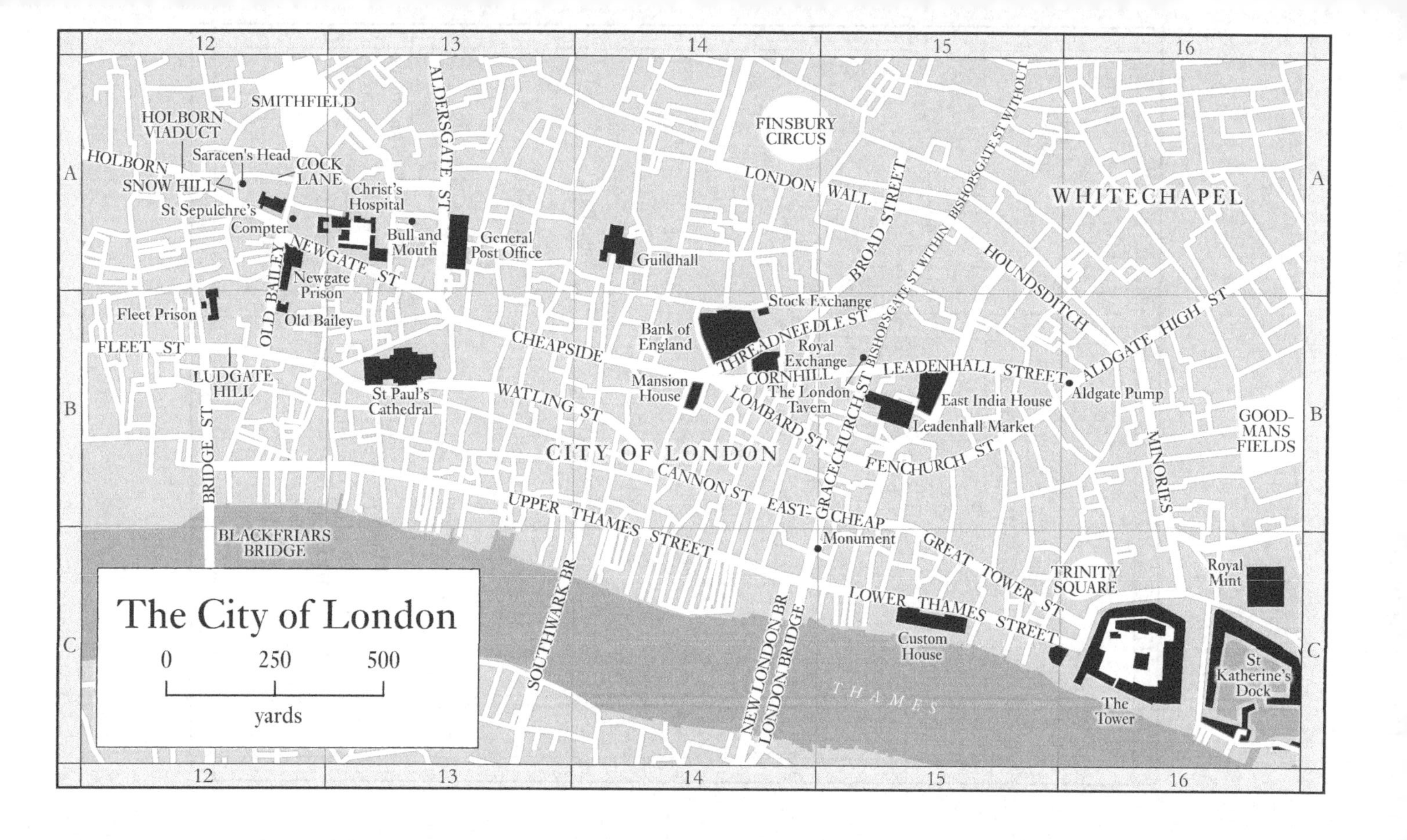
The City of London
0
250
500
yards
12
13
14
15
16
A
B
C
SMITHFIELD
HOLBORN VIADUCT
HOLBORN
Saracen's Head
COCK LANE
SNOW HILL
St Sepulchre's
Compter
Christ's Hospital
Bull and Mouth
ALDERSGATE ST
General Post Office
NEWGATE ST
Newgate Prison
OLD BAILEY
Old Bailey
Fleet Prison
FLEET ST
LUDGATE HILL
BRIDGE ST
BLACKFRIARS BRIDGE
St Paul's Cathedral
CHEAPSIDE
WATLING ST
Guildhall
FINSBURY CIRCUS
LONDON WALL
BROAD STREET
Stock Exchange
Bank of England
THREADNEEDLE ST
Royal Exchange
CORNHILL
Mansion House
The London Tavern
LOMBARD ST
CITY OF LONDON
CANNON ST
UPPER THAMES STREET
SOUTHWARK BR
EAST-CHEAP
GRACECHURCH ST
BISHOPSGATE ST WITHIN
BISHOPSGATE ST WITHOUT
Monument
NEW LONDON BR
LONDON BRIDGE
LEADENHALL STREET
East India House
Leadenhall Market
FENCHURCH ST
GREAT TOWER ST
LOWER THAMES STREET
Custom House
THAMES
WHITECHAPEL
HOUNDSDITCH
ALDGATE HIGH ST
Aldgate Pump
MINORIES
GOOD-MANS FIELDS
TRINITY SQUARE
Royal Mint
The Tower
St Katherine's Dock

17 18 19

Perth
Glasgow
Edinburgh
SCOTLAND
Ayr
Dumfries
Newcastle
Carlisle
Sunderland
Belfast
Barnard Castle
Greta Bridge
Scarborough
Boroughbridge
YORKSHIRE
York
Blackpool
Kingston upon Hull
Bradford
Irish Sea
Liverpool
Manchester
Sheffield
Trent
ENGLAND
Chester
Nottingham
Newark
Grantham
Tutbury
Severn
LEICESTERSHIRE
Norwich
Stamford
Birmingham
WALES
Coventry
Cambridge
Eton Slocomb
Stratford-upon-Avon
Ipswich
Oxford
Swansea
LONDON
Cardiff
Bristol
Reading
Rochester
Bath
Guildford
Godalming
Chatham
Canterbury
Taunton Vale
Winchester
Hindhead
Brighton
DEVONSHIRE
Exeter
Southampton
Ryde
Portsmouth
Bournemouth
Dawlish
CORNWALL
Plymouth
Penzance
English Channel
0 25 50 mi

Eel-Pie Island, Twickenham
Petersham
Ham House
Moseley Hurst
Thames
Kingston upon Thames
0 1 mi

A B C D